Black Manhood and Comm
1900–1930

NEW PERSPECTIVES ON THE HISTORY OF THE SOUTH

UNIVERSITY PRESS OF FLORIDA

Florida A&M University, Tallahassee
Florida Atlantic University, Boca Raton
Florida Gulf Coast University, Ft. Myers
Florida International University, Miami
Florida State University, Tallahassee
New College of Florida, Sarasota
University of Central Florida, Orlando
University of Florida, Gainesville
University of North Florida, Jacksonville
University of South Florida, Tampa
University of West Florida, Pensacola

Black Manhood and Community Building in North Carolina,

1900–1930

Angela Hornsby-Gutting

University Press of Florida

Gainesville/Tallahassee/Tampa/Boca Raton

Pensacola/Orlando/Miami/Jacksonville/Ft. Myers/Sarasota

First cloth printing, 2009
First paperback printing, 2010

Library of Congress Cataloging-in-Publication Data
Hornsby-Gutting, Angela.
Black manhood and community building in North Carolina, 1900-1930
/ Angela Hornsby-Gutting.
p. cm.—(New perspectives on the history of the South)
Includes bibliographical references and index.
ISBN 978-0-8130-3293-1 (alk. paper); ISBN 978-0-8130-3679-3 (pbk.)
    1. African American men—North Carolina—Social conditions—
20th century. 2. African American men—North Carolina—Race
identity. 3. Masculinity—North Carolina—History—20th century.
4. Middle class African Americans—North Carolina—Social conditions—20th century. 5. Community development—North Carolina—History—20th century. 6. Community organization—North
Carolina—History—20th century. 7. Racism—North Carolina—
History—20th century. 8. North Carolina—Social conditions—20th
century. I. Title.
E185.93.N6H67 2009
305.38'8960730756—dc22   2008044515

The University Press of Florida is the scholarly publishing agency for
the State University System of Florida, comprising Florida A&M
University, Florida Atlantic University, Florida Gulf Coast University,
Florida International University, Florida State University, New College
of Florida, University of Central Florida, University of Florida, University of North Florida, University of South Florida, and University of
West Florida.

University Press of Florida
15 Northwest 15th Street
Gainesville, FL 32611-2079
http://www.upf.com

New Perspectives on the History of the South
Edited by John David Smith, Charles H. Stone Distinguished Professor
   of American History
University of North Carolina at Charlotte

To my grandparents, Mandy and Signal "Bo" Lockhart,
Lillie and Alton Parker Hornsby Sr. and for all my family

Contents

Figures

Acknowledgments

Many individuals and institutions have made indelible imprints on this book, forwarding its interpretations, progression, and completion. Jacquelyn Hall expressed her faith in the project and its author at numerous junctures. Her careful reading of multiple drafts always disclosed an essential revelation that needed further exploration. She continues to be a model of scholarship and humanity and serves as a reminder of both the joys and challenges inherent in historical research and writing.

For her encouragement and support, I thank Jerma Jackson, whose enthusiasm for the book and its tenets proved infectious when most needed. Reginald Hildebrand offered sound critique of embryonic chapters. Peter Filene's expertise in gender and cultural history and Joel Williamson's solid repertoire in southern history and race relations also forwarded the narrative's analytical trajectory.

I wish to extend thanks to the able staffs of several research libraries and institutions, including the North Carolina Collection and the Southern Historical Collection, both at the University of North Carolina–Chapel Hill; Robinson-Spangler Public Library, Charlotte; Traci Thompson, reference librarian, Edgecombe County Memorial Library, Tarboro, for help with Masonic materials; Sheila Bumgardner, Charlotte Public Library; Zoe Rhine of Asheville-Buncombe Public Library, Asheville, for assistance with Heritage of Black Highlanders literature; and Pat Rickman and Marilyn Schuster, Atkins Library, University of North Carolina-Charlotte. The book's research aims were also advanced substantially by the Most Worshipful Marvin Chambers, who allowed unrestricted access to records chronicling North Carolina's Prince Hall masons.

Fellowships and grants supported travel and research expenses and allowed time for writing. The Erskine Peters Fellowship at the University of Notre Dame proved especially germane to the project's development. Two critical chapters were drafted at this time. I owe a big thanks to Gail

Bederman, who made extensive commentary on the work in progress and provided good humor and comraderie. I'm also thankful for suggestions and support offered by Hugh Page Jr. and Richard Pierce of Notre Dame's Africana Studies Department. The University of Mississippi's College of Liberal Arts provided summer funding that facilitated expanded research and revisions.

The book has benefited from several commentators, readers, and conference participants who, collectively, honed my arguments, encouraged me to think more critically and expansively about themes raised, or suggested additional research avenues. They include Gail Bederman; Elsa Barkley Brown; Prudence Cumberbatch; Allison Dorsey; Bobby Donaldson; Gregory Mixon; Laurie Maffly-Kipp; Jacqueline Rouse; Alton Hornsby Jr.; Steve Estes; Sarah Thuesen; Kathryn Walbert; Katie Otis; Cristina Nelson; and Ken Zogry. The two anonymous readers for the press made very helpful comments and recommendations. I'm particularly grateful to University of Mississippi colleague Nancy Bercaw, who read the entire manuscript and provided novel, intricate ways to conceptualize the book's key themes.

I'm appreciative of the encouragement I have received from family, friends, and other loved ones. I owe an immense amount of gratitude to my parents, especially, for their support of my career ambitions. Finally, Edward Gutting's deliberative critiques of the manuscript helped advance its arguments in creative and nuanced ways. His steadfast support of me in all things (historical and otherwise) has been unwavering. I owe him a debt of gratitude.

Introduction

In January 1900, Congressman George H. White, representative of North Carolina's Second Congressional District, joined a coalition of other leading blacks from thirty-six counties to oppose a proposed disfranchisement amendment. The stripping of the franchise, White stressed, would "blunt our aspirations, ruin our manhood, and lesson our usefulness as citizens."[1] James Shepard, founder of North Carolina College in Durham (now North Carolina Central University) expressed similar concerns. Invoking the rhetoric of manhood, he stated, "We cannot see that the best way to make a good man is to unman him."[2]

The turn of the twentieth century signaled disfranchisement for most of the state's African-American men. In the 1890s, a Fusionist Party ticket comprised of black Republicans and white farmers who were disaffected with Democratic politics seemed to foreshadow increased opportunities for the black middle class. In 1894 and 1896, Fusionists won majorities in both the state legislature and Congress. Republican Daniel Russell won the governorship in 1896. Several other Republicans and Populists, including blacks, were elected to positions in local and state government. In the Second Congressional District in North Carolina, a Republican and black stronghold, four blacks (including Henry Cheatham and George H. White), were elected to the U.S. House of Representatives between 1874 and 1898.[3] Increasingly concerned about the Fusionists' growing political power, Democrats launched a virulent white supremacist campaign. By playing on fears of "Negro domination," Democrats hoped to sway white farmers away from the Fusionists. The campaign resulted in the Wilmington race riot of 1898, in which a mob of prominent and armed businessmen who opposed power-sharing—particularly an integrated city council—rioted in the streets, effectively driving black and white Republicans from the city. Three white men were wounded and eleven blacks were killed in the incident. A successful disfranchisement amendment campaign followed in 1900.[4] Faced with suffrage restrictions such as poll taxes, literacy

[handwritten margin note: Dissatisfied w/ people in authority + no longer willing to support them]

tests, and the grandfather clause, black men were effectively driven from electoral politics.

After passage of the disfranchisement amendment, George White exclaimed, "I cannot live in North Carolina and be a man." Another black leader compared disfranchisement to the "shock of an earthquake," adding that some black men "are only waiting to see just how greatly they are damaged, before making a move."[5] During the first decade of the twentieth century, 27,827 African Americans fled the state; over half were men. The subsequent decade saw 29,162 blacks depart but with a smaller percentage of black men.[6] Indeed, several of North Carolina's black men, including George White (the last black elected to Congress from the South until after the modern civil rights movement in the 1950s and 1960s); race leader John C. Dancy, port authority officer in Wilmington; and newspaper editor Alexander Manly, whose fiery editorials in defense of black manhood and womanhood presaged the Wilmington race riot in 1898, joined the migration. In explaining the exodus of many of the state's "best men," Congressman White blamed "the institution of jim crow cars, the passage of the disfranchisement amendment, and the bitter political campaigns of 1898 and 1900." J. W. Smith, editor of the *Star of Zion* in Charlotte, also saw the specter of Jim Crow laws as responsible for black men's departure. "The world is wide; trains are running in every direction, and there are places where the honest and industrious Negro can and will go to be a man and not a beast of burden." The "Negro," Smith declared, was "on the move."[7]

North Carolina's deteriorating racial climate prompted the exodus of about 57,000 black North Carolinians in the first three decades of the twentieth century. Much of the traditional scholarship on Jim Crow has reflected the gravity of such migrations. Stressing black victimization and accommodation, such accounts have denied black men and women agency and self-determination.[8] Yet despite innumerable obstacles, both sexes determined to remain in the South and establish themselves as dynamic race and civic leaders.

While historians of women and gender generally have focused on black women's subversion of Jim Crow through their social, religious, and political activities (including interracial alliances with white women) within their communities after disfranchisement, the localized grassroots work of black men during this period has received less treatment.[9] This lack of emphasis can be attributed, in part, to the tendency of some scholars to view black men's identity through a narrow prism, that of formal politics. Historians such as Glenda Gilmore, Deborah Gray White, and others have eloquently and convincingly shown how black women stepped forward after disfranchisement to lift up the race, build community institutions, and serve as ambassadors to the white community. Building on their work, *Black Manhood and Community Building in North Carolina* peers into the institutional lives of North Carolina's "best" black men to further illuminate this ongoing narrative by documenting and comparing men's activities to that of black women.

Though numerous scholars have investigated African-American male identity from ideological, sociological, and historical perspectives, these studies have lacked the community-based moral emphasis attached to black women's work. Rather than situate black men alongside black women in community-centered politics, scholars have assumed that black men, whose identities were moored in political ideology, stepped aside in deference to their female counterparts. As black men confronted the cumulative strains of racial violence, segregation, and the loss of the vote, black women shouldered the race problem in this narrative. At the turn of the twentieth century, the narrative continues, black women believed themselves the key to ensuring the moral uplift of the race. "Woman's Era" signaled women's superiority concerning the moral welfare of the black community but the equality of men and women in all other matters.[10] Supporters of social welfare work argued that it suited black women since it required nurturing and altruism; where men could be belligerent and aggressive, women's work was generally more humane and constructive. Black clubwomen's dominance in community work, while not explicitly excluding black men from this arena, nevertheless made black women's contributions more visible.[11]

It is black men and women's collective engagement in community building work, however, that helped define their gendered selves. While the period 1880–1920 has been hailed as a "great age for women in politics"[12] through their social welfare activities on the local level, this interpretation does not take fully into account the ongoing uplift and ambassadorial activities of black men. Indeed, racial reform for black male intellectuals during Jim Crow was framed as a project of manhood resurrection. Kevin Gaines posits that within a middle-class ideology of uplift, "civilization, manhood, and patriarchal authority" dictated race progress. Prominent leaders W. E. B. Du Bois and Booker T. Washington emphasized the importance of educating black men, preparing them for participation in economic systems and forwarding their role as household breadwinners.[13] Yet within these goals were competing motivations and objectives influenced by men's gendered position within communal institutions and their direct engagement with black female race activists. Historians Elsa Barkley Brown and Stephanie Shaw have made this point, emphasizing the importance of internal gendered dynamics within the black community as key to black women's emergence as prominent race activists. They point to the long tradition of shared civic and political activism in African-American communities that allowed black women's entry into politics well prior to women's "great age." Houston Baker, too, acknowledges the multiplicity of meanings applied to black public spaces. He asserts how African Americans refashioned notions of the public sphere to suit their particular circumstances. In doing so, they redefined "public" to encompass not a singular sphere, but a "plurality of spheres."[14]

Moreover, Brown's work on the black community in Richmond, Virginia, and her theoretical essays demonstrate the necessity of placing black men and women within the same sphere of analysis. Brown and sociologists such as Andrea Hunter support using feminist methodology (which attends to women's role as "kin keepers," culture carriers, and stewards of morality)—which has broadened our understanding of black women's everyday lives—to black men. They suggest that questions be raised about black men similar to those posed about black women in the fields of gender and feminist studies.[15] Black men and women, these scholars assert, should be placed in dialogue with one another with the understanding that they occupy similar historical and cultural ground.[16]

This book borrows from feminist methodology and insights to show how North Carolina's black men and women were equally engaged in community-based activism during the Jim Crow era. Central to this investigation is an examination of men's appropriation of communal spaces—generally labeled public and private—to promote gendered agency, cooperation, and, at times, sexual dominance.

Interrogating community space is key to understanding the gendered complexity of African-American communal politics within the early-twentieth-century South. With gender and spatial constructs as the lenses, what emerges is a complex portrait of gender cooperation, tension, and negotiation between the sexes and among African-American men during an era of heightened racial repression. North Carolina's black men and women used multiple institutional spaces for distinct and, at times, parallel uses. Changes in men's conceptualization of these spaces altered how manhood was defined within them. When North Carolina churchmen demanded new roles as religious social service workers, they appropriated positions typically understood as womanly tasks. Men's comfort in securing this role underscored their ease in realizing gender nonconformity while still cutting a manly figure. Thus, black men's immersion in this type of politics signaled an elasticity of conceptions of manliness and leadership roles that was premised on dialogue and community constructs of kin keeper and caregiver.

The evolution of different articulations of black manliness and leadership in the South is resonant before the imposition of Jim Crow. Correlations between manhood and manhood rights (suffrage) have tended to dominate the scholarship for this period. Literature generated in the 1960s and 1970s that focused on the antebellum era cumulatively sought to rescue black men from an emasculated identity (which some observers deemed evident in the structure of the contemporary black family) while distinguishing their identity from slave women. Historian Herbert Gutman and others asserted the centrality of black men in their communities and home life. Gutman argued that slave households were less matrifocal, emphasizing that during the Civil War slave men protected their wives and children when threatened by slaveholders or Union troops. As another example of men's centrality in African-American families, Gutman notes that often slave children were named after their fathers.[17] Other scholars emphasized the dominant roles played by men, who occupied managerial and artisan positions, instructed in the cultivation of domestic garden plots, and provided extra food for their families. Once considered dominant, black women are now seen by some scholars as largely subordinate and sometimes submissive.[18] As such, they have increasingly become marginalized in scholars' projects to resurrect black manhood.[19]

The recent anthology edited by Craig Thompson Friend and Lorri Glover, *Southern Manhood: Perspectives on Masculinity in the Old South*, also seeks to reinvent antebellum black manhood by rejecting static definitions that put the planter elite and ideals of honor at the center of southern manhood.[20] The historians who contributed to this collection document competing definitions of manhood as fashioned by non-elite yeoman farmers, urban workers, Native Americans, and enslaved and free black men. Black masculinity, which scholars deemed had weakened during slavery, takes on renewed meaning in the light of this new scholarship. Unlike the portrayal of black men in some of the revisionist slave literature, in these essays, black men's identity proves more expansive as slave men play a variety of roles that include assuming roles as community caretakers or asserting an "extremist individualism," including abandoning family and community responsibilities. Varying cultural contexts and social relations, then, are critical to formulations of African-American gender identity. But we must complement these factors with contemplations of spatial politics, including the dynamics between black men and women in local communities.

While *Southern Manhood* does much to forward multiple renderings of Old South masculinity, scholarly assessment of New South masculinity lacks similar complexity or breadth. Just as slavery and white supremacy were assumed to emasculate black men in the nineteenth century, the evolution of Jim Crow laws allegedly did the same. Yet just as antebellum black men constructed their manhood both around and separate from white hegemonic standards, this book argues that African-American male activists during the Jim Crow era had to negotiate issues of black female identity and communal spaces when marking their man -hood.

Martin Summers addresses the notion of gender elasticity in his Jim Crow study on middle-class black manhood, though largely from a nationalist bent. Probing such organizations as the United Negro Improvement Association (UNIA), North Carolina's Grand Lodge of Prince Hall Masons, renowned Harlem Renaissance writers, and college protests at Hampton and Fisk colleges, Summers reveals the import of simultaneously acknowledging and rejecting dominant cultural ideas when documenting black masculinity.[21]

Shaping black men's activist agenda in the early twentieth-century South were prevailing notions about what it meant to be a man in society. Men's gendered perspectives reflected a cultural interdependency that cut across the black/white racial binary. As American and black men, they adopted and experimented with values and broader trends from a variety of "cultural fields."[22] White Protestants' masculinization campaigns, the influence of which is treated in Chapter 1, were but one example of such cultural sharing.[23] "Civilization" as a racial and gendered construct for the aspiring and elite classes also held currency among North Carolina's black men. To be manly and civilized meant the display of self-control and self-restraint, characteristics that on the surface privileged class status over race. However, the trope of civilization also became the marker of race supremacy as whites appropriated the term and used Social Darwinist thought to cast blacks, and in particular black men, as primitive. When white men charged black men with the crime of rape against white women, they affixed labels of "barbaric" and "savage" to the banner of black manhood. The concept of civilization whites held fed the propagandizing of American imperialism. White and black religious institutions, moreover, felt it their duty to civilize other peoples domestically and internationally. Black middle-class men were thus shaped by broader rhetoric about manhood and other cultural imperatives of the day, which, among other things, called for high moral character and conduct, less individualistic material consumption, and separate spheres of activity for men and women.[24]

Rather than arguing that black men succumbed to hegemonic discourses of manhood, however, Summers endorses a cultural hegemonic trope of manhood, wherein African Americans express distinct identities while in relationship with dominant cultural tropes. In doing so, they "engaged in their own gender identity formation, a process that was shaped not only by their race and ethnicity, but by their class, age, and sexuality as well."[25]

North Carolina's middle-class black men, in turn, formulated a communal manhood to boost their identity and demonstrate their faith in agency/progress, which was at odds with the South's segregated social order and is still at odds with historians' traditional interpretation of Jim Crow as predominated by black subjugation and accommodation. Communal manhood also provided a social and psychic reservoir from which black men governed their affairs and molded respectable identities. As visible community activists, black women figured directly in men's self-imaging.

The turn of the twentieth century, which historian Rayford Logan characterizes as the nadir in American race relations, presented gender and race challenges to black men and women in the South. The new century brought lynchings, black peonage, disfranchisement, race riots and white supremacist ideology. Between 1889 and 1922, the National Association for the Advancement of Colored People (NAACP) estimated that of the 3,436 people lynched in America, most were African Americans and all but 83 were men. This era of race relations also popularized the image of the "black beast rapist," that rationalized violence against black men for presumed sexual assaults on white women. Between 1900 and 1931, North Carolina mobs lynched thirty-six people, all but three of whom were black. Throughout the Jim Crow era, blacks were maimed, jailed, intimidated, and otherwise terrorized for racial dissent.[26]

Moreover, the first Jim Crow laws to codify racial segregation were passed in February 1899, affecting steamboats and railroads. Legislation mandating segregated streetcars passed in 1907.[27] In March 1907, North Carolina's legislature approved a law sanctioning the separation of blacks and whites on streetcars. Within a month, streetcars in such cities as Charlotte, Asheville, and Durham had complied with the order. In the 1880s, aspiring and elite blacks were confident that class status would trump race as they strove to achieve the desired triumvirate of property ownership, educational attainment, and moral propriety. The streetcar legislation shattered such expectations, as it made no differentiation between acculturated middle-class blacks and the masses.[28]

Regardless of class status, African Americans found themselves compromised politically, occupationally, educationally, and legally under Jim Crow legislation. Besides segregation in public and private establishments, African Americans were subjected to poll taxes, literacy tests, and property qualifications that served to keep blacks disfranchised and dilute black political strength. "Grandfather clauses," in which voting requirements were waived for those whose fathers and grandfathers had been qualified to vote in 1860, also proved effective in disqualifying most blacks from the franchise. Occupationally, vagrancy laws, crop liens, and work contracts kept blacks either in perpetual debt or in prison. Most states provided for separate schools by 1885, and in 1896, the Supreme Court's ruling in *Plessy v. Ferguson* provided that states could utilize law enforcement agencies to enforce race segregation so long as separate but equal facilities existed for the races. Other rights withheld from blacks included the right to sit on juries and hold public office. Economic reprisals such as blacklisting of black businesses, violence such as lynching and threats of violence stripped African Americans of their claims to citizenship and political life.[29]

Confronted with a racially defined middle-class status that restricted them occupationally, politically, and legally, black elites formulated a Victorian moral economy that stressed privilege based on moral standing and patriarchal conventions within black communities. Both men and women of the black middle class subscribed to white beliefs regarding separate spheres ideology, a belief system inscribed in the South's racial and gender hierarchy. In addition, black men worked to counter the effects of urban amusements and street culture upon the youth of the race. North Carolina's black men also demonstrated their compatibility with the modern age through exhibits at state fairs and Emancipation Day celebrations that demonstrated the progress of the race. To be African American and a man meant reconciling external forces such as white oppression with the needs of the African-American community.

For young black men coming of age during the Jim Crow era, serving the race entailed active engagement in the social regeneration and redemption of its people. This particular mandate, as articulated by Eugene Harris, a Fisk University professor, stressed "new ambitions, new purposes, new motives, new ideals," the result of which would be a new social status. Because of the imbalance of existing power relations, Harris urged his audience to labor and wait. In his reformulation of manliness, manly strength need not be aggressive: "It is not *aggressive*, but *submissive*. Its triumph is assured, not because of the violence of its fury and the might of its arm, but because it puts away bitterness and wrath with all malice; and is kind and tenderhearted and forgiving." Harris preached a version of manhood that, while compliant with white supremacy, encompassed "new purposes and ideals." Not unlike black clubwomen during Jim Crow, he stressed internal rather than external race improvements given the degree of racism present. At the same time, he envisioned a place for young black men in the race's "social regeneration" by placing them at the center of religious and educational work.[30] While Harris deemed such activity passive, it did not function to emasculate black men in his view. Within the racialized boundaries of Jim Crow, he reassured black men that strength is *submissive*.[31]

The notion of a compliant black manhood was tested by events such as the Spanish-American War, World War I, and the rise of the Garvey movement. At the conclusion of the Spanish-American War, black servicemen had lost patience with the limited opportunities and the racism and paternalism of white officers. That war bolstered white supremacy in its conflation of the concepts of "nation" and "whiteness." During both the Spanish-American War and World War I, the U.S. government sought to relieve oppression abroad while allowing it to remain on the home front. At the same time, in both conflicts manliness was defined by the values of independence, citizenship, and patriarchy. All of these geopolitical events shaped the context in which black men attempted to define a respectable male identity.

North Carolina soldiers in the Spanish-American War's all-black Third Regiment hoped that their service in the war would "prove themselves worthy of the rights and obligations of citizenship." Yet the regiment, which never deployed, stood on duty in Knoxville, Tennessee, as the Wilmington race riot erupted. Once back in North Carolina, the men of the regiment were regarded as pariahs rather than heroes. In 1899, just as the Third Regiment was returning home, the North Carolina General Assembly passed legislation that eliminated blacks from the state guard.

Scholars have argued that in response to World War I, some male activists reasserted and revised notions of black manhood by adopting a more militant approach toward racial inequity.[32] My research focuses on another response to the regional and national changes in race relations after the war by examining the changing strategies of male leaders of longtime African-American public rituals such as black state fairs and Emancipation Day celebrations. Another venue for reworking African-American masculinity was freemasonry. Within the all-black Prince Hall Masons, ideas about loyalty to self (not racial deference), the meaning of citizenship, and patriarchy converged to produce a new version of masculinity and racial pride.

Garveyism also informed conceptions of African-American manhood and relations with black women nationally and regionally. Scholars have studied the masculinist sentiments of Garvey's United Negro Improvement Association (UNIA) and the way it circumscribed female roles and identities. The extent to which black men sought to balance the tug of militancy and a black nationalist ethos with desires to accommodate the needs of their communities and community partners, including black women, has been less studied. This balancing act is evident in the links between the national Garvey movement and its regional work. Mary Rolinson has documented how southern black rural women figured prominently in the UNIA as grassroots organizers and "micromobilizers." They, she contends, expanded the UNIA's reach to other communities, hosted UNIA meetings, and held offices. The historical sexual exploitation of black women by white men in the South led to rural support for Garvey's race purity platform via its antimiscegenation agenda. Interest in maintaining racial purity, ostensibly for the protection of black women's bodies, involved the embrace of black patriarchy, not only by black men but also by women, whose numbers in the UNIA were considerable.[33]

The UNIA was also strong in North Carolina's urban centers, though to a lesser degree than it was in the countryside. Blacks in the state learned of Garveyism through such journals as the *Star of Zion*, an American Methodist Episcopal Zion publication that reported on UNIA conventions, and Garvey's steamship company, the Black Star Line. In fact, North Carolina claimed the largest urban and middle-class black constituency within the organization. Rev. W. M. Allen, president-pastor of Raleigh's UNIA division, proclaimed it the "stronghold of Garveyism in the state of North Carolina." UNIA men drilled in the African Legion uniform while Raleigh's UNIA women served in the Black Cross Nurses auxiliary. Though Allen claimed that his UNIA division was the largest, Winston-Salem's branch was larger. Meetings were so well-attended that they had to be held in the city's Symphony Hall. Women had prominent roles in the Winston-Salem UNIA; Mrs. S. S. Womack served as the division's "lady president." Garvey ideology (racial pride, pragmatism, struggles for citizenship, patriarchy, and economic progress) and war conflicts thus ushered in complex deliberations on the local level as North Carolina's middle-class black men sought to promote a proper black manhood and womanhood and build solid institutions.[34]

While the disfranchisement campaign and the subsequent institutionalization of legalized segregation inspired leading black men to leave North Carolina, it also motivated African-American men who stayed to affirm a manly identity and expand their community role. Though the pervasive nature of racial segregation limited the power of blacks, it also gave them an opportunity to redefine their existence, including their gendered selves.[35] Rather than accept black congressman George White's lament that he could "no longer live in North Carolina and be a man" after the disfranchisement amendment was passed, the state's black men articulated a communal manhood whose meaning changed within varying spatial locations. This process was mediated by distinctions between private and public and by daily interactions and rhetorical exchanges with African-American women.[36]

The men who worked to reshape masculinity included Charles B. Dusenbury. Born in 1861 in Lexington, North Carolina, Dusenbury's labors both in and outside the church garnered him a reputation as one who, though overworked, devoted his life to faithful service to others. To one observer, "He was one who just didn't give up. If he had something to do, he'd just do it."[37] Dusenbury's habitual walks up and down Asheville's hills were a familiar sight to the city's residents, who welcomed his routine pastoral calls. Dusenbury founded Asheville's Calvary Presbyterian church in 1881, the Catholic Hill School in 1891 and the Presbyterian Parochial School in 1894. After fire destroyed the Catholic Hill School in 1917, killing seven students, Dusenbury successfully petitioned Asheville's school board to build its replacement, Stephens-Lee High School.[38] Dusenbury also played an instrumental role in founding the Young Men's Institute (YMI), a social, educational, spiritual, and cultural haven for blacks. White citizens dubbed him a race diplomat, and many proclaimed him a "peace-maker and peace-keeper."[39] Biltmore estate owner George Vanderbilt, prompted in part by his friendship with Dusenbury, financed construction of the YMI building in 1893. In 1906, Dusenbury joined a coalition of black leaders who bought the YMI for $10,000. Shortly thereafter, Dusenbury began the popular YMI band. His son Paul followed in his footsteps, becoming leader of Stephens-Lee High School band in 1941.[40] In all that he did, his wife shared in his work. Dusenbury's union with Lula Martin Dusenbury, a graduate of Scotia Seminary in Concord, produced seven children. They reputedly worked "side by side in complete sympathy." Though Dusenbury's life had been hard, his life's work had been a delight. Towards the end of his life, he remarked "I feel my work is finished."[41]

For North Carolina's middle-class black men, racial uplift encompassed several dimensions and approaches rooted in a commitment to community and the fostering of a respectable manhood. The pliable nature of gender roles predicated by changing times and evolving needs dictated that black men define and display their manhood in various and seemingly contradictory ways. Community proved central to this dynamic. Manhood is often viewed from a binary perspective: men versus women or black versus white. But the dynamic between men and different community spaces is also conceptually rich. How does community function in diverse places? And how do these spaces shape expressions of manhood?

This book explores the construction of male and female gender roles in African-American communities in the early twentieth-century South and expands our knowledge of elite black manhood beyond the canon of great African-American leaders (Du Bois, Washington, Garvey) or "best man" ideology that has obfuscated alternate meanings of politics, manhood, and leadership. The individuals and institutions this book examines challenge the notion that cultural experts, or elite leaders, are shaped from the top down.[42] This study resists narrow definitions of black intellectualism and looks at how local communities produced leaders from the bottom up. African Americans used a number of cultural institutions to voice and claim authority. While they were surely influenced by nationalist propaganda (both internal and external) that distilled race and gendered prescriptions for racial progress or preservation, it is evident that such dictates did not prevent local community leaders from debating salient issues and fashioning their own expert solutions.

Because black manhood is still a problematic concept in America today, *Black Manhood and Community Building in North Carolina* provides historical context that is useful to current debates about the "endangered" state of African-American males.[43] As evidenced by the Million Man March of 1995, performances of African-American manhood resound loudly. At the march, which was led by Nation of Islam minister Louis Farrakhan, speakers emphasized the need for manhood, self-respect, respect for women, devotion to family, and repentance. The march prompted lingering questions over why women were not invited to participate and is a reminder of the potency and divisiveness inherent in gendered activism among African Americans, which is a reflection of their position within and outside black communities.[44]

The chapters that follow examine African-American men's inner and outer worlds through their community-building work. Chapter 1 examines North Carolina Baptist Convention leaders' efforts to make their churches and themselves more manly. Fearing that their churches were becoming feminized, they sought to weaken black church women's home missionary work. At the same time, black men campaigned to assume more of "women's work" by engaging in social service activity. The rhetoric of masculinization within the church influenced the dialogue and activity of North Carolina's black men and women as they fought to assert and redefine the influence of their respective genders within their churches.

Chapter 2 examines how black men groomed black boys into industrious and respectable men. While histories of African-American life under Jim Crow have revealed in great detail the rhetoric and strategies black women used to enhance the morality and respectability of young black girls, less attention has been paid to the collective and similar efforts of both sexes to bolster the character and gender identity of boys. Indigenous religious, educational, and social movements spearheaded by black men aimed to relieve the "boy problem." The Baptist State Sunday School Convention; schools such as the Mary Potter School in Oxford, North Carolina; and the Young Men's Institute sought to tend to boys defined as drifting. Such boys were considered passive and malleable. While drifting boys had the potential to be shaped into respectable men, in an unsavory environment, they could also turn bad.

To fend off this consequence, black men offered boys wholesome diversions, counseled temperance in thought and behavior, and instructed them in how to lead virtuous and manly lives. Part of this project of masculinization sought to reinforce black boys' fidelity to domestic concerns. Men's work in public institutions addressed private issues as men such as George Shaw, principal of the Mary Potter School, helped his male students overcome broken home environments. Men like George Shaw believed that both men and women shared the responsibility for crafting wholesome domestic spaces.

Chapter 3 assesses the construction and contestation of black manhood within private male-dominated spaces. The proceedings of North Carolina's Grand Lodge of Prince Hall Masons reveal the importance of gender to men and how it was retooled over time to allow for uplifting images of black manhood. This task proved challenging for Prince Hall Masons. They struggled to define what constituted respectable manhood amid the perceived threat of rival factions within their ranks, the growing calls for fraternity men to embrace a more militant politics, and, most notably, conflicts with women in their auxiliary (the Order of the Eastern Star) over work autonomy.

Chapter 4 explores the institutional efforts of North Carolina's leading black men to promote racial pride, progress, and a dignified manhood within the black race while fostering interracial dialogue with whites. Though black men dominated the public events as spokespersons, black women played critical roles in these communal enterprises. Interracial gatherings at Emancipation Day and state fair events spoke simultaneously to black and white audiences, often producing multiple and conflicting messages about the meaning of racial progress and equality. Over time, strategies for racial progress within these institutions evolved from a philosophy that emphasized good feelings between the races to one that endorsed more militant and uncompromising approaches. The self-help leadership preferred by men such as Charles Hunter thus fell into disfavor after World War I and the rise of New Negro ideology in the 1920s.

While this book stresses the community work of black men alongside black women, it also recognizes the continued viability of black men in formal politics after disfranchisement. These men remained invested in voting and sought elected positions. In spite of great odds (in Charlotte, African-American voter registration plummeted from 2,200 in 1902 to 51 in 1903), some blacks registered and voted in the general elections. Additionally, black men persisted in the political development of their cities and state, even if on a much reduced scale. In Charlotte, black Republicans advertised a caucus meeting in 1902 to consider issues important to them. Black newspapers also commented in varying degrees on political campaigns and candidates on the national level. Moreover, black physician Manassa Thomas Pope, having found a loophole in the state disfranchisement law, voted in the same district as staunch disfranchisement proponent and racial demagogue Josephus Daniels. Pope also ran unsuccessfully for Raleigh's mayor in a 1919 election that, until recently, has lacked scholarly attention.

Black men also demonstrated their lingering interest in traditional political matters by holding membership in black political clubs. The Twentieth Century Voters Club of Raleigh and the Colored Voters' League of North Carolina are but two examples. While black men retained their voice in the political system, the stress of this book remains the cultural terrain inhabited by black men, a terrain that has been obscured historically due to the emphasis on traditional politics for black men and the effects of disfranchisement and Jim Crow on that terrain. While it is true that black men mobilized themselves politically in response to these blows, that is only part of the story of their efforts during the Jim Crow era. The ongoing campaign by black men to reclaim the franchise and citizenship rights did not, in and of itself, define them or their manhood. Men's political goals accompanied rather than superseded the impulse for social and cultural uplift initiatives.[45]

Black men's imperative to serve the interests of the whole of black society was complicated by an equally strong impulse to promote a gender consciousness that placed their manhood front and center. Boxed in by myriad ideological pressures arising from within and outside the black community, black men's ongoing dialogue with black women activists produced moments of consensus and tension as each group campaigned for similar goals: the uplift of the race and their sex.

1

What Can He Do?

African-American Churchmen Confront
the Black Women's Era

At the 1908 general meeting of the North Carolina Black Baptist Convention, corresponding secretary Calvin Scott Brown addressed the tender subject of women's position within the church body. The question of women's place had generated considerable debate among the churchmen in their proceedings. Discussion had focused on whether women should function primarily as assistants, or "help-meets," to men's religious and social vocations or whether they should conduct an independent work. As part of his report to the convention, Brown expressed growing frustration about the autonomy of the women's activities. "It purports now to be contributory to this body, but in reality no organization was ever more independent in its work," he claimed.

A year later, Baptist convention leader John Alston Whitted expressed an opposing view. "It is the opinion of some that the women should not have a definite work and make that work their task," Whitted said. "We differ with such an opinion. If the women find they can better do a definite work . . . in the name of God, we bid them go on."[1]

What explains the complex attitudes of these black churchmen toward black women's church activism—their calls for women's deference, on one hand, and autonomy, on the other? And what does such rhetoric suggest about black men's racial leadership and roles as men and Christians during a period of both increasing racial hostility toward and anxiety about a "women's era"?

Between 1880 and 1920, many middle-class white men in America began to see the Victorian gender system that touted women's ability to cultivate moral citizens as a threat to their manhood. In the early days of the American Republic, white middle-class Protestant Americans energetically paired woman's presumed religious nature with men's "innate" business acumen to craft a moral capitalistic society.[2] This union between women's moral strengths and men's business interests was designed to temper men's selfish pursuit of private gains. The shift from an entrepreneurial economy to a corporate consumer culture that emphasized greed and materialism, however, prompted fears among white middle-class men that they were becoming emasculated by feminine appeals for self-restraint. Women's efforts to use their moral activism as a catalyst to extend their influence beyond the domestic realm only fed men's anxieties. These turn-of-the-century tensions generated a crisis of masculinity. In response, men launched masculinization campaigns that sought to recode church work as manly.[3]

These broader cultural debates over male power and privilege struck close to home for many middle-class black churchmen in North Carolina, where they were ensnared in an environment of disfranchisement and legalized segregation. Some black men saw a gender framework in which black men and women worked together for racial uplift as appropriate and necessary. This perspective placed primacy on a legacy of racial oppression and discrimination that both sexes had endured since slavery. While these black men did not abandon all belief in a gender hierarchy within the church, they were willing to expand the vocabulary of gender and racial leadership to include women. But others, ever conscious of the rhetoric of a crisis in masculinity swirling about them, perceived threats to their manhood as triply endangering—to their status as men, as black men, and as Christians. As white male Protestants, such as those in the Men and Religion Forward movement, sought to pair a "muscular Christianity" with an emergent business and consumer culture, so too black Baptist men endeavored to reconcile a manly religion with the rise of Jim Crow and what they perceived as a surge in black women's influence. Like Protestant white men, black Baptist men tried to lure more men into the church as members and preachers, worked to increase men's presence within social service work, and fought to control churchwomen's finances.[4]

The gendered conversations among black Baptists in the early half of the twentieth century were part of a larger internal dialogue in the black community about the relationships between gender, public space, and community activism. Such struggles played out in other southern black religious denominations, such as the Colored Methodist Episcopal Church.

In that context, black Methodist leaders tussled with churchwomen over the meaning of independent activism. Black Methodist women openly challenged male dominance by lobbying for equal rights for women parishioners. Such agitation on the question of woman's rights began in 1909.[5] North Carolina's black Baptist men hoped to reassert a potent manhood, to a large degree through suppressing (including replicating) churchwomen's autonomous work.

The Black Baptist State Convention, which was organized in Goldsboro, North Carolina, in 1867 by ten black ministers, rose slowly to prominence within the state.[6] The black Baptist convention initiated its mission after securing advice and financial support from North Carolina's white Baptist association as part of a much-heralded cooperation movement wherein black and white Baptist men worked together to promote Christianity and better racial understanding. The goals of the black Baptist convention included providing financial assistance to Shaw University, educating young men called to preach, promoting education for all the state's residents, providing missionaries to Africa, bringing the Gospel to "destitute" parts of the state, encouraging "the proper care of indigent orphan children and destitute and aged ministers of the gospel," and forming cooperative alliances with the American Baptist Home Mission Society and the Foreign Mission of the United States, both of which were white-dominated national organizations.[7]

The Women's Baptist Convention was formed in 1884. In its constitution, black women stated that their organization sought to establish and improve Baptist home mission societies in all Baptist churches and destitute portions of the state, support the Grant Orphan Asylum at Oxford, awaken interest in Bible study and other "good books at home," establish fireside schools in every home, and influence families to attend Sunday school and church services.[8]

Inherent in the missions of both conventions was a claim to self-government. This democratic principle informed all their work, from publicizing and distributing information for larger communities of people to implementing church-supported programs. The freedom to represent and voice individual interests within the conventions, moreover, gave both black men and women power to negotiate with each other regarding stewardship of the church and church bodies.

While it was multifaceted and grounded in democratic principles, the public sphere of the Black church became contested as men and women aspired to own and cultivate a "definite work."[9] Throughout these gendered deliberations, which were informed by Victorian ideology, Christian theology, broader political and cultural changes such as disfranchisement, and a discourse intent on "masculinizing" religion, black Baptist men were challenged by a dual desire to satisfy the needs of the race and those of their gender.

Seeking Common Ground, Defining Place

The violent racial politics of the 1890s reinforced the black community's need to work together for racial uplift. During the 1890s, southern states passed laws or constitutional amendments depriving African Americans of voting rights. Jim Crow laws were later passed, instituting segregation and discrimination in virtually every facet of life. In response, blacks came to value association in formal and informal groups. Black clubs, lodges, and societies sprang up in North Carolina as the impulse to organize gained renewed currency. In these settings, members could speak out on important issues and stretch their leadership abilities. Black community life coalesced around churches, lodges, and fraternal groups, all of which fostered the growth of individual and group character.

Following Reconstruction, black churches played a fundamental role in the communal life of North Carolina. Between one-third and one-half of all black North Carolinians attended church during the period 1877 to 1900. Within this milieu of association and cooperation, many black churchmen supported coeducation for black women and the proposition that women's public activism and racial uplift were symbiotic activities. Augustus Shepard, who spoke about the "Opportunity and Responsibility of the Christian Woman" at the 1909 meeting of the North Carolina Baptist Sunday School Convention, was one of many men who spoke of the need for black men to support their women. "God never made a great man without making a great woman. . . . The men of the race need never hope to rise while the women are down."[10] Speaking on the subject of "The Education of Our Girls: Our Relation to It," Dr. A. M. Moore addressed the importance of women's education. "Womanhood and motherhood are the foundation of all races and people," he said, "and a woman properly educated will be reverenced and respected by all."[11]

Nicholas Frank Roberts, president of the state's black Baptist Sunday School Convention, even went so far as to proclaim that the group "ever recognized the equality of woman with man." He boasted that his religious organization, unlike others that he refused to identify specifically, respected the abilities of its "noble woman" by appointing them as delegates and officers within the convention.

> Not very far back in this closing century woman was not needed in some of our religious bodies save to furnish fans and handkerchiefs to the consecrated delegates, sweating over points of order, and to have the meals ready at the close of a prolonged session in which nothing was done except to elect a moderator, with a motion to elect some of the other important officers pending.[12]

Yet many black middle-class men and women understood and subscribed to white beliefs regarding separate spheres ideology, a belief system inscribed within the racial and gender hierarchy of the South. In an increasingly hostile racial climate, black men and women in the late nineteenth century called upon all black women, particularly those in the middle to upper classes, to behave in a manner appropriate for a "lady."

Race leaders had long considered the bolstering of black women's status as "ladies" essential to realizing the goal of racial equality. Even women's rights supporters such as Frederick Douglass stressed that black women's proper role was as wives and mothers, a perspective that was similar to that expressed by white men and reflected hegemonic conceptions of male superiority. Faced with the economic and political limitations imposed by segregation, the black middle class began to place increasing social and political value on boosting the race's morality. J. C. Smith, editor of *The Messenger* newspaper in Charlotte, believed that "woman is the noblest piece of God's work" and that women should "occupy their proper sphere— next to the angels." His wife, Annie Blackwell, concurred, saying that woman's place was in the home and that black women should "follow the example of our best white women and let them not do things or go places white ladies of standing don't visit."[13]

The elevation of the home as the center of black life refuted theories of racial degeneration that portrayed blacks as morally corrupt and "uncivilized." As part of North Carolina's disfranchisement campaign, white supremacists used the home as a weapon against blacks' claim to equal citizenship. Brandishing rhetoric that accused black men of a lack of manly restraint toward white women, architects of disfranchisement also lambasted black womanhood by casting aspersions on the ability of black women to make good homes. The debate about black morality, particularly the morality of black women, became part of white society's preoccupation with Victorian values. In the nineteenth century, white men constructed a desexualized womanhood that ennobled white women and placed them on pedestals of purity and virtuosity. Whereas white men asserted that black women were sexually voracious, they stripped white women of sexuality and transformed them from "sinners to saints."[14] To have black women appear in public spaces designated as male only, to have them interact and linger alongside men, raised doubts in black and white minds about the legitimacy of black women's claim to true womanhood and led whites to question black men's fitness for and understanding of politics.[15] Efforts by the black community to purify the "defective" home thus became laden with political and gendered import.

Black men and women who subscribed to the discourses of separate spheres undermined an African-American historical tradition that viewed public spaces, especially black churches, as sites of active engagement for both sexes. While it is important not to oversimplify this racial tradition, it was in these public spaces, protected from the harsh reality of Jim Crow politics, that black men and women strengthened communal bonds, nurtured race unity, exercised democratic principles, and plotted racial strategy.[16] The black church's location as a public sphere for both sexes allowed for the airing of an array of ideas, complaints, and emotions, either orally or in correspondence, without undue sanction. As a civically minded structure that encouraged free and open debate, the church facilitated the engagement of black churchmen and women in collective problem-solving.

This complex mix of racial ideology found expression in other church denominations. For example, William Fonvielle complained of an excess of women delegates at the A.M.E. Zion's general conference. "Some of them are good friends of mine," he said. "But it is but fair for this writer to say that he does not believe in women delegates to the General Conference. It looks like a bad precedent, as was beautifully demonstrated, several times during the sessions. There seems to be nothing in it for the Church."[17] His perspective found validation in the broader debates about male authority and woman's place that occurred at the turn of the century. In his essay titled "The Taint of the Bicycle," Fonvielle vigorously admonished the twentieth century's New Woman. He borrowed from the rhetoric of Frances Willard, who, in her book *A Wheel within a Wheel: How I Learned to Ride the Bicycle* (1895), linked the technological wonder to expanding opportunities for women beyond traditional boundaries. Willard believed that by mastering the bicycle, women could master the world. Yet for Fonvielle, the bicycle,

> called into existence that modern monstrosity, the New Woman. The new woman goes out of her home at unreasonable hours of the day and night. She refuses to be a wife and a mother in the home; feeding her husband on baker's bread and canned goods. She makes up her bed at night and sweeps and dusts when she gets ready. She neglects her children and dresses like a man. What with stiff hat and laundried shirt, high collar and four-in-hand tie. She wears low cut vests and cutaway coats. Dressed in this garb, plus a substitution for pantaloons, she rode and pretended to be happy in her new role imitations of man. Perhaps she was happy.[18]

The black church has historically assumed multiple identities—as a safe haven for the black community and as a space where men and women could devise and plan political strategy, sustain social cohesion, nurture race consciousness, and advance education. At the onset of the Jim Crow era, the black church provided the race with the power to idealize, authenticate, and represent itself in opposition to prevailing ideas of white supremacy, white male privilege, and existing racist institutions. Women found the ability to represent and transform themselves against the grain of patriarchy within church walls as well, part of a broader history in which black women exercised autonomy and self-reliance. Churches provided nontraditional sites for women to develop intellectual and leadership abilities. Yet paradoxically, the black church has reinforced codes of social propriety and behavior among its members by stressing a hierarchy in which men dominated. Scholar Cheryl Townsend Gilkes says this paradox explains why "while black religion is patriarchal, it sometimes exhibits an ambivalent patriarchy." She posits that the duality and conflict inherent in black women's roles is representative of the "multiple consciousness underlying issues of gender, race, and their intersection."[19] The term "partner" thus at times carried conservative meanings. While North Carolina's Baptist men acknowledged the need for activist black women in their work, many sought to prescribe the manner in which such activity was conducted.

When the Baptist State Convention convened in Raleigh in 1884, President Lizzie Neely and Secretary Sally Mial of the Women's Baptist Home Mission Convention sent a letter to the men outlining their organization's proposed plan of work. Their later stated that

> we, the sisters of our denomination, having organized ourselves into what is known as the Woman's Baptist Home Mission Convention of the state of N.C., for the purpose of aiding you in the work of Missions, especially among the women, therefore, we ask your prayers in our work, also your hearty co-operation that we, as your weak sisters in the Lord, may be able to do some of the small things that will honor Jesus. We offer our beloved sister, B. E. Green, our traveling Missionary, to aid you in stirring up the sisters of the churches and organizing them into Christian work. Dear brethren, please pray unitedly for us. Be sure that you have our united prayers that God may be with you in this session to bless and enable you to do more for Christ than ever before.[20]

The women's invitation to cooperate, laced with a delicate appeal for independent authority, would be repeated often in women's exchanges with black Baptist men. Invoking gendered descriptions such as "weak" and "small," Baptist women sought to carve out public space for their own ambitions without appearing to transcend their "sphere." President Pattie G. Shepard said that she didn't intend to "take charge of the pulpits and preach, but we want to preach to the children around our fireside." Appropriately, the black Baptist women's convention took as its motto "A Christian in Every Home."[21] Interestingly enough, North Carolina's Baptist Educational and Home Missionary Convention's first missionaries were men. Four of the convention's "ablest men," a general missionary and three district missionaries, were sent throughout the state to hold Ministerial Institutes and do "house to house" service. Their activities helped challenge counter-narratives that held that the "Negro Baptists had no men of note." Such work also presaged black women's future church activity, which took its initial inspiration from men.[22]

Yet black Baptist home missionary women such as Sally Mial (Raleigh, N.C.) and Roberta Bunn (Selma, N.C.) ultimately felt emboldened to heed a higher authority that sanctioned their work beyond traditional borders. These women believed themselves "called by God" to assume the special work of converting their people at home and abroad to a Christianized, and thus elevated, world view.[23] For many black foreign missionaries, American intervention overseas provided a "door of opportunity" whereby occupied peoples such as Haitians, after having been exposed to civilizing agents, could ultimately govern themselves. They felt that examples of successful black self-government abroad might indicate to American white society the capacity of American blacks for civil engagement in the political arena.[24] Black Baptist women, especially, felt confident in their ability to impart lessons of moral living to the "uncivilized." Their gendered interpretations of biblical texts and endorsement of feminist theology reinforced women's unique ability to Christianize homes and educate the masses. The spread of Christianity also meant an elevation in the race's womanhood. As culture carriers, black women exercised intelligence and morality in the home that set a standard for the race as a whole. These women believed that through their activism they were responsible for not only the evolution of the race but also the evolution of civilization.

Black women's religious activity found inspiration from secular women's rights groups, and religious work informed and underlay much of black clubwomen's activity. Administering community clean-up days and visiting the sick provided invaluable organizational and leadership experience. Additionally, home mission work allowed women to hone their networking and fund-raising skills. For black women and men, church and race work were synonymous rather than dichotomous concepts. While they might not have made brazen attempts to "take charge of the pulpits," black churchwomen did not underplay their "god-given" talent and aspirations to spread the faith and improve the race.

Black Baptist women in North Carolina accepted their tasks with zeal. Convention records annually chronicled women's successes and travails with home missionary work. These vivid testimonials reflected an unwavering faith that they were the best ones to spread Christianity among their sex. "Spent all of my time away back in the country where the women knew but little of our work and many of them had not heard of our convention," testified Mrs. Sessoms. "I find that the christian women, even in these destitute places are willing to work, but just don't know where to begin. There are many weights that must be put aside, yet we believe the light is coming, if we who are on the field do not get discouraged. We are making appeals for the dark corners of our own State."[25]

In addition to bringing light to downtrodden women, members of the convention also tried to indoctrinate the most impressible. The Cradle Roll Department of the women's convention sought to interest mothers in the early religious training of their children and to recruit babies into the Baptist Sunday schools. Cradle Roll Department superintendents encouraged mothers to read Bible stories with their children. Babies were also given certificates signed by the pastor, the Sunday school superintendent, and the Cradle Roll superintendent confirming their membership within the organization. Another group, the Sunshine Band, instructed children in mission work and Bible study.[26]

Men also seemed eager for women to assume their religious work. Rev. Hill reiterated God's desire for "individual service—each one in his own place. I am with you in all your work, in mind and heart, if not in person." In language that blurred gender distinctions further, Rev. Crow added, "I am with you and feel that I belong to the [women's] convention, because we all belong to God."[27] Speaking to the women's convention in 1906, J. A. Whitted said that he was "very much interested in this convention, and I am anxious that you should enlarge your borders by getting into every home." Whitted noted the importance of women's contributions to home training, situating their work within the broad reach of African-American experience. "As much as they stood in need of education, as much as they needed property, the greatest need of this people emerged from slavery with all its stains, and greatest need for many years thereafter was home training."[28]

Many black women viewed it their womanly duty to inoculate the home against outbreaks of moral deficiency and to build character and integrity within black youth. The importance they attached to sustaining good homes increased at the turn of the century as whites intensified their efforts to denigrate the race by denigrating the honor of black women. White intellectuals such as Howard Odum, a professor at the University of North Carolina at Chapel Hill, argued that the weak moral fiber of black women was responsible for the race's poor home life. Black clubwomen began a Better Homes campaign to counter attacks on black womanhood and assumptions about black debauchery by stressing better, cleaner, and purer homes among the black masses. Such campaigns also reflected class divisions within the black community as middle-class black women encouraged their working-class counterparts to become "respectable." As a result of these and other activities, some black women declared themselves equal to men since they assumed primary responsibility for a key aspect of the race's betterment—the cultivation of a respectable black manhood and womanhood. As Sarah Dudley Pettey, a grade-school teacher in New Bern and a columnist for the A.M.E. weekly *Star of Zion*, observed, "Men go from home into the world to execute what women have decreed."[29] Women such as Petty saw the home as a vehicle for asserting black women's equal standing with men and a location from which to extend women's activism into the community. Operating within religious, civic, and social service organizations, black women buttressed "good homes" rhetoric to campaign against the scourge of alcoholism and to lobby for better sanitation and educational facilities.

Besides providing the foundation for black women's domestic activism, the home functioned to boost black manhood. Home, which functioned as a refuge where black men could exhibit dignified, respectable behavior without the threat of white reproach, provided the foundation for the race's political virility. Owning homes and eliminating domestic chaos and disorder, black social critics urged, was critical to fitting African Americans for public governance.

The concept of the home as a male sanctuary and instrument for race elevation resonated among the race's prominent citizens. Rev. Richard Carroll of South Carolina believed that it would be difficult for African Americans to govern the country if they could not govern their homes. He claimed that "the house is the greatest institution on earth for good or evil; you can't make a great, good, patriotic and intelligent race if you live in low, wicked, filthy, and ungodly homes."[30] At a meeting of the Tuskegee Women's Club, Mrs. Booker T. Washington described the home as a safe haven for men, "a place into which any man might enter without fearing for his life."[31] C. C. Spaulding, an executive with the North Carolina Mutual Insurance Company and a Baptist Sunday school leader, stressed that "there is a great need of our emphasizing the importance of better homes."[32] He recalled an interview conducted with a 92-year-old black man, who, when asked what he thought "the most beautiful word in the English language, replied 'Home.'"[33] Domesticity, race uplift, Christianity, and gender were closely connected and were priorities for both sexes.

Black Baptist men outlined the particular burdens women carried as home missionary workers. Rev. A. B. Vincent encouraged sisters to set "the standard high and strive to live and bring our families up to it." J. A. Whitted also advised that the women conduct themselves in a manner commendable to the church and its members. "Brother" Richardson told women that in addition to their temperance work, they should "not fail to give the divorces a blow."[34] Women, often with men's support, felt that their sex should "nurse the sick, raise the fallen, strengthen the weak, comfort the bereaved and rear the orphans."[35]

Yet intense discussion over exactly what role Baptist women played in relation to men remained a constant of convention proceedings. If this was indeed a "women's era," black men felt compelled to steer its direction. Church paper titles such as "The Relation of the Woman's Baptist State Convention to the Convention," "What Woman Can Do?" "Woman's Part in Kingdom Development," and "The Women's Work among Us," made the subject of churchwomen's work a focus. The record of women's activities and dialogue about their role within the North Carolina Baptist Convention suggest a complicated union of race, gender, and Christian identity. If the convention provided space where black women could amplify their voices and create spheres of independent influence, more often than not they found themselves in a perpetual state of negotiation with men for that authority.

A Call for Cooperation

The black Baptist State Convention of North Carolina began the twentieth century with a renewed call for cooperation and unity. Church spokesmen appealed for more unity among the convention's affiliated societies, including the Women's Baptist Home Mission Convention.[36] Beginning in 1900, membership in the general convention began to decline as many men left the state following the racially charged politics that accompanied the passage of that year's disfranchisement amendment. "A political upheaval such as the State had not known before was felt everywhere," recorded J. A. Whitted, adding that "much of the enthusiasm of previous years was lost.... The work so fairly under way was greatly retarded."[37] To compensate and boost morale, black Baptists proudly proclaimed the era one of organization and cooperation between men and women. President

Albert Witherspoon Pegues, addressing the convention in 1901, remarked that Baptists must "die out of self for the good of others; and the man who is not willing to die out of self never accomplished much for Christ." He continued, "The man who undertakes to do anything by himself will fail. The social, co-operation principle should be cherished. We live and succeed by working together."[38]

Within the black community, calls for cooperation were part of the historical role of the black church as a promoter of nation-building and democracy. The black church, which E. Franklin Frazier called a "nation within a nation," situated itself both within and apart from the dominant white society and its racist institutions. It constructed itself as an institution that fostered collective well-being. It became a protected communal space where black men and women could confront and contest race inequities. And yet North Carolina's leading black Baptist men manipulated the meaning of cooperation to emphasize black manhood. They waged a counterattack within their own community against what they deemed as major threats to their gender interests. Many churchmen increasingly felt their masculine authority spinning out of control as they witnessed the emergence of rival factions rise within their ranks. One of these factions they identified as churchwomen.

By the turn of the century, the growing influence and competence of Baptist churchwomen had begun to gnaw at the confidence of churchmen. The women's convention had been presented with its first missionary, Sally Mial, and was taking on increased administrative roles and organizational oversight. Male convention leaders increasingly felt that the achievements of Baptist men were lagging behind those of Baptist women. In an address to men at the general convention in 1910, J. A. Whitted said with chagrin, "When compared with the women in their convention considering our advantages we are far behind."[39] While the men's convention had recently raised $1,700 for the church, the women had raised $2,300, despite the fact that fewer resources were available to them. As Whitted remarked, "They have undertaken specific work and they are carrying out their obligations to the letter, and yet I am told that their president comes to this convention from year to year without a cent of compensation and without her railroad fare." His parting shot, meant to arouse his male brethren from their complacency, warned that "if you do not wake up[,] your sisters who are regarded the weaker vessels will leave you far in the distance."[40]

Baptist male leaders also considered "disastrous" a movement to inaugurate a rival black Baptist convention in the state. The exact nature of
the controversy is not explained in church minutes, but the dispute so
concerned church leaders that they attempted to reconcile with the new
faction. "We could hardly believe that our brethren would attempt a thing
so fatal to the peace and welfare of our great Church [as a rival organiza-
tion]," C. S. Brown bemoaned. Brown spoke to a mass meeting of brethren
he felt had gone astray. There he officially protested a proposed plan that
would establish a separate Baptist convention. In the meeting, he noted
that the group had lodged no official grievances with convention leaders
and that there was no indication that Brown and other state leaders had
treated them discourteously. Despite his warning as "the recognized head
of the Missionary Baptist Churches of the State" that "any effort to destroy
its supremacy could be regarded with nothing less than an open rebellion,"
plans continued to institute the rival convention. Church records indicate
that the issue remained unresolved, apparently for years. Little additional
context was needed when a 1912 correspondence report read: "This convention, be it said to its credit, has offered every honorable proposition for
harmony, but the opposition has preferred to continue hostility. It is self-
evident that no two conventions can occupy the same territory without
friction and ill-feeling."[41]

In response to this threat to unity, the convention called for cooperation
across all its affiliated bodies. These included the Baptist Sunday School
Convention, the Baptist Young People's Union, and the women's convention. As part of its structure, the male-led general Baptist convention saw
itself as the head of all these organizations. However gender-neutral cooperation purported to be, the women's group remained the focus of black
Baptist leaders' attention as they worked to enforce the principle of unifica-
tion and project a manly leadership. The general convention's "committee
to adjust relations" met with representatives of the women's state convention in 1901 to discuss the plan of cooperation. The committee members
found that the women were "anxious to co-operate with us in our work and
have agreed to refer the question of plans to their executive committee for
adjustment." One of the plans the committee proposed sought to have the
Educational and Missionary Convention appoint a board of supervisors
to "advise" the women in their work.[42]

Two years later, public space within the religious body was reconfigured to reflect a revised power-sharing agreement between the sexes. Male Baptists increasingly sought to control what occurred within the women's organization by instituting constitutional clauses stipulating that the "Advisory Board to the Woman's Convention of North Carolina shall keep in touch with the Woman's Convention, shall advise them whenever necessary and shall make annual reports and recommendations to the Educational and Missionary Convention of North Carolina, respecting the work of the women." Outwardly, at least, women seemed to concur with the democratic sentiments behind the concept of cooperation. The General Baptist Convention's constitutional objectives included a willingness to "cooperate with the Chicago Women's Baptist Home Mission Society and the Missionary and Baptist Convention of North Carolina to send the gospel to Africa."[43] Addressing the men's convention in 1904, Roberta Bunn described relations between Baptist men and women as that of brothers and sisters. Though there might occasionally be points of misunderstanding, the bond was "indestructible. It is so very close until you cannot touch the one without touching both."[44] The metaphor of a united supportive family inserted the private realm into public space. The use of familial language, however, also reinforced a paternalistic hierarchy between men and women. But Bunn believed that Baptist women could naturally merge their domestic role, which included Christian love and support of men, with a public role as civilizing agents. Saying that her group of Baptist women only sought to help the men, Bunn drew from the scriptures as she justified women's "rightful" place in church work.

> Sometime ago the brethren took fright, thinking the women wanted to preach; so they began to preach from almost every pulpit, using as a text, 1 Cor. 14:34–35: "Let your women keep silence in the churches," etc. If the brethren will read Ezekiel 22:30, they will see where the WORD says: "I sought for a man among them that should make up the hedge, and stand in the gap before me for the land, that I should not destroy it; but I found none." And then brethren turn to Ezekiel 23:2 and see that he found two women.[45]

Roberta Bunn's gendered interpretation of biblical texts provided a theological justification for women's church work. Just as black male ministers invested religious texts with new meaning to affirm racial equality, black churchwomen appropriated religious language to further their work.[46] They were also influenced by the secular women's movement, which sought to dismantle the artificial barrier placed between women's home life and the public world of business and politics. Bunn and other Baptist women's inversion of traditional theology to satisfy personal and professional objectives illustrate what Evelyn Brooks Higginbotham has called the "multivalent" meaning of texts.[47] Such textual interpretations are rich with social and radical implications. As Rita Felski has observed, "Radical impulses are not inherent in the formal properties of texts; they can be realized only through interactions between texts and readers, so that it becomes necessary to situate the . . . text in relation to the interests and expectations of potential audiences."[48]

Despite their appropriation of biblical texts, Baptist women in North Carolina were reluctant to break free from the church's gender hierarchy. For example, they did not challenge the exclusively male composition of church clergy. Rather, they attempted to observe what Rosemary Ruether and Eleanor McLaughlin have termed a "radical obedience."[49] While believing themselves to be loyal and faithful stewards of the men's religious mission, churchwomen sought to maintain the independence of their work.[50]

Black Baptist women increasingly questioned whether their male counterparts were sincere about the principle of cooperation. Dr. S. N. Vass, speaking before the women's 1905 convention meeting in Lumberton, suggested that women send more delegates to the general convention so that the men could be better informed of their work. At the same time, he praised the women as "colaborers" and suggested that they could direct their own activities without undue interference from men. "I believe women should be free and not driven to anything, Vass said. "I think you should have something to do with the State work. The women have a large share in making things just as they should be in North Carolina." In response, "Sister" S. C. Johnson shared her reservations about more women attending the general convention. "We would like to go, but the brethren treat us so coldly, we do not like to get in their way." Sally Mial and Lizzie L. Walker attempted to soften Johnson's blunt critique by acknowledging the support from some of the male brethren for their work, adding that "we should not do any thing to drive them from us." In a sharper critique, women's convention president Pattie Shepard spoke of men's shortcomings in the moral instruction of youth. "Why is it that our men do not respect their women?" she asked. "Must be that *we* fail to teach our sons to respect other girls when out of their home" [emphasis mine]. Women's duty, in this instance, involved taking more responsibility for securing race progress. As Shepard noted, "Congregations have been swayed with men's eloquence, and yet where are we?"[51]

The diversity of the remarks of Mial, Shepard, and others is indicative of the fragile tightrope Baptist women traversed as they worked to satisfy the ambitions of the race, in part by demonstrating racial and gender unity (bolstering black manhood) and in part by becoming community and moral leaders through their work. The women's position was supported by their reading of Christian theology. In their view, Christ's teaching affirmed submission to governmental laws, in this case the male hierarchy of the Baptist church. At the same time, they believed that the principles of Christianity included the right to autonomy. Following this logic, black churchwomen felt obliged to engage in activity that encouraged self-definition and self-representation. Baptist churchwomen were thus never completely in agreement with their men and each other regarding their relationship with black churchmen.

Some black Baptist men were dubious about women's devotion to cooperation. C. S. Brown, an active member of the Baptist convention who had been a staunch proponent of cooperation since the concept's inception in 1895, routinely criticized the women's convention for failing to uphold the principle. Brown served as corresponding secretary of the convention. In that capacity, he was charged not only with directing the convention's work but also with addressing and proposing solutions to any defects that threatened to retard the organization's progress. He often relayed the challenges of what he termed the "hardest, most exacting" work to his constituents. "This is not always a pleasant thing to do," Brown confided, "for in doing this duty conscientiously one is likely to find himself compelled to oppose some pet schemes of persons whose friendship he values, but whose policies must be condemned. This has frequently happened in my experience; but, by God's grace, I have never flinched in giving facts as they appear to me." Brown did this work for a quarter of a century and was absent from the convention's annual meetings only three times during that period.[52]

Brown was born in Salisbury on 23 March 1859 to Henry and Flora Brown, mulattos of Scots-Irish descent. Aided by the Freedmen's Association of Philadelphia, Brown began his education at Salisbury. After completing his coursework at age 16, he took a federal government job guarding a national cemetery for Union soldiers in the city. On his salary of $20 a month, he managed to buy land and build a cabin home for his widowed mother and siblings. Brown then began teaching in the public schools of Stokes County. At the age of 17 he had professed his conversion to Christianity and joined the Baptist church in Salisbury. In 1880, he matriculated at Shaw University. Thanks to financial support from Shaw president Henry M. Tupper, Brown finished his education as valedictorian in May 1886 with a bachelor's degree in theology. (Brown later served as Tupper's private secretary.) While in college, he traveled widely across the state, doing mission work and leading revivals. He organized the Baptist Minister's Union for the state. The black press noted his efforts. One publication called him "one of the hardest working men in the state" and a "real leader of all the people of the Negro race in the State as any other man in North Carolina."[53] After Brown was chosen as secretary of the Baptist State Convention, he was offered a position as pastor at the rural Pleasant Plains Negro Baptist Church near Winton at a salary of $150 a year. He served the church for twenty-five years.[54]

After Brown graduated from Shaw, his work accelerated. Politically, he denounced the state's proposed disfranchisement amendment, a position that required the temporary posting of armed guards around his house. He also participated in several Republican Party political campaigns. Despite this, he did not envision himself in formal politics, even when afforded such opportunities. He twice refused to serve as a delegate to the National Republican Convention and turned down a nomination for Congress. He did, however, serve two years on the County Board of Education and in this manner fulfilled a lifelong goal of "preaching, teaching and lecturing." His more noteworthy accomplishments and duties included pastoring five country churches and baptizing more than 2,000 people; presiding over the Lott Carey Foreign Mission Convention, which sponsored missionary work in Africa; moderating the West Roanoke Baptist Association, which raised $3,000 for education projects each year; acting as corresponding secretary of the Baptist Convention; and editing *The Baptist Sentinel* in Raleigh. Brown's influence was also felt within the state's black secret societies. He served as grand secretary of the Masons, grand auditor of the Odd Fellows, and finance committee member of the Knights of Pythias.[55]

While endeavoring to fill the "hearts of men" with the Bible, redirect souls from "darkness to light," care for the sick, and redeem the "heathen" world, Brown's "pre-eminent desire" was to foster unity within the black Baptist Educational and Home Missionary Convention. "The marvellous results so evident among us, the activity along all lines of Church work, and the advancement in educational enterprises are attributable largely to the awakening occasioned by co-operation," he said. The loyal Baptists of the state, he continued, had for the past eight years united what had previously been a disharmonious and ineffective organization. Baptists had been "wonderful in numbers, but impotent in strength; great in multitudes, but weak in action." But cooperation had given the religious body "broader ideas of duty, and revealed possibilities unthought of. We know ourselves better, and are ready to undertake great things. Whatever course the future may suggest as practicable, we should never cease to appreciate the value of co-operation."[56] Cooperation had also stimulated "manhood and self reliance."[57]

However, black Baptists such as Brown were wary of the ability of cooperation to curb the growing independence of churchwomen. Many attempts had been made shortly after the organization of the women's convention to unite their efforts more closely with men. However, J. A. Whitted felt that "for fear of the change of the autonomy and a final submerging of their Convention [the women] would never consent to the change." While men such as Whitted at times felt that the women accomplished more "existing separate and apart," Brown disagreed.[58] Within his annual reports, he routinely raised doubts about the religious and financial integrity of the Women's Baptist State Convention. In his 1908 report, Brown chastised Baptist women for conducting "heretical proceedings." He prefaced this indictment by endorsing the potential of the women's work, if properly directed. "We desire nothing but the highest welfare of our Woman's Convention, but duty demands me to say that reports indicate their meetings to be nothing short of holiness convocations, mixed largely with Christian Science theories."[59] These gatherings would compromise the health of the entire Baptist body, he believed, until "every Baptist Church will be converted into a Christian Science Temple." Brown's fears about the dilution of the Baptist faith and women's place within it were perhaps not misplaced, given the meaning of Holiness practice for some southerners. Some Holiness followers, for example, tested racial boundaries and provided opportunities for female leaders. Christian Science adherents also challenged gender restrictions as part of their religious doctrine.[60]

For Brown, the bonds between theological and gender heresy were intrinsically linked. He urged Baptists to intervene to assure that Baptist women were "positively commanded to assume their rightful relations to this body as our help-meets." Drawing parallels between the hierarchy of the church and that of a traditional family unit, Brown lamented that the women's convention was not "bound to respect the wishes of the [male] parent organization."[61]

Brown's portrait of Baptist women gone awry served a larger goal of highlighting the dangers inherent in a feminized church structure. Baptist women had revealed themselves, from Brown's perspective, to be soft and emotionally vulnerable to the spreading of subversive doctrine. Brown's rhetoric argued that while black churchmen sought to unify, black churchwomen could only divide.

While admitting that he was discouraged about women's lack of cooperation (read deference to men), Brown refused to be dejected. He proposed a plan to stir the ministry to action and "systematic, co-operative and mutual action . . . among the Convention's State bodies," including, but not exclusive to, the women's group. Yet a note of pessimism crept into his oratory as he challenged men to take up the duties before them. "Are we really Baptists?" "Why are our preachers so indifferent?" "Are they mistaken as to their calling?" "Let us determine here and now to take up the unfinished task like men."[62]

Questions about the merits of the ideal of cooperation thus perplexed Baptist men and women. Were men courting women's support or enticing them to submit to their control? Could black men be blamed for wanting to organize and present a united front? Did protection of their manhood and religious integrity necessitate the suppression of black women's autonomous contributions to church work?

Baptist missionary women such as Sally Mial attempted to defend their work and assuage black men's unease about women's growing visibility. Mial stressed that "we have not outgrown you. We have been given to you to help you. We dare not leave you. You have opened our hearts, and given us increased privileges in the churches, and many of our women are being strengthened for the Masters' use."[63] Mial told her male audience that she and other women had a "peculiar" work to do. "We can go where you can not afford to go. We teach the women to love their husbands, to be better wives and mothers, to make the homes better." Mial appropriated racialist assumptions that black women had greater agency than black men (who, within the southern white supremacist lexicon, were defined as both political actors and beastly rapists) in their community-building and outreach efforts. However, the proposition that black women were somehow less vulnerable to racial violence during Jim Crow and that they had greater leeway than black men within the public sphere is incorrect, as scholars continue to document.[64]

If black women were prepared to go where their brothers dared not tread, some black men aimed to retard their momentum. For black men expressed confidence that they too had been called to do a "peculiar work." Several black men countered the loss of their manly right of suffrage by emphasizing the unique responsibilities (or obligations) that befell them as manly Christians. They focused on the need to cultivate and support more male ministers. Albert W. Pegues touted the education of ministers as "most helpful in uplifting the people." He raised funds to aid Shaw's Theological Department. Pegues reminded the brethren that as "God's ambassadors" they were responsible for recruiting young men into the ministry. "God wants drill masters all over the State, and not recruiting officers and stations," he said.[65]

Rev. A. L. E. Weeks also recognized "the duty and the responsibility devolving upon us. We come as men to assist in developing this great work." Assuring those in Durham that they wouldn't regret having hosted their convention, Weeks insisted "you will see none of us godly men going around with cigars in our mouths, but with the Bible in our hands, anxious to uplift humanity. We are not here to dispute, but to do business for God."[66] The ministers' ability to appropriate a high moral authority heightened in importance when faced with women's claim to do the same. The burden on ministers to be worthy moral stewards did not escape them. "Every preacher that is guilty of immorality, sins not only against God and the church, but he is actually injuring his race in the eyes of the whole world and emboldens the vicious and immoral elements in our race to continue their sinful lives," warned Albert W. Pegues. "We urge . . . our churches and Associations to raise the ministerial standard higher than ever before and all of us here pledge ourselves to visit upon them such punishment as they deserve, when guilty of immorality and we urge our churches to discipline all their members strictly for immorality."[67]

The urgent appeals by black Baptist men to raise moral standards carried gendered as well as racial import. Weeks's anxious plea that men "do business with God" was a none-too-subtle call for manly church work and echoed other movements that sought to defeminize the church. White male Protestants sought to institute manly church work in response to a burgeoning business and consumer culture. To accommodate this new social and commercial order, Protestant men constructed their churches to reflect the manly world of business. Advertising campaigns, both on billboards and in print, announced that the Men and Religion Forward movement was in step with the consumer world and was "Making Religion Efficient" and "Going After Souls on a Business Basis."[68] North Carolina's Baptist men sought to distinguish their work from women's work by staking claim to a business ethos. In their proceedings, Baptist churchmen often referred to their skillful use of "intelligence and business methods."[69] Despite many discouragements, the lingering taunt that the "Baptists have no men," was fast losing currency from the perspective of some Baptist men. Sentimentality, they claimed, was being replaced in the pulpit and pew by Christian intellectuality and efficiency. "From the mountains to the seashore the Negro Baptists are sending men of whom they feel justly proud," Whitted said. "Every known section of the State" was "dotted with secondary Baptist schools," and Shaw University was "in the midst of them, the pride, not only of the Baptists, but the entire race of the country.... The day can not be far distant when every country church, as well as the brick structures of our cities, will be filled with men of intellectuality as well as the Divine Spirit."[70]

"Our Opportunity"

While some black churchmen supported increasing the number and quality of male ministers, others sought to assume "women's duties" as their own. Several black ministers began to decry the absence of their brothers in community affairs, citing their disproportionately small numbers when contrasted with black women.[71] Men such as O. J. Allen, auditor of the Baptist State Convention, proposed a new job title for ministers, that of social services worker. Rather than having ministers strictly attend to the religious needs of the people, Allen welcomed efforts to reach deeper into communities, especially among young people. "Many of us stand off and advise what the young people shall not do—but never advise what is best to do or, in other words, never outline a program in which all the members can participate and receive benefit."[72] Allen pointed to the inspiring work of Dr. J. W. Hariston of Spencer as worthy of emulation. Under Hariston's guidance, Allen said, a "Community Social" was being held each Friday at which old and young met and socialized for two or three hours. These moments of "real pleasure" netted several converts to the church. "Unless the church shall bestir herself and no longer seek merely to be ministered unto and supported simply because she is the church," he cautioned, "but set out to minister in such a way as will make her need and influence felt by making her presence in the community vital, she will soon become the neglected spot in the community."[73]

Within Social Gospel ideology, social welfare activity traditionally had found broad appeal among women, who internalized social "salvation" as their special domain. The Social Gospel movement sought to merge the salvation of the individual with the saving of society. The sacred and secular elements of Christianity were therefore joined in an effort to reproduce a Kingdom on Earth. Black Baptist men's rhetoric about social service work resonated with larger religious masculinization campaigns, which manipulated Social Gospel ideology to produce a more manly church work and sever the close association of women with missionary activity. For white Protestant men, the Social Gospel's call for a religiously inspired social activism meant a transformation in the urban environment. The Social Services Committee of the Men and Religion Forward movement, for example, fashioned a social service work that was distinctly masculine. To counter their fears about appearing "soft" on social matters, middle-class white Protestants asserted control of their communities by shutting down prostitution rings, improving housing and sanitation, and addressing labor unrest. They also worked to recruit young boys in the church under the banner of a "muscular Christianity."[74]

The black church historically had practiced the tenets of Social Gospel teachings. Because of racial restrictions the black community confronted beginning in the late nineteenth century, black churches featured secular as well as religious programming. Consistent with a racial philosophy that stressed self-help, these institutions offered an array of services designed to affect the total person. These included vocational training, health clinics, recreation centers, and libraries. With the rise of industrial capitalism and its attendant problems of child labor and slums, the reform impulse took hold. Progressives sought to cure these social ills by proposing and passing laws that would mediate the excesses of capitalism.

Histories of black churchwomen emphasize the attraction social reform work held for them during this time. Mary Lynch, who was a member of the colored branch of North Carolina's Christian Temperance Union (WCTU) argued that women yearned to vote against the ill effects of the saloon and gambling house. From Lynch's perspective, WCTU members were working to put an end to the base appetites of men. Lynch and other black temperance workers worked to eliminate gambling and the use of alcohol and chewing tobacco among their people. In doing so, they strove to fulfill both Victorian ideals of self-control and race-conscious goals of self-help and respectability.[75] National Baptist churchwomen such as Nannie Helen Burroughs reminded ministers often of their obligation to incorporate social Christianity within their church mission, denouncing those that didn't as "unprogressive" and "sleek, lazy and 'jack leg' preachers."[76]

National race leaders such as Robert R. Moton, Booker T. Washington's successor at Tuskegee, stressed the need for the race to "stop the ravages of disease among our people" and argued that the race needed to be "united to keep black boys from idleness, vice, gambling, and crime; united to guard the purity of black womanhood and I might add, black manhood also." Black spokesmen felt that patrolling the sexual behavior of both men and women was critical to projecting a wholesome moral image. Racial theories addressing black deficiencies in sexuality and reproduction spurred reformist responses from the black community. Beginning in the late nineteenth century, reports of unstable birthrates and high rates of infant mortality increased speculation about black people's degeneracy and ultimate demise. The advent of professionalized medicine brought with it "scientific" evidence of the impending extinction of African Americans due to poor health, lack of child hygiene, and venereal disease. Eugenics and Social Darwinist theories suggested that black men and women were incapable of reproducing or creating healthy babies due to impure sexual activity or an absence of virility. The alleged reproduction woes of African Americans raised questions about the impact of sexuality on the collective advancement of the race.

The sexuality of African Americans during and after slavery was a much-discussed topic among southern whites. During slavery, they castigated black women as sexually wanton and promiscuous and black men as sexually voracious and bestial. During the Jim Crow era, lynching rhetoric designated black men as rapists. Both before and after Reconstruction, black women were victimized by rape at the hands of white men. Thus, "preventing the ravages of diseases" proved a particularly salient topic among African Americans. Leaders stressed the importance of marriage, the establishment of patriarchal households, and the eradication of sexual vice.[77]

Thus, the authors of *Progress of a Race or The Remarkable Advancement of the American Negro*, a paean to black advancement and achievement, emphasized black men's need for self-sacrifice and innovative behavior. "The days of chance are gone, it is only the man who does not wait for things to turn up, but turns up something, that succeeds. Young man, do something; attempt something that will be a benefit to your race. Something ennobling, something enduring; something to elevate manhood and win men to noble, virtuous, upright lives, and your life will not have been lived in vain."[78] This New Negro Man, as advertised in national black periodicals, was bright, conscientious, progressive, and, above all, a doer. New Negro Men, proclaimed the *Voice of the Negro*, were "known according as they do less theorizing and more actual, practical work; according as they turn their vast learning and wealth into simple, kindly helps to the poor, distressed and suffering; and in proportion as they make the play and music and revelry of the high head, the common enjoyment of all."[79] John Campbell Dancy, editor of the *AME Zion Quarterly Review*, also counseled the race to embrace progressive reform. For Dancy, the "man of the hour . . . will keep in touch with all great movements looking to the betterment of the world, and the institution of reforms which will popularize improved conditions in the home, in charities, in school and church life and in the uplift of the world."[80] Black men, Dancy continued, should think less of themselves and more about the community around them. Real men should assume roles as Good Samaritans by alleviating the suffering of others. "There are plenty of men who pose as men who never regard other men's destitution or misfortune as worthy of the slightest consideration, so long as all goes well with them."[81]

North Carolina's black Baptist ministers needed little outside prodding about their responsibility to better social conditions. For black Baptist churchmen, the pursuit of social service activity furthered their objective of injecting more virility in church work. Through social service activism, they aimed to debunk the notion that home mission work was largely the province of women. This is clear in their addresses at annual conventions. Rev. G. W. Bullock, speaking on the "Signs of the Times," proclaimed a new era in black Baptist missionary work. "We must prepare for the new day that is now upon us," he said. "We have thought for a long time that it was right to let the women do the Missionary Work of our Churches, but we are going to find in this new era that Missions is not a job for women alone but a man's job as well." Bullock urged men to measure up to "our opportunity."[82]

Charles Clinton Spaulding agreed as he appropriated the motto of the Women's Baptist State Convention by speaking on the topic of "Christ in Every Home." Alongside emphatic pleas to support black businesses, he asked reflective questions such as "What are we doing to better the condition of our homes?" "What kind of homes are we maintaining?" "What are we doing to inspire our boys and girls?" Black women activists had long been occupied by issues of morality and domesticity, and as convention proceedings attest, so were men. The question of what to do with black youth was highlighted in the proceedings along with black men's particular responsibility to inculcate black pride among boys. "I want my boys to love their race," Spaulding said. "I want my boys to have confidence in our people.... We have got to come to ourselves as a race."[83]

Spaulding's public activities supported his argument that black men needed to take charge of their communities. In the 1920s, Spaulding and William Kennedy, also of the North Carolina Mutual Insurance Company, worked to establish black branches of the YMCA in Durham. Kennedy was a trustee of the Oxford Orphanage and pressured North Carolina's state legislature to establish a facility to rehabilitate black male delinquents. As a result of his efforts, the North Carolina legislature approved the Morrison Training School for Negro Boys in 1927. A longtime North Carolina Baptist, reminiscing in 1911 on his forty-year association with the religious body, advised that ministers "are not fully alive to the proper care and training of their children" and said that "the preacher is the best substitute for the parent. God has put us here in the world for a special purpose. What is God's purpose for putting us under the influence of this splendid civilization? Let's inaugurate a layman's movement in the church, not out of it."[84]

Black Baptists worked hard to get and keep black boys in the church. "In many [churches] not a single young man was to be seen," Whitted remarked in 1908 after reviewing Baptist State Convention data for that year. "This was true not only in the Sunday School, but largely in the day school. In fact the Convention itself was largely composed of young women."[85]

The impulse to reassert a manly presence in the church extended to other African-American religious denominations. "Unfortunately, the average man is not taking as much interest in the church as he should. The attitude of many men is one of indifference; others regard the church contemptuously, while others are positively antagonistic," reported Rev. Thomas B. Neely, corresponding secretary of the Sunday-School Union (Methodist Episcopal Church). While he did not discuss at length the causes of this religious malaise (he did cite the church's failure to properly address the concerns of boys and young men and an inability by ministers to sufficiently "stir" men with their preaching), Neely outlined its effects, which he termed "most injurious."[86]

Black men's lack of involvement in the church, Neely argued, meant the absence of the vigor that men foster in human organizations, a lack of financial strength, and a lack of male influence in the church community. "While many of the best workers in the church are women," Neely observed, "it is no disparagement to them to say that the church needs also the masculine element, and, of all classes, women should be the most profoundly interested in this question of men and the church, for, if men are not under churchly influences, they are under worse influences, and the injury wrought by these anti-churchly influences in turn afflicts mothers, wives, sisters."[87]

Concurrent with discussions about men's integration into "women's" work were attempts by some male secular and religious leaders to fortify a still-fragile partnership between the two sexes and bolster race unity. J.A. Whitted's presidential address to the convention in 1909 argued that women should be included in race work more equitably. Whitted said that some convention members had branded leaders of the women's convention as "unruly," but Whitted gave "no heed to the admonition of the brethren. . . . Our opinion, after careful consideration, has wholly changed, and at no period have they shown any but the most humble and Godly spirit." He continued,

> The two conventions better understand each other; and while there may be little features creeping in now and then which the leaders of the women's convention themselves are not pleased with and are endeavoring to modify, and even to change, let us hope for the better, knowing that the sun in the heavens is not perfect, and give every encouragement in our Churches and Convention we can give, to encourage our sisters.[88]

Addressing the meeting of the black Women's Baptist Convention in Washington, N.C., that same year, Whitted took as his subject "The Outlook for Woman's Work in North Carolina, and How We May Unite Our Forces." He lauded women for their home missionary work and affirmed that "the responsibility resting upon the leaders of the Convention is great upon both men and women; and there never was a time when the women held the power in the State as now." Whitted hoped that women would use their power in a way that uplifted both sexes. "Whatever our opinion," he urged, "let us still be brethren; let nothing separate or place a barrier between us."[89]

Baptist women had repeatedly urged men to increase their cooperation with them. They counseled men about their obligation to support and affirm "women's work." Roberta Bunn, corresponding secretary of the women's convention, delivered a strong message concerning what the pastors "owe to the women" in their work. "It is with you to help or to hinder. . . . We are trying to create a missionary spirit among all our people." Miss S. A. Johnson of the Parent's Conference also pleaded for men's assistance in establishing a reformatory for delinquent girls. "Give us a push," she implored. Sister Bunn repeated her appeal in 1904 as she backed Corresponding Secretary Hannah Stannard's discussion of "Woman's Work— It Needs Our Encouragement." Following her remarks, Stannard donated $50 to the general convention from her group.[90]

The symbolic gesture did not go unnoticed; male Baptists expressed thanks for the "tangible exhibition of cooperation between the two organizations." Financial support was one way Baptist women could demonstrate increasing cooperation with men. In 1903, the general convention agreed at the request of the Women's Baptist Convention that the women would share in the financial support of a foreign missionary. At the 1907 convention in Reidsville, it was agreed that the women would pay the salary of North Carolinian Cora A. Pair to labor as an evangelical missionary in Africa. Women's convention members paid Pair's salary of $267 for the first quarter of the following year.[91]

This financial aid reflected a tradition of Baptist men supporting women's activities within the convention. The 1904 general convention resolved to give two hours to representatives of the women's convention. In a show of mutual exchange, a similar resolution stipulated that women give a portion of their program over to the men. Even C. S. Brown paid homage to women's work, albeit indirectly. Brown called the Sunday School Convention's efforts to raise money for the education of indigent worthy girls deserving of the brethren's "highest approval. More should be done in this direction; for the womanhood of the race is a matter of great concern to us as a people."[92]

For some members of the ministry, the conciliatory gestures toward women distracted the church body from loftier matters. Speaking to the general convention in 1923, President O. S. Bullock expressed regret about the "individual selfishness" that still obstructed the convention's work. "Too much of our energies and efforts have been taken up in petting and coaxing and pacifying the adjusting bodies that call themselves auxiliaries to the great State Convention," he said. "This ought not to be. This energy and effort ought to be spent promoting the objects of the Convention."[93]

Revolt(ing) Matters

In the 1920s, mild disagreements and open hostilities between the two sexes intensified. Rev. G. W. Bullock, speaking in a context of increasingly militant woman suffrage activism and assertions of black civil rights in the aftermath of World War I and the race riots of 1919, characterized the time as one of revolt. Bullock noted that an increasing number of men who had previously accommodated themselves to a lesser lot in life were now demanding "independence and freedom." This movement had global dimensions, stretching into India, Russia, and South Africa as well as Great

Britain and the United States. Bullock used these larger movements for independence to express his dismay at the ongoing "revolt" against principles of unity and cooperation within the Baptist church. "The different organizations that have been established were organized in the church only to assist the church in its functions," he remarked. "They cannot exist apart from the church, no more than a branch or a vine can exist separate from the trunk."[94]

Heeding Bullock's admonitions, Baptist men and women once again agreed to a plan of cooperation in 1922. It included having their work directed by a joint committee comprised of members of the two organizations, opening up financial records for inspection by both bodies, providing for participation of men and women on the programs of both conventions, aiding as much as possible the financial projects of the two organizations, and agreeing that the objectives of the groups would be "one and the same." In a remarkable show of conciliation, Baptist women extended an olive branch to one of their harshest critics, C. S. Brown. The women and Brown had consistently battled over whether the women should control their plan of work and financial coffers. Several of the sisters presented a bouquet of flowers to Brown in recognition of his many years of service to the Baptist cause. Brown, reportedly wearing a broad smile, responded "I am profoundly grateful."[95]

Yet correspondence addressed to the men's 1922 convention revealed grievances that "wounded . . . hearts" of some women. "We have been misrepresented, handicapped and insulted by some of the leading men of your Convention," the women wrote. At issue lay the treatment of women's convention leader Pattie Shepard at the hands of Secretary Brown, who reportedly belittled her in front of an audience that included Baptist men and women from other states. Recurring remarks by Brown within the Baptists' *Union Reformer* about the women's alleged mishandling of finances also sparked the women's ire. Such accusations had done much to undermine the progress of work in the state, the women claimed. At a gathering in Winston-Salem in 1922, the women's temperature again rose. There, Dr. A. A. Graham apparently used language so demeaning to the women that they "felt chagrined and disgusted." Baptist women resolved afterward to bar Graham and Brown from addressing them until they had offered apologies for their "unchristianly manners."[96]

Throughout their letter, the women invoked the rhetoric of protection as they challenged the validity of convention leaders' declaration of man-hood. Male relatives and pastors should exhibit a level of chivalry that was now absent, they said. "The women who oppose the State Convention, many of them, have husbands, brothers, fathers, and sons, who will not stand for the treatment we are receiving at the hands of some of your lead-ers," the women wrote. Women Baptists deemed their men, not the "hea-thens" abroad, in need of evolved thinking and behavior; in short, Baptist black men required civilizing. "We assure you, brethren, we are ready and willing to work and work and work, but we have learned that money is not everything. And until we are civilized and Christianized and know how to treat our brothers and sisters at home, we need not bother about those in foreign lands."[97] Baptist women thus articulated demands that were con-sistent with both Christian and race uplift ideology. Respect for women meant that male Baptists should do their Christianly duty and protect them. From a racial perspective, black women's effectiveness in home mis-sion work as well as their pronouncements to white society that they and the race were respectable were enhanced by black men's affirmation of their status as "ladies." Moreover, believing themselves equal in the sight of God (religious doctrine and the clergy typically promoted the idea that all Christians were equal), black women Baptists recoiled at the prospect of male stewardship of their work. At the same time, the women were deeply influenced by a racial history that necessitated activism by both sexes.

Brown's version of protection mandated that women merge their re-sources with male Baptists in a united "brotherhood." Responding bluntly to Baptist women's allegations, Brown expressed feelings of betrayal and dismay. Addressing the "delicate" question of women's place within the Baptist Convention hierarchy, Brown declared that "it [the Women's Bap-tist State Convention] must be auxiliary, or nothing. . . . I am sure that they form a part of our church work, and therefore must come under our direct supervision."[98] Brown found the women in breach of the contract entered into at the general convention in Wilson, N.C., in 1922. The motto at that convention had been "All doing the same thing at the same time." Brown interpreted this to mean that black churchwomen had to devote their financial resources to black men's priorities. For some women, this interpretation of the church's motto spoke not to unity but a to men's de-sire to take away women's power to control their own fiscal resources.

Brown argued that Baptist women had broken their agreement with

Baptist men by withholding monies earmarked for a Shaw Day rally to raise funds for Shaw University. The women had reportedly collected $5,000 for the year yet had "failed to appropriate a cent." Moreover, Brown was disturbed by the fact that the women planned to hold a separate fundraiser from the one organized by the men. The men's fund-raiser included all Baptist-affiliated churches and groups. "We are grateful for the crumbs that our sisters give us from time to time, but they must remember that they belong to us, and must get their support from our churches," Brown said.[99]

The familiar dance of discord, resistance, and attempted reconciliation between North Carolina's Baptist men and women began again in 1924 as male convention leaders formulated another plan of "united work."[100] That year, representatives of all the boards of Baptist state bodies met at the First Baptist Church in Raleigh with the goal of more completely uniting the work of the convention. Among those in attendance were convention president Dr. O. S. Bullock, Corresponding Secretary C. S. Brown, C. C. Spaulding, and women's convention representatives' Mary Burrell, Pattie Shepard, and Hattie Shepard.[101] It was ultimately agreed that within five years, the convention's various bodies would collectively raise an endowment fund of $100,000 for Shaw University; do Christian educational work together (aid indigent girls, help worthy young men prepare for the ministry); jointly engage in local and state home mission work, both in destitute places and among women of the churches and race; and require that all receipts and disbursements be combined and made public each year in a single report.

A Board of Promotion comprised of five members each from the men's and women's Baptist conventions, the Baptist Young People's Union, and the Sunday school bodies was organized to oversee the united work plan. C. S. Brown, who was appointed secretary of the Board of Promotion, seemed optimistic that the plan could be implemented successfully. "We have evidently been seriously handicapped by permitting our various organizations to operate on independent lines," he said. "The blending of our state organizations into co-operative action under a Board of Promotions is certainly a hopeful sign, and we must decide to stand by this board in its plans to push our work."[102]

This "united" plan proved an oxymoron for black women missionaries, however, as it called for a systematic dismantling of their work. The proposals that home mission work be done jointly by both sexes and that women's financial accounts be merged with men's would effectively destroy any semblance of autonomy for the churchwomen. Like men in the white Protestant movement who disbanded churchwomen's boards without consulting them and combined them with churchmen's groups, black Baptist men sought to sever black women's attachment to a "definite work." Unlike the white Protestant movement, however, black Baptist men aimed to do this with churchwomen's permission. Ironically, black women Baptists in North Carolina were given a "voice" in the reorganization plan, and unlike the Protestant and Methodist movements, black women's position in the church body as subordinates to churchmen was still not definitively resolved by 1930.[103]

While convention minutes do not reveal details of the discussion between Baptist men and women about the plan, they do suggest its ultimate failure. Brown found himself making the same appeal for unity four years later. He argued that "co-operation among our several state organizations does not seem feasible at present, because of the mistaken notion that they are independent and co-ordinate. Each seems determined to collect, spend their money, and plan their work with little or no regard for the parent convention."[104] Yet in that same year, convention president J. S. Brown made a point of praising the women's work. He particularly paid tribute to women's convention president Pattie Shepard and Corresponding Secretary Mary Burrell for their mission work. Additionally, he praised Burrell for having been chosen to plan the upcoming All-Baptist Celebration. Brown concluded, "May I urge our pastors to visit and give encouragement to their sisters in their local circles that their work may go forward."[105]

In 1930, convention president R. R. Cartwright again called upon men and women to work together for "the Master's cause." In the context of the Depression-era pressures on church finances, he strongly urged "united, unselfish action." "I would advise that every man and woman when going to great meetings like this, leave at home all selfish interests and contentions; go or come up to the grand settings with nothing in view save that which is pleasing to God and beneficial to mankind," he said. "The General Convention is the one great head of the whole Baptist family in the

State. This is the only right and plausible way for it to obtain the greatest good."[106]

The "right and only plausible way" for men and women of the Baptist State Convention of North Carolina remained a puzzling conundrum. As men sought to bring together the diverse bodies of the church into one united organ, as they worked to repair and promote their manhood, some women found their ambitions and gender identity stifled. For women leaders of the junior division of the Women's Baptist Convention, their motto effectively became "She has done what she could."[107]

Black Baptist men then, not unlike Baptist women, found themselves negotiating a thread of gender identity that was easily frayed. Indeed, the rhetorical refrain of "What can he do?" likely lingered in the minds of many southern black men, who found themselves in the position of asserting their manliness while at the same time affirming the contributions and identity of black women. Celebrating black women's independence and activism in race work, proclaiming them indispensable instruments in efforts to end Jim Crow legislation, and affirming them as New Women encouraged race solidarity and an equal status between men and women in public affairs. Yet they felt that these policies also eroded masculine authority and security. In response, black male leaders within North Carolina's Baptist State Convention worked to make their churches more manly. Influenced by the masculinization rhetoric and strategy of the larger church, they plotted to recruit more black men and ministers to the church and weaken black women's home missionary work. They also sought a more visible place in areas such as church outreach and other social welfare work—activities black women deemed suited to their sex due to the work's nurturing and altruistic characteristics. The fact that churchmen attempted to claim feminine territory as their own suggests that defining manhood was a complex endeavor for African-American men during this period. Their repeated assertion that home mission work should be done jointly by both sexes validated the legitimacy of women's work. Yet, that legitimacy was undermined by men's attempts to co-opt women's religious enterprises. Black churchmen's appropriation of traditionally feminine roles illustrates their embrace of a dual gender consciousness. From the perspective of churchmen, no contradiction existed between using women's work identity to forward masculine pride and dignity.

While church members bickered, sometimes vehemently, over their differing visions of gender and race work, the freedom to repeatedly air such dissension in public spaces remained protected for both sexes. Baptist men might have exercised authority over black churchwomen, but they could not silence them. These dialogues were in a way uplifting in that they encouraged an ethos of collective problem-solving by an engaged African-American citizenry. And yet this broad-based inclusion of ideas also inspired colliding truths, multiple meanings, and differing approaches among church men and women. This process divided Baptist men and women along gender lines.

As North Carolina's black Baptist men and women negotiated the meaning of race work for their gender identities, other black men began concerted efforts to groom the next generation and in the process to reassert their masculinity. After the onset of Jim Crow laws and the disfranchisement of black men, the answer to C. C. Spaulding's emotional plea of "What are we doing to inspire our boys and girls?" was a statewide endeavor to address the "Boy Problem."

2

Solving the Boy Problem

Fashioning Boys into Respectable Race Men

We must save our boys. The glory of any race is the manhood of that race.
—JOHN C. DANCY

The boys are the only beings out of which we can make men.
—NICHOLAS F. ROBERTS, NORTH CAROLINA BAPTIST SUNDAY SCHOOL CONVENTION

The meeting of the Y.M.I. Sunday afternoon will be for men only. The women will hold their mass meeting at St. James A.M.E. church.
—ASHEVILLE CITIZEN, 10 MARCH 1904

"Bad Atmosphere"

In a 1909 address before the North Carolina Baptist Sunday School Convention, President Nicholas Frank Roberts discussed the boy problem. "Is he bad?" he asked. "Is he worse now than he was forty years ago? Has the boy changed?" Roberts responded emphatically that the environment, not the boy, had been adversely altered. "Bad atmosphere makes bad boys," he concluded.[1] He defined atmosphere as the place where the boy lived, moved, and situated his being. Parents' indecisiveness as to how to raise the boy produced a home environment where "everything is harsh and snappish and crabbed," he said. As a result, boys sought more congenial surroundings; they frequented "low places" such as pool and gambling rooms, barrooms, and dime theaters. While Roberts conceded that much attention had been given to the question of girls' environment and how that shaped their moral, physical, and spiritual well-being, the plight of boys' welfare had, lamentably, not received similar attention. "I am of the opinion that many parents have made a great mistake in bestowing all their care upon the girls and none upon the boys," he said.[2]

Confronted with the "bad atmosphere" of race prejudice in the early-twentieth-century South, several of North Carolina's race men changed

their strategies and turned their attention to preparing the next generation of race leaders. Religious, educational, and social movements aimed
at relieving the "Boy Problem" took place at the same time as the white supremacy campaigns that produced disfranchisement and race riots in such
southern cities as Wilmington (1898), New Orleans (1900), and Atlanta
(1906).

North Carolina's middle-class black men sought to rectify what they
perceived as their generation's compromised public ambitions by instill-
ing community-based lessons of self-pride, etiquette, and industry among
boys and young men. If there was to be a solution to the "Race Problem,"
the black men of tomorrow needed to help fashion it. As John C. Dancy
said, "We need to teach the boys that the future destiny of the race is in
their hands, and on their shoulders."[3] Boys, he felt, needed to be infused
with self-pride and respect for law and order; they should exhibit "rugged"
honesty, avoid criminal conduct, restrain unsavory appetites, and grasp the
importance of work and responsibility. With the proper training, Dancy
advised, "like Moses, [the boy] will be singled out by omnipotence to lead
his people out of darkness, another form of slavery, into the glorious light
of liberty and manhood."[4]

Proscriptive literature within the race identified clear causes and offered
solutions to many social ills affecting the race's youth. Boys were unshaped
clay and could be turned into men if they were properly handled. Rejection
of feminine behaviors was key to boys' development into men and for the
uplift of the race. To replicate girlish behavior equated to unmanliness. It
was unnatural and bolstered contentions that black male identity had been
emasculated due to slavery and the racial oppression that followed. The
stress within the prescriptive literature on heteronormativity is also indicative of the class bias inherent in such tutorials. *Floyd's Flowers*, a manual to
uplift the race as much to groom boys and girls into adulthood, captures
in its rhetoric the sentiments of African Americans who sought individual
and collective progress through the sexual patrolling of the race.[5] Floyd
offered 325 pages of anecdotes and sketches to convey moral instruction to
black children. He endeavored to produce boys and girls who "shall turn
out to be good men and good women."[6]

As part of that objective, he identified general and specific behavioral
traits for boys and girls. He observed that girls had the potential to be
"almost as bad as some boys." Girls' penchant for "fast" behavior, relishing

of "trash" literature, and immodesty led to deficient character. Inattention to delicate and modest behavior, Floyd related, produced the "loud type" of girl, who is "regarded with dislike, distrust, and even disdain, by the better class of people."[7] Boys could be rowdy and "bad." The rowdy boy cut class, smoked cigarettes, proved "saucy and impudent to older people," was a bully, and attended Sunday school infrequently. "Bad Boys" were more than mischievous; they were "bad in heart and in deed." They could be found in chain gangs or wearing disheveled clothes on street corners. They smoked cigarettes, rolled dice, and sought leisure in saloons, "drinking, playing pool and playing cards."

These boys, he claimed, needed intervention to accomplish the transition to manhood. He desired them to attain a respectable identity as "manly little boys." By categorizing them as both "manly" and "little," Floyd established their identity as distinctive from yet resembling traits representative of adult manhood.[8] Floyd outlined the process for "making a good man out of a bad boy." Boys could be reclaimed and reformed through alterations of their bodies and minds. Attention to hygiene was key to assuring boys' purity. Clean bodies and clean clothes would affect a boy's habits, morals, and character. Purification of a boy's environment—physical, spiritual, and mental—was the essence of producing a good man. Boys who read good literature, avoided "bad company," and paid attention to their spiritual natures would develop proper characters and evolve into good men.

Floyd's definitions of male and female identity, though they were framed by the principles of racial uplift, may also have been informed by a desire to stress the distinction between African-American boyhood and manhood. In contrast, historians of masculinity note the softening of the difference between middle-class white boys and men during this time period. At the turn of the century, in response to what they considered weakling males, white men began to cultivate the manly traits of competitiveness, passion, and impulsivity among boys. The Victorian manly model of self-control and restraint faded as middle-class neurasthenia increased.

African-American men in the South, however, saw little benefit to obscuring age difference. They (and the race) still faced struggles to separate their identity from that of children. Socioeconomic conditions and racial etiquette blurred categories of boyhood and manhood, placing males of disparate ages in frequent contact. Black boys often had to negotiate adult worlds because of racial, economic, and social inequality. Planter elites insisted that schools close part of the year to make sure they would have a black labor force. In 1900, almost half of all black boys in the South between 10 and 15 worked for wages, compared to 22.5 percent of white boys. Racial deference, as encoded under Jim Crow, also served to infantilize black men, who were often called the pejorative epithet "boy." Such designations impressed upon black men the need to distinguish their identity from that of their youthful charges. The path toward respectability for black men thus lay in their concomitant embrace and distance from black boys.[9]

Gender differences were critical for understanding boyhood, according to Floyd. A strong opposition between male and female helped draw distinctions between boys and men because of the ambiguous relationship of boys to feminine qualities. Unlike real men, the gender identity of boys was still in flux and was susceptible to developing effeminate traits.

Gender-specific identities offered by men such as Floyd were seldom followed that precisely among the black middle class in North Carolina.[10] African-American men's performance of gender identity in different spaces showed how subjective that identity really was. As Chapter 1 illustrates, churchmen and women did not always conform to strict gender roles. Churchmen sometimes tried to assume women's work roles, although they retained their manliness in their campaign to assume roles in the area of traditionally feminine social work. Though women conducted their work independently, black churchmen nonetheless felt emboldened to assert themselves as women's primary authority figures because the church was a patriarchal as well as a sacred space. Within its structure, the male-led Baptist State Convention saw itself as the head of all its organizations, including women's groups. Men could thus appropriate feminine and masculine roles simultaneously.

Men and women who sought to solve the "boy problem" devised similar strategies to reform their boys. These gendered partnerships tended to reinforce rather than compromise black goals of racial uplift. As men and women worked together in youth outreach, they were also bound by the growing need to solidify their class status, which was built upon respectability and an unassailable home environment.

Historians' focus on women's roles in the moral uplift of the race, however, has reduced clarity about how boys' well-being was a significant part of that effort. Indeed, some race women deemed it appropriate to give more attention to boys than to girls. Mrs. Rev. J. S. Brown of the Women's Baptist State Convention spoke of the importance of saving young people, "especially the young boys." Mrs. Peebles said, "I have several children, and I am as careful about my boys as I am with my girls."[11] Women such as Charlotte Hawkins Brown dispensed do's and don'ts to men as well as women at her finishing school in Sedalia. While North Carolina's leading black men expected black women to patrol the moral habits of both girls and boys in and outside the home, they were also involved in the racial upbringing of their young men.

The Baptist Sunday School Convention, schools such as the Mary Potter School, and the Young Men's Institute (YMI) sought to keep boys from drifting by providing wholesome diversions, counseling temperance in thought and behavior, and instructing them in how to lead virtuous and manly lives. Though black men and women both accepted the challenge of "saving our boys," largely adopting similar ideologies and strategies, the investment of some black men in this type of uplift was informed by a desire to reify their manhood. When it was necessary, they crafted a gender identity separate from that of black boys and black women. This process occurred at the YMI, which became renowned as an inclusive community organization. Like black Young Men's Christian Associations (YMCAs), Asheville's YMI welcomed the whole black community. Men and women, young and old rented meeting space, attended mass meetings, did business, and socialized at the institute. The manipulation of public space by YMI's leaders, however, also taught lessons about gender. Within a community-centered organization, YMI members created a gender hierarchy principally governed by men.

Shaping black men's instruction to male youth in the early twentieth century were the results of modernization: urbanization and consumerism. Male and female black activists framed responses to these developments and the emerging norms they produced.[12] Black women activists were conscious of the deleterious effects of urban youth culture on black womanhood. The sight of black women openly socializing with black or white men in public spaces strengthened white judgments that black women were morally weak and sexually deviant. North Carolina's Bureau of Race Welfare, which was launched in 1925 with support from philanthropist Laura Spelman Rockefeller, focused on the sexuality of black girls. Bureau Director Lawrence A. Oxley deemed the sexually active young black woman to be "the most difficult of solution," blaming her circumstance in part on the actions of sexually irresponsible black men. Commenting on North Carolina's social welfare program for blacks, Oxley wrote, "The prey of unprincipled men of both races, the Negro girl stands as a most pathetic figure in world history." In cities and rural areas, "the maladjusted Negro girl is left free to wander from place to place, leaving in her wake a trail of disease and human suffering as the heritage of the future generation of both races."[13]

Black men also considered at length the consequences of urbanization on their gender status. They especially believed that urban or "street" culture stunted the growth of boys into respectable men by disrupting the traditional home environment and subverting Victorian-inspired values of self-control and restraint. Grooming subsequent generations of race men thus required acknowledging changes in the racial atmosphere of the South and alterations in the region's economic and cultural landscapes.

North Carolina (and the South more broadly) became increasingly urban and industrial in the latter half of the nineteenth century. While agriculture had traditionally defined the region's economic identity, industries that capitalized on local raw materials soon became too profitable to overlook. In the 1880s, southern boosters began to forecast a profound yet beneficial transformation for the region. Within the next two decades, key industries such as textile factories, coal mines, and lumber mills developed across the Piedmont. In addition, mechanization modernized how the agricultural staple of cotton was produced. While the possibilities of industry lured many blacks outside North Carolina's borders, thousands of others migrated to its urban centers.[14] By 1900, North Carolina blacks accounted for 40 percent of urban dwellers (compared to 31 percent in the entire South). Blacks migrated from rural to urban areas for a variety of reasons. They wanted to escape the racial intimidation and violence prevalent in the countryside, take advantage of educational opportunities, and enjoy city life. Many others felt for the first time the freedom that unrestricted movement engendered.[15]

White anxiety over blacks' migration into urban areas precipitated legislation that segregated neighborhoods and institutions. In response to hardening Jim Crow policies, black business districts developed in urban areas across the state, among them the Hayti districts in southeast Durham and in Raleigh. Raleigh's black Second and Fourth wards included two elementary schools; six churches; Shaw University; the Colored Masonic Hall; the Institute for the Colored Blind, Deaf and Dumb; and an assortment of businesses, boardinghouses, and hotels. Upwardly mobile black North Carolinians settled in middle-class enclaves such as Raleigh's

Oberlin and Method neighborhoods. In Charlotte, business boomed for black merchants and professionals as black consumers recycled dollars within their communities. Between 1898 and 1915, the number of black-owned grocery stores in the city doubled, the number of black-owned restaurants tripled, and the number of black physicians quadrupled.[16] The Mecklenburg Investment Company began operations in 1921 in response to the economic boom.

While urbanization made a self-sufficient, economically prosperous black middle class possible, it also bred a consumer culture that offered consumers opportunities that challenged the thrift that some black leaders recommended. The black middle class struggled to reconcile a Victorian value system that emphasized stability, thrift, and refinement in manners with a new value system that emphasized spontaneous, free-wheeling leisure-time activities. Amusements such as the dance hall and nickelodeon threatened the claims of the race to moral progress. The urban arena afforded blacks the space and anonymity to experiment with new identities beyond that dictated within the stiff rubric of Victorianism, which remained a central component of race uplift ideology. The freedom to mingle in an unregulated environment with men and women of varying classes and ages provided a public forum for private activities such as courting and legitimized "criminal" conduct such as gambling and saloon-hopping. Black rural migrants, unaccustomed to city life, were deemed by black middle-class reformers as especially susceptible to falling prey to these "death traps."

While organizations led by business and professional black men such as the black YMCA saw their mission as rescuing rural migrants who found themselves "easy prey to the vicious and deadly influences" around them, the black middle class also sought to preserve the integrity of black manhood.[17] As W. E. B. Du Bois put it, young middle-class black men needed protection against the dangerous class of "criminals, gamblers, and loafers." The demographic and economic shifts of the early twentieth century spawned several black middle-class business and residential districts, whose member sought to distinguish themselves both commercially and culturally within black communities. Within the context of youth reform work, the quest by middle-class African-American men and women for "respectability" meant pursuing an identity distinct from that of working-class and poor blacks. Terms such as "uplift" and "respectability" illustrate the classist presumptions embedded in the community initiatives of men's and women's community issues.[18]

Concerns about the urban environment transcended race; whites also worried about the effect of city pleasures on the moral compass of youth. Jane Addams, for example, blamed the "gin palaces," five-cent theatres, and dance halls "to which hundreds of young people are attracted" for the moral downfall of young people. Urban entertainments such as dance halls "require[d] five cents to procure within [them] for five minutes the sense of allurement and intoxication which is sold in lieu of innocent pleasure."[19] The popularity of amusement parks in the early 1900s grandly showcased attractions that seemed to threaten long-standing cultural values.[20] Both races voiced dismay at the new urban amusements, but while black leaders were attuned to the consequences of such entertainments on the values of African Americans, they also reflected on the meaning of urban culture for the advancement of the race.

The embrace of Victorian manners by America's best black men and women had been the yardstick by which the middle classes measured their racial progress. Respectability "constituted a counter-discourse to the politics of prejudice" by demanding that every black, regardless of class background, assume responsibility for his/her own behavior and self-improvement.[21] The success of individual self-policing would determine the image of the race as a whole. Though ineffective in eradicating all racial discrimination, consistent displays of controlled and dignified behavior by blacks debunked racist portrayals of a childlike immoral race and helped forge partnerships with sympathetic whites. Building bridges across race held the promise of transgressing skin color as the dominant marker of citizenship by debunking stereotypes that rationalized the exclusion of blacks from democratic processes and protections.

Exhibition of morals and manners by the black community also validated the race's claim to self-definition and self-representation, or the power to shape and project its own identity separate from white constructions. Displays of race etiquette were motivated by the black community's evolving external and internal needs. Externally, such displays seemed to demonstrate a passive mode of resistance to Jim Crow practices in that blacks tended to hold their individual behavior, rather than governmental bodies, accountable for solving the race problem. Middle-class blacks' demand for respectable behavior across the race reinforced a conserva-

tive assimilationist agenda that was antithetical to the cultural practices
of working-class and poor blacks. Viewed another way, however, the black
community's self-regulated behavior helped shift the emphasis away from
scientific theories that justified race prejudice and made possible a wider
interpretation of blacks' capacity for equal citizenship. Internally, the issue of moral rectitude elicited a fluid debate among African Americans
about community standards and values in the midst of Jim Crow laws and
growing class stratification. After disfranchisement and segregation, prov-
ing one's moral worth became more critical for black Americans, especially
as new urban environments seemed to promote values that were hostile to
the work of some members of the race to cultivate respectability. For some,
"street" culture came to symbolize black depravity at its worst.

North Carolina black men who were anxious to solve the "boy problem"
worked to quell this rebellion against the values of self-respect, discipline,
and middle-class respectability by devising a standard of innocence for
black boys. One of the state's most prominent agents in this task, the Baptist
Sunday School Convention, articulated a desire to produce "consecrated"
black men, in part by promoting wholesome entertainment. Throughout
this process, convention leaders grappled with how to avoid compromising their evangelical identity as they proposed alternative places for young
black men to spend their leisure time. As part of this work, churchmen
also sought to assert their status as men by stressing traditional gender
roles.

The "Boy Problem": The Dilemma of Churchmen

North Carolina Baptist Sunday School Convention leaders despaired over
the absence of boys in Sunday schools; in their view, the Sunday school
was the key site for shaping black youth.[22] Boldly proclaiming time and
again that the Sunday school was "the best place to train and evangelize
the boy," Sunday School Convention leaders were alarmed by its declining
membership.[23] In his bid for an "increase membership movement," A. W.
Pegues noted that of the state's 240,000 Baptist members, only 50,000
attended Sunday school. "There are churches with a membership of 500
and a Sunday school enrollment of 40 or 50," he said. Nicholas Roberts
conceded, "It can hardly be denied that the average young man and woman
are not as religious as in former years. They care less about the Sunday

School, less about the church, less about any kind of religious meeting.
Why are they less interested?"[24]

Many blamed a bad atmosphere, within and outside the church, for
black boys' religious and moral malaise. Some Baptist men pinpointed a
weakened home environment as the heart of the boy problem. They felt
that it was critical to shore up traditional gender roles in which mothers presided over the domestic sphere. Others blamed urban amusements.
Still others cast Sunday schools and their teachers as derelict and in need
of reform. J. A. Whitted, on the other hand, castigated his Christian brethren for alienating youth through discipline that was too stringent. "Many
churches have driven the young people away from them by their destruc-
tive discipline," he said. "By this we mean constantly holding them up to
ridicule and discouraging them in their efforts." He encouraged ministers
to use the "right discipline" with young people and to give boys the "proper
encouragement."[25] C. C. Spaulding added that only love, not "abuse and
threatening," could save young people.[26]

The need to attract more youth to churches became more important at
the turn of the twentieth century as secular influences grew with increasing
urbanization.[27] As Silas Ford noted at the inaugural meeting of the Negro
Young People's Christian and Educational Congress in Atlanta in 1902, the
"problems of commerce and finance" had wrapped themselves around the
greater issue of the "destiny of the young men now growing up and projecting their lives into the great currents of society and business."[28] Citing
the fact that only 27 percent of 12 million young men between the ages
of 15 and 25 attended church regularly, Ford lamented that there seemed
to be "more of downright brotherhood, fellowship, fraternity in the average saloon than there is to be found in the average church."[29] Moreover,
where "shameless women preside you will likewise find the young men,
night after night and day after day, sucking the poison of hell from the lips
of 'strange' women." Another observer described the status of many black
boys:

> It is a common sight in the public streets to see at all hours of the day
> and night small boys, some of them even in knee pants, half-grown
> boys and boys just merging into manhood, puffing cigars and ciga-
> rettes, ejaculating the large-sized oaths they have learned, breathing
> out the fumes of cheap liquors, exhibiting the swagger of the dead-

game sport, and retailing with great gusto their bar room experiences and their disgusting revelry in houses of ill-repute.[30]

J. A. Whitted agreed that black Christian men were responsible for producing moral and useful black boys. Whitted reasoned that just as Christian mothers nurtured and trained their daughters to be rich in chastity and virtue, so too did Christian fathers. He argued that "the spirit of the Bible combined with Christian fathers for the right development of the sons, will necessarily produce men of the proper stamp."[31] Ford also saw the church as the social and moral wellspring for black boys. "It is the duty of the church to take the lead in insisting that young men shall be as moral as young women," he said.[32] John Dancy also felt that boys were in need of uplift. "There are . . . boys in poverty and distress, who need a helping hand, a suggestion of counsel and adviser," he said. "Let us see that it is given and that a wall of despair is turned into a song of triumph and of rejoicing. To the rescue then."[33] The church's present and future usefulness was thus defined in part by its ability to recruit, nurture, and retain young men within its hierarchical structure.

The urgency North Carolina's black religious leaders felt during the Jim Crow era was not unique or new. The "boy problem" had begun in the nineteenth century. Statistics and scholarly "boyology" studies all concluded that young men were weak and sickly and that those under twenty were responsible for two-thirds of crimes committed nationwide. Florida's white Baptists were distressed to learn that by age 15 or 16, most boys had left Sunday school and the church. Though they were concerned about the effects of alcohol, masturbation, and other social ills on young men, clergymen also felt that the absence of male role models was an important piece of the puzzle. They noted how much their churches had been feminized; more women than men were members of churches and Sunday schools. Boys, these religious leaders claimed, needed male mentors to help them assert their masculinity.[34]

In response, Sunday school teachers turned their attention to boys in their classes. Weekly lessons focused on male heroes who behaved with honor and dignity and who shunned sinful indulgences such as tobacco and alcohol. By the early twentieth century, several Sunday school boards had changed their names and added young adult societies. Though white churches were clearly concerned about the boy issue, the situation seemed to be most grave in black communities. At North Carolina's interdenominational Colored Sunday School Convention, international Sunday school spokesman N. B. Broughton "dwelt on the absence of boys and young men from Sunday schools and churches," noting that the problem proved "especially noticeable in the colored Sunday schools."[35]

Yet the traditional stance of black religious leaders of denouncing such activities as dancing, card playing, movies, and sports as evil had convinced many young people that the church was fundamentally irrelevant to their lives. Declaring the church the "broadest expression of organized Negro life," Charles H. Williams, director of physical education for men at Hampton Institute, concluded that the church was out of step with the needs of young people. Williams wrote that the opposition of ministers to community centers and their indifferent support for the YMCA, the YWCA, the Urban League, and other social work agencies was evidence of a lack of "social vision." In a survey of leading black churchmen across the country, Williams observed two divergent trends within black churches. While one element of the church judged it "not its business to amuse people," a more progressive wing of the church felt that it should "encourage and promote playgrounds, ball teams, track sports, and dramatic clubs that offer Christian drama, oratorios, and cantatas. It believes that orchestras, bands, and social, literary, and debating clubs should also be organized."[36] The survey demonstrated to Williams that black church ministries were becoming more liberal in their administration of institutional work but that "there is still much work to be done."[37]

At Baptist State Sunday School and Baptist Young People's Union conventions in North Carolina, church leaders participated in the debate about the relationship of youth to the church. Convention leaders devoted considerable time to discussing ways to recruit and retain the interest of young people, particularly boys. For many churchmen, this meant reevaluating and reformulating the church's religious values. They hoped to strike a balance between their Christian ideals and the modern world.[38]

Sunday School Convention members increasingly began to question the relevance of the church in a modern age. "This is an electric age in material things," submitted Dr. W. T. Coleman of the Baptist Convention in 1913. "Men have become birds and fly in the air. All of this progress is being made by the world. We naturally ask ourselves the question: Is the Church keeping pace with the times?"[39] An unsigned editorial in Durham's *Carolina Times*, a black weekly, also bemoaned the church's difficulty in looking forward. "Religiously, men do not change easily and often, and any man or

group of men who dares to propose a reform, or even a change, is tread-
ing upon dangerous ground." Noting a proposal raised in two churches to
form a baseball club for teenage boys, the editorialist reported that "need-
less to say the older heads for the most part rose up in arms and defeated
the movement. . . . The church afforded only one attraction for them and
had only one way of presenting it which wasn't sufficient for active young
minds, hence the church lost them, maybe forever."[40]

In his critique of the ability of Baptist Sunday schools to stir youth, C.
C. Spaulding observed that "the reason a boy will sit outside of a baseball
park and look through a knot hole for two hours to see a game is because there is something going on in the park. He is interested." Spaulding
continued, "Until we pay more attention to our Sunday School programs,
keeping always in mind the importance of creating and holding the atten-
tions of our children, our services will be more of a drudge than a success. We must create a desire within the pupil to go to Sunday School;
then drive the truth home."[41] Longtime Baptist Dr. Moore agreed as he
lamented the fact that thousands of freshly minted Baptist theology school
graduates were seldom "strong in the faith" and often were alienated from
the church. "It is certainly high time for us to turn our attention towards
our young people, and efforts should be made to save, train, educate them,
and use them for the uplift and promotion of our great denomination," he
said. "Our pastors have largely neglected the young people, forgetting that
it is also their duty to 'feed the lambs.'"[42]

Convention leaders were also chagrined at the inroads the YMCA and
boys' club/scout movements were making with black youth. Founded before the Civil War, YMCAs were organized to infuse Christian character
in men. African-American men, who were considered chattel at the time,
were excluded from the mainstream "Y" movement. The first black YMCA
branch was established by a former slave in Washington, D.C., in 1853.
After the Civil War, freedmen were encouraged to start their own segregated YMCA branches. After the national YMCA hired two black men,
William A. Hunton and Ohio minister Jesse E. Moorland, black branches
were established in New York, South Carolina, and Pennsylvania for the
"mental, moral and spiritual improvement" of the race. Between 1900 and
1920, the number of black YMCAs grew from 21 to 44 in cities while the
number in colleges and universities blossomed from 53 to 113.[43] Such organizations were needed, their supporters claimed, to fortify black manhood

against racial caste and prejudice. YMCAs indoctrinated young men with the principles of "true manhood."

Echoing John Dancy's pronouncement that "the glory of any race is the manhood of that race," YMCA leaders paired the tenets of traditional Victorian virtues with muscular Christianity in their training of black men and boys.[44] Members were groomed to be industrious, self-reliant, pious, honest Christian gentlemen who were also physically fit. Through their immersion in athletics, hygiene instruction, and religious and educational programs, men and boys would acquire a Christian character capable of withstanding both the demands of an industrialized society and racial discord. YMCA supporters believed that members of white society would come to see black men who displayed rugged individualism and a Christianly deportment as their equals. While black YMCA leaders' endorsement of manly Christianity was in part shaped by their external environment, they also likely adopted such values in response to their own needs and concerns.[45]

Black YMCA advocates also dealt with the perceived problems of urban migrants. Scholar Nina Mjagkij stresses that black architects of the YMCA, unlike their white counterparts, cultivated a masculine identity that looked to the future instead of resurrecting the past. Blacks' development of "true manhood" emphasized self-determination, a quality that ultimately could break down racial barriers. In this sense, the new manhood that emerged in the early years of the twentieth century was forward thinking. This analysis, however, understates the extent to which black leaders from the YMCA and elsewhere shared in whites' anxieties about modernity. YMCA leaders feared that without proper supervision, single black men who had no religious or home ties would be unable to resist the temptations of urban life. And yet, they maintained, ministers were too distracted with their efforts to build larger churches to develop the social programs that could attract young people. As a result, young men were alienated from the church. It was easy for black YMCA officials to see the church as "a dreary place" for young people.[46]

For these reasons, influential black leaders looked to the YMCA as an effective solution to the race and boy problem. W. H. Davenport, a graduate of historically black Livingstone College in Salisbury, North Carolina, spoke at the anniversary of the college's YMCA on the topic "Tread of the YMCA in the South." He began by linking the YMCA's growth in the region with the spread of Christianity and asserted that the YMCA ensured the eventual eradication of racial caste and hatred. "Who can dispute the rights of manhood when the soul is illuminated by the light of the cross and the heart pulsates in harmony with the meter of the Psalms?" Davenport asked. "As this organization advances much will be done towards modifying Southern sentiment against the bronzed American."[47] Asserting that much "depends upon the young men in the settling of this race issue," Davenport argued that the work the YMCA was doing to provide young men with a Christian education and cultivate a sense of manhood was crucial. While the black church had done much in this direction, "the Association treads upon territory where the church does not move. It secures the Christian membership of young men that never before attended church. It furnishes their rough hewn natures, enthrones good feeling and causes men to be regarded as men."[48] Rev. D. J. Sanders, president of Biddle University, a co-educational Presbyterian school in Charlotte, also testified to the good work the YMCA was doing. "The series of meetings recently held under the auspices of the Association," he noted, "resulted in the conversion of a goodly number, and greatly revived the spiritual life of the community."[49]

The development of black boys' clubs as an antidote to juvenile delinquency and idleness also undermined claims that Sunday schools provided the proper training ground for young black males. C. C. Spaulding felt that the Boy Scout movement was a countermeasure to the delinquency problem. He described it as a "fine, Christian, manly program" that emphasized Christianity, citizenship, character, and culture. These four principles, Spaulding believed, produced well-rounded boys who understood their obligation to God and their fellow man. The Boy Scouts helped develop "the ability of boys to do things for themselves and others" and taught them "patriotism, courage, self-reliance, and kindred virtues."[50]

North Carolina also sponsored boys' conferences designed to teach boys piety, self-control, and problem-solving skills. The state's third annual black Older Boys Conference took place in Durham in 1927; previous conferences had met in Greensboro and Raleigh. Held under the auspices of the state association of the YMCA headquartered in Charlotte, the local committee on the Colored Older Boys' Conference began a vigorous letter-writing campaign to enlist community support for the enterprise.[51] In correspondence addressed principally to local church leaders,

W. F. Witherspoon, general chair of the conference, and W. J. Kennedy Jr., North Carolina Mutual Insurance Company president and chair of the conference's registration and entertainment committee, requested that housing arrangements be made for the estimated 300 to 400 boys who would descend upon Durham's Hillside Park High School on 4–6 November. Noting that it was "custom . . . that the good church people of the city furnish homes for the boys," the conference chairs urged ministers to appoint a person or committee to provide shelter for at least twenty-five boys. Though records do not indicate the degree of cooperation achieved through the committee's appeals, correspondence after the conference, which had as its theme "Youth's Craving," described the occasion as successful.[52] The conference featured religious services, music, an address by C. C. Spaulding, Sunday school attendance, and a group session for "problem discussion." Boys were encouraged to make the conference "worthwhile" by demonstrating respectable behavior. They were to try to know and be obedient to the will of God, strive toward punctuality at each session, not allow "selfish pleasures" to distract them from their obligations as conference delegates, and to be judicious about "conduct in the place where you are entertained and with your room-mate."[53]

Stung by the inroads of groups such as the YMCA and boy's clubs and by criticism of the church's inadequacy in shepherding young men away from immorality and vice, the leaders of North Carolina's Baptist Sunday School Convention proclaimed its position as the premier institution for the moral and religious training of black youth. As a supporter of boys' clubs, C. C. Spaulding challenged his religious brethren to go beyond lip service in the battle to help black boys become men. The neglect of church and Sunday school workers of youth had caused "welfare, social societies, YWCA's and YMCA's to do the work that Christ commissioned us as Christians to do. *Jesus Christ* was a social worker—he went about *doing*, not *saying* good." Rev. Robert Bruce McRary called the black church "the highest exponent of our social, civil, moral and religious status."[54] Dr. J. A. Tinsley also noted the unique role of Sunday school in advancing the physical development and moral well-being of its students and the race. "The Sunday-school has the child when its [mind is] soft and pliable and can be bent in any way," he said. "The Sunday-school should be a great agent in reducing the mortality of the race." Nicholas Roberts deemed it the responsibility of the church and Sunday school not only to "win the young people to membership, but train them for useful service. . . . It is a mistake to have people join the Church, and soon after drop their names, because the proper influence has not been exerted to hold them."[55]

As part of a Sunday School Forward movement, Baptist churchmen responded to the boy problem by outlining ideas and programs to increase the membership and participation of young boys. They attempted to make boys feel welcome and useful, proposed wholesome amusements, sought to strengthen home environments, and worked to improve the quality of Sunday school instruction in their efforts to prevent boys from turning to street culture. In all these activities, they stressed conventional gender roles.[56]

Acknowledging the "difficult problem" of reaching and keeping the boy in Sunday school, Nicholas Roberts was one of many men who urged his brethren to display greater sympathy in their outreach efforts. "We must not only notice him in the Sunday School, but wherever we meet him shake his hand and say a kind word," he said. "Every boy that goes astray is not mean at heart, but becomes discouraged, and like one of old, says in his heart, 'No one careth for my soul.'" Teachers, he advised, should be more tender and patient in their discipline of boys. "When he gets him in Sunday School do not scold him for his absence, but encourage him to come again. We must learn to be fishers of boys to be successful teachers."[57] While Rev. A. S. Croom suggested that Sunday school rooms should be made as "beautiful and attractive as possible," he also encouraged teachers to offer an affirming environment such that the boy would feel "the school cannot get along very well without him." In response to a question posed by a minister, "How to hold the boys in Sunday School after they get about thirteen years old?" Sunday School Convention president Dr. A. M. Moore thought it best to sympathize with the boy and give him "something to do."[58]

In their effort to foster a welcoming environment, some churchmen thought boys could best be lured with a "live bait." For "boys are like fish, birds and animals, and will come close to you if you give them something they need," instructed Dr. Ray of Raleigh's Deaf, Dumb and Blind Institute. The speech was afterward described as one of the most helpful addresses given at the convention.[59] Henry M. Houston, founder and editor of the *Charlotte Post*, baited children with sweets. His Crusaders Organization, formed to help deter criminal behavior among blacks, focused on drawing young people into Charlotte's churches. The plan worked as follows: "For several Sundays, all of the children who went to Sunday school received some candy," he said. After the children got in the school, it was the "work of the church to keep them there. Then we offered prizes to the Sunday school having the largest number of new members on a certain Sunday." Another observer, writing in the *Star of Zion*, noted a Sunday school superintendent who "wins his children by spreading party feasts for them."[60]

Black Baptist Convention women also explored the question of how to attract young women. The subject of "How to Obtain and Retain the Interest of the Teen-Age Girls" was discussed at one meeting. There Mrs. Washington suggested that the Sunday school needed to touch the "every day life of the girl" by providing picnics, lawn parties, and other amusements and "socials of the right kind."[61] In her address "Young Women," Mrs. Cora B. Long counseled that "girls' attention may be won by giving them such books to read as will inspire self-respect. Then, too, the Sunday School should cultivate the social natures of the scholars by occasionally giving socials and invite all classes of young women to attend and feel a welcome."[62] Writing to "our girls" in the *Star of Zion*, Sarah Dudley Pettey noted that girls who focused on "trashy stories of fiction become gay, giddy and oftentimes unbalanced. . . . Therefore you should not cultivate the habit of reading light literature."[63] Churchmen and women thus proposed solutions for the problem of youth alienation, such as social meetings, that were applicable to either sex. But some Baptist women such as Mrs. Weeks determined that although some behavior might be wholesome for boys, it was off limits to girls; she was pleased to report how she "broke up a baseball game on Sunday."[64]

Male leaders of North Carolina's Baptist Sunday School were unhappy about some of the youthful amusements the urban environment offered, and they expanded the structure of their institution to compete with those entertainments.[65] They took their cue from other progressive black ministries in the South, many of which offered free lunch rooms, gymnasiums, amusement halls, and reading rooms. Other churches, however, tried more unorthodox measures. A nondenominational black church in Durham, for example, hosted a young man's club, which contained a smoking compartment in addition to providing social meetings and a reading room. And J. H. N. Waring, principal of the Colored High and Training School in Baltimore, disclosed that, most remarkably, "one good bishop of a great church has recently given his approval and sacerdotal blessing to a liquor saloon which some people regard as very little different from the ordinary grog-shop and whose great and distinguishing merit, as widely advertised, lies in the fact that only *pure* liquors will be dispensed therein" [emphasis mine].[66]

Sorting pure from impure amusements became a delicate task for North Carolina's black churchmen as some attempted to move between two seemingly dichotomous but related worlds. They acknowledged that new ideas and approaches were necessary to stop the moral freefall of the race's young men, but they also clung to the ideals of moral and cultural refinement that were intrinsic to their religious mission. For many churchmen, adherence to values such as temperance and thrift formed the structural core of their religious beliefs. Strict disciplinary measures, such as church censure, were often used with church members who failed to regulate their behavior in and outside the church. The tensions and contradictions present in churchmen's evolving value system thus abounded as they struggled to formulate acceptable behavior and activities for young black men. While some men sought to fight modern temptations with modern means, others preferred more conservative religious ideology and practices.[67]

Shaw University's theological department, for example, made only modest adjustments to its quarters. A reading and reception room was added to Convention Hall. The men's theological programs were reorganized so that they appeared less "technical" or stiff. "Slight modifications of the usual meetings, it is thought, will provide both entertainment and instruction," Shaw's F. B. Holt surmised.[68]

For Nicholas Roberts, the key to getting and "holding the boy" also lay in "better conditions, better surroundings." He applied the concept of social environment broadly. He believed that modern houses of worship should come equipped with attractive rooms, good libraries, and classical literature and should host social gatherings, lectures, reading circles, and clubs—"everything that will interest and attract the young."[69] The judicious construction of wholesome attractions such as these, he thought, would not only provide young men with intellectual stimulation but would also foster a collegial environment in which appropriate forms of social contact and expression could occur.

Other entertainment devices used to "hold and keep the boy" were less novel. North Carolina Baptists endeavored to increase Sunday school attendance by boosting their musical offerings. Mr. M. W. Williams submitted that music was "the most valuable" tool for the Sunday school. Miss

Hicks of the Baptist Young People's Union concurred, saying that "no Sunday school is complete without music, and church services would never seem complete without music."[70] She recommended that a program be started for students to perform alone or in quartets to "make the Sunday School more interesting and to develop the musical talent of boys and girls."[71] Educator Ezekiel E. Smith also believed that music "drives the evil passion out of the child, and inserts high ideals."[72] Church members' praise of music as a socializing tool for children was validated in larger racial discourses. W. K. Tate wrote in the *Southern Workman* that "music should be placed in the first rank as a socializing activity. . . . When people sing together they can usually do a great many other things together. Singing should be taught in the schools and should have a part in every social gathering or entertainment." Music as a source of recreation for black youth had several benefits, according to its supporters. It enlightened young people about their own possibilities; instilled them with goals, purposes and direction; and promoted racial solidarity and fellowship.[73]

While there was broad agreement that amusements of some sort were needed to recapture black boys' interest in sacred things, judgments were mixed about what to offer. Rev. Jordan, for example, urged a conservative course. He told attendees at the 1930 Baptist Young People's Union state convention to "help close up the Sunday movies, golf courses, and many other evils that are open to the young people on Sunday afternoons."[74] Other men seemed to agree with Shaw University's F. B. Holt, who agreed with the view that modifications were needed to stir young men's interest but judged that they should be "slight."[75]

Ministers speaking from other southern pulpits were even less enthusiastic about alterations in the mission of the church. Rev. Silas Ford, for example, denounced the "multiplicity" of uses that some sought for the black church. "The day has gone by when it needs to be an entertainment committee, a lecture bureau, an intelligence office, and a business association," he said. Rather, he preferred that the church assume its basic and "legitimate" duty of ministering to the spiritual and moral needs of the community.[76]

As North Carolina churchmen continued to define and institute pure amusements for boys, they worked to repair a weakened home environment, symbolized by women's departure from traditional gender expectations, which in their view, underlay the boy dilemma. Home, most religious leaders agreed, provided the building blocks for a child's social-ization. "Home is a child's social model," declared C. C. Spaulding. "What he eats, sees and hears in that period, when the plastic mind is taking on its most enduring impressions, will almost invariably be adopted as his life's standard of his relationship to his fellowmen and his God. He goes out from the home a living exponent of the principles and teachings of that home. Therefore, much grace and wisdom is needed in the heart of the home maker."[77] Mr. E. A. Johnson, speaking to the North Carolina State Teachers' Association meeting, defined the home not simply as an edifice where one lived but a place of "purity, right living, honesty, industry and all things grand and pure." Moral "looseness," in contrast, "causes children to leave their homes."[78]

Spaulding linked the home's "looseness" with the growth of commercialism and black women's labor outside the home. "Mother and father are not on good terms," he said. "They are not agreed as to what the boy shall or shall not do." The advent of mass advertising, upscale retail shopping, and installment buying were potentially damaging to racial uplift ideology and the project of cultivating an appropriate manhood as an ideal for black boys to follow. New values that stressed extravagance had replaced older ideals of self-sacrifice and thrift, key components of the Victorian framework that black church leaders had incorporated into their strategy of racial advancement and in which black women played a prominent part. Spaulding continued, "Large numbers of mothers are leaving their children at home unprotected and undernourished while they go out to labor during the day in order that they may help keep these luxuries up," he explained. "Then we wonder why our children are getting away from us."[79]

Henry Houston of Charlotte also thought that black children's "bad beginning" stemmed from black women's employment. "They leave the children early in the morning and return late at night," he said. Despite this "great handicap," Houston remained optimistic that recreational and educational programs for young people would help.[80] Such pronouncements exposed the class and gender biases of middle-class black men and their conscious willingness to ignore the reality of black women's experiences. Extensive scholarship has recorded how pervasive racial discrimination against black male workers propelled black women into the labor force in order to support their families. Yet from the perspective of middle-class black men, women's waged labor undercut their men's roles as breadwinners or the patriarchal protectors of their households.[81]

Leaders in the National Baptist Women's Convention also voiced displeasure at women's reliance on modern conveniences, arguing that it stunted race progress and individual character. The convention preached aggressively against the installment plan. Women were encouraged to save their money and invest in "more of the old-fashioned comfort . . . clean walls, bare floors, a few rugs, and a good library with the best books and magazines."[82]

The expectation of black men that black women should play a major (and traditional) role in the home training of black youth was not lost on North Carolina Baptist women. Miss C. A. Moore remarked that the reputations of black women rested squarely within the home, which she termed a "great center of influence." "The training of children or parenthood is a profession," she said, "and should be learned like any other profession, so that the mother might know how to train them the right way, for she has the greater part of training and making of our home, and with her rests the happiness or fate of a home, state or nation."[83]

This stress on individual responsibility espoused within the politics of respectability led to a situation in which women were blamed or blamed themselves for the moral lapses of the race. While black men could be excused from childrearing responsibilities, distracted as they were with worldly matters, black women were roundly criticized when they pursued worldly interests. As Mrs. Garland Penn noted in 1902 at the Negro Young People's Christian and Educational Congress, "It is no unusual occurrence to see fathers so full of ambition, so much in love with the things of the world, that they have no time nor heart for the religious instruction of their children," she said. "But how strange and unnatural, yes, how shameful it is to see a mother so much absorbed by fashion and things of the world that she has no time to gather the little ones about her and warn them against sin and its punishment."[84] At the North Carolina Sunday School Convention in 1914, Rev. O. E. Askew said that the Christian woman shouldn't squander her obligation to "train moral men." He had "no patience with woman trying to get the ballot because she is the head of the stream and it will go as she directs, thus she should train the men right!"[85]

North Carolina Sunday School corresponding secretary A. W. Pegues felt that the quality of Sunday school instruction was more important than the home environment for shaping young boys. "It is pure folly to expect boys and girls to go to Sunday school Sunday after Sunday and sit for an hour unless there is something for them," he said. "It is no use to put the blame on the parents, or lack of home training and such like. Of course, there are exceptions, but as a rule if the teacher can and will make the hour of interest, the children will stay in school and will get more satisfaction in than out of the classroom."[86] Dr. A. M. Moore agreed, arguing that obtaining morally upright Sunday school teachers was critical, adding that "tattlers, dancers, card-players and gigglers" were unfit to teach. A more rigid selection process of Sunday school teachers was thus needed, not unlike that required for lawyers, doctors, engineers, and other professionals, for Moore found it distasteful that "we entrust the lives and souls of our children to Sunday School teachers who are often not even Christians."[87] Rev. J. L. Holloman's address "How Can the Sunday-School Be Made Attractive to Young Men and Young Women?" emphasized that instructors needed to be both earnest and devout. Teachers must "believe what they teach" and "must love those whom they teach." Professor Benjamin G. Brawley of Shaw University informed the 1924 Baptist State Sunday School Convention that to make Christian men and women, "the teacher must have character, his teaching must be vital and dynamic. He must present the lesson so that it will make a lasting impression on each boy and girl."[88] For Rev. I. S. Riddick, Sunday school teachers needed to believe that no other agency but the Sunday school was capable of "doing a greater good in moral, spiritual and educational uplift of humanity. . . . The word taught should not be considered as an abstract theory, but as a divine personal utterance," he said.[89]

The structural organization of the Sunday school also merited attention, according to convention leaders. "We sometimes speak of the boy problem and the girl problem," said President A. M. Moore. "In great part they have their origin and settlement in the . . . improper classification and government of the school." He felt it was a mistake to use 40-year-old methods in the modern Sunday school. Moore suggested that separate primary departments for boys and girls be developed with competent teachers placed at each helm. Sunday School Convention president C. C. Spaulding also lamented a "noticeable lack of system" within Sunday schools. Similar teaching methods were being used to instruct adults and children. No "scientific" plan existed to properly classify and grade pupils. Spaulding also noted that little connection seemed to exist between Sunday school teachers' lessons and the children's environment. Based on these observations, Spaulding concluded that "no incentive is offered children to go to Sunday School."[90] He recommended that Sunday schools be classified into cradle roll, kindergarten, primary, and adult departments.[91] This classification system would assign importance to each stage of an individual's religious training and provide children strong associations with the church at their earliest stage of mental and physical development. Dr. James Shepard, president of the North Carolina College for Negroes in Durham, also offered direction for "reaching the unreached." Citing the ages of 4 to 18 as the "stormy period in young people's lives" and thus a critical time for indoctrinating children in the church, Shepard advised parents to enlist their small children in the cradle roll department. That affiliation would associate children's earliest memories with attending Sunday school. Shepard also suggested beefing up the Home Departments of Sunday schools to promote and strengthen religious values within the family unit. "This done and it will not be long before the home will be [made] into the Sunday school," he said.[92] Dr. A. M. Moore suggested that boy "scholars" be grouped according to their age and intellect. "The long-pants boys should be separated from the short-pants boys. The young men from the long-pants boys and so on." Separating older and younger students, Moore said, would make boys feel that they had a special and unique place in the Sunday school.[93]

Although the sources do not reveal how boys reacted to the various "lures" set before them in North Carolina Baptist Sunday schools, it seems clear that such entertainments failed to sustain broad appeal because convention leaders continued to grapple with the "boy problem" well into the 1920s. Churchmen's attempts to provide youthful amusements signaled efforts to strike an accommodation between the traditional and the new. To adherents of conservative religious values, modest, self-restrained conduct was appropriate. For churchmen amenable to implementing modern attractions, "everything that will interest and attract the young" was potentially useful. Finding wholesome amusements for black boys was hard work for churchmen, and their quest to mold the character of black boys and at the same time uphold the spiritual integrity of their churches was challenging. As churchmen worked with boys, they also labored to maintain their status as men by affirming a gender role structure that subordinated women.

Minding Morals and Manners: Fashioning Respectable Gentlemen
in Cultural Schools

Education facilities such as the Mary Potter School in Oxford, North
Carolina, sought to clarify the path of respectability for boys. One newspaper called it "one of the important institutions for colored youths." Potter was founded in 1890 by educator and minister George Clayton Shaw,
who ran the private Presbyterian elementary and high school for forty-
five years. Shaw, born in Louisburg and educated at Lincoln University,
was first led to Oxford in 1888 by Mrs. Mary Potter of Schenectady, New
York, who advised him to do religious work in his native North Carolina.
After a disappointing survey of the black community of Wilson, North
Carolina—out of its 2,000 residents, not one claimed to be Presbyterian
or to have ever seen a black Presbyterian minister—he decided to pastor
there. Upon reflection, however, he sought out the counsel of a local white
Presbyterian minister, who recommended he consult with one of his black
church members, Mrs. Mary Howell. It was Howell, Shaw claimed, who
marked his life's "turning point." As he recalled, "She said: 'Why certainly
you can organize a Presbyterian church here [in Oxford, North Carolina];
that is what God sent you here for. I have been praying for years that God
would send us a colored Presbyterian minister. Why, man, God sent you
here, you can't go away.'"[94]

Shaw, thus inspired, began his "continuous labor," preaching the "doctrine of pure homes, pure churches, and a pure ministry."[95] Mary Potter
School, which occupied land valued at $95,000 and typically enrolled 400
to 500 students, offered a mix of literary and vocational courses designed
to train students for "life's duties."[96] Girls were taught domestic science
and boys were instructed in manual training. On the campus's farm, located just outside the corporate limits of Oxford, young men absorbed
lessons in agriculture and agricultural theory.[97] The Mary Potter School
promoted itself as having faculty who were able and "devoted to their calling." It claimed that its location and setting proved healthy and inspiring,
a place where "fine fellowship" meant stimulating intellectual and social
opportunities.

Besides their immersion in academic and vocational courses, students
were exposed to what the school referred to as the "wholesome traditions"
of musical training, debating clubs, and athletic activities such as football, baseball, tennis, and basketball.[98] Assessing the school's legacy, Shaw

proudly remarked "If there is any one thing that gives us delight . . . it is the many young men and women who came to us in the crude and went out refined, cultured and polished—and have gone on to serve even as they were served." The Mary Potter School, Shaw boasted, excelled in "developing character."[99] Though George Shaw was careful to illustrate the activities of and goals for both girls and boys at his school, his written reflections largely focus on the rehabilitation of boys and their successful transition into a respectable manhood. Partnering in this effort was his wife Mary Shaw, who in her written tribute to her husband's work also identified with the particular challenges boys faced and, like George Shaw, sought to ameliorate them.

For Shaw, respectability manifested itself in a drive for self-improvement, not only in appearance but also in vocational pursuits. Supporting oneself through work, regardless of how menial, signaled that one had assumed responsibility for oneself that was critical not only to self-development but to the development of the race as well. As Stephanie Shaw observed in her study of black professional women workers during the Jim Crow era, black community leaders lived by an ethic of "socially responsible individualism," an expectation that the individual achievements of blacks would dovetail with a commitment to race progress. The welfare of the self and society were therefore inextricably bound.[100] In his annual reports, Shaw routinely praised the numerous graduates who worked in the fields of nursing, teaching, the ministry, medicine, and farm work. He paid particular attention however to the school's boys, whom he often spotlighted as symbolic of his school's pedagogical approach and success.

Reflecting on the Mary Potter School's modest beginnings, Mary Elizabeth Lewis Shaw recalled how she and her husband had observed the short shrift boys were initially given at the school. She wrote of boys' placement in substandard housing in the early years of the school. The school's board of directors had approved the construction of a new administration building in 1912 to replace Recitation Hall, and boys were given the old building as housing.[101] "Our boys always had to have the leftovers," Mrs. Shaw lamented. "The recitation building made a poor dormitory but it was larger than the one we had and we made the best of it." Fate apparently intervened in the boys' behalf when the subpar dormitory succumbed to fire on a Sunday morning in 1924.[102] "We felt sorry for the boys," Mary Shaw recalled, and because of that the Shaws quickly took heart as they absorbed the manly image the boys cut dressed in their "best Sunday clothes." Because of the importance of religion for George Shaw, who preached the doctrine of "pure homes, pure churches, and a pure ministry," the Shaws would have been attentive to the boys' deportment on Sunday. Promotional materials about the curriculum at the Mary Potter School cited heavy student involvement in the YWCA and YMCA and a course offering on the "English Bible." Given the school's objective that students leave Mary Potter "refined, cultured and polished," the Shaws were duly impressed at the boys' effort to be at their "best," both spiritually and in their appearance.[103] That affirming display on the Sunday after the fire, Mary Shaw noted, "decided our boys' building." The following fall, Pittsburgh, or Pitt, Hall was built. Though some school officials wanted to give the beautiful building to the girls, Mrs. Shaw remarked that "our boys had never had a real break and as it was built for the boys it was and is our boys' building."[104] It must have pleased the Shaws to no end, in the context of their collective effort to redeem and bolster young men, to brag with gusto about the personal and vocational advances of Potter boys.

Shaw's narratives of the evolution of particular boys into confident, self-assured, and socially responsible men were often rags-to-riches stories. As he told these stories, Shaw typically assumed the roles of rescuer and protector as he described his random encounters with "forlorn, ragged" boys. One such "ragged" pupil was Henry, whom Shaw met while walking Oxford's streets. As was his custom, Shaw invited the boy to attend Sunday school. He later learned about the unstable family life that had led Henry astray. The boy's father had died at the age of 2, and his mother, after remarrying, passed some four years later. Henry's stepfather also remarried, a situation that apparently proved untenable as the boy soon learned that the only use his stepfather had for him "was to bring his dinner."[105] After some time, Henry began attending Sunday school regularly. As Shaw recalled, "From our missionary box he was made to look respectable during the week, and more so on the Sabbath." Henry studied hard to make a way for himself in life, and as he grew older he was appointed superintendent of his Sunday school. After he graduated from Potter, he earned a theological degree from Lincoln University and worked a Sabbath school missionary in Oklahoma. Henry's domestic life proved exemplary as well when he chose to settle down with another graduate of the Mary Potter School.[106]

Another student worthy of Shaw's admiration was Walter Hughes, who also came from humble roots. Hughes's troubled background included his father's infidelity, which ultimately led to a broken marriage and dissolution of the family. When Hughes was accepted at the Mary Potter School, he proved himself an "unusually good and smart boy."[107] After graduating, he earned degrees at Lincoln University in Pennsylvania and Meharry Medical College in Nashville. Hughes was hired by the government to administer health clinics in Memphis. After World War I, he became a member of North Carolina's state Board of Health, headquartered in Raleigh. In that capacity, he traveled throughout the state to lecture black communities on venereal disease. Shaw recalled a conversation between Hughes and a white health official that demonstrated Hughes's penchant for exuding and receiving respect. The official, Dr. Knowles, asked the young doctor to also provide lectures to white citizens in Oxford. Knowles went to Oxford to hear the young instructor's lecture, which featured a film presentation. Hughes gave one talk to black women at 3:30 p.m. and another to white women at 4 p.m. "As the reels were run through the colored show, there was a boy there to take them immediately to the white show," wrote Shaw, who noted with great satisfaction, "The colored people for one time were first!"[108] Dr. Knowles was impressed with Hughes's performance, remarking that he was the "best informed man that he had in the work," black or white. Hughes is a good example of male graduates of Mary Potter School who exhibited the qualities of self-help, respectability, industry, and socially responsible individualism that Shaw touted as the benchmarks of character and manhood.

Like Shaw, educator Charlotte Hawkins Brown sought to reform and transform the "crude" at her Palmer Memorial Institute in Sedalia. In addition to academic training, she provided training in racial etiquette befitting black boys and girls.[109] Brown, who founded the private finishing school in 1902 at age 19, expected her students to abide by a strict code of Victorian moral conduct. She worked to smooth "the rough edges of social behavior" by producing graduates who were educationally sound, religiously sincere, and "culturally secure."[110] This training was partly accomplished through small discussion groups for boys and girls. Adult male and female counselors led these groups and gave students individual attention in matters of etiquette. The discussion in one boys' session centered on how best to obtain "culture" along with clean minds and bodies. The girls, meanwhile, were instructed in the true meaning of friendship and how to act and think responsibly. In some instances, the curriculum of the small circles transcended gender differences. Younger Boys' Circle advisor Robert Nicks felt that lessons learned in the girls' circle could be used to "good advantage with the boys."[111]

Students also participated in "wholesome" fitness activities designed to nurture habits of self-reliance, self-control, and fair play. Palmer girls played basketball and volleyball. The sports repertoire for young men was more expansive, including basketball, football, baseball, and track and field. Brown wanted the athletics to strengthen boys' self-confidence and foster courteous behavior, discipline, and fair play. Football, in particular, achieved a balance in male behavior that suited Brown's cultural tastes. According to her, football did not result in boys' rough or coarse behavior. Rather, the "clean" sport encouraged temperance through its "constant operation of courage and gentleness, daring and sympathy, strenuous endeavor and just consideration. These contrasted forces are constant and vital in producing the highest type of man."[112] Brown's vision of the highest type of gentleman, as extolled in her curriculum, was a balance of contrasts.

Perhaps Brown's most noted contribution to her student's cultural education was her etiquette manual, *The Correct Thing, to Do, to Say, to Wear*, where she succinctly defined good manners and behavior for boys and girls. Mirroring the perspective of Sunday School Convention president Nicholas Roberts, Brown dismissed the idea that boys didn't need cultural training. She felt that otherwise intelligent people "make all kinds of plans for the proper training of their girls and so nonchalantly express their attitude in these words: 'Oh, the boys will get along all right.'" And yet while black girls were taught how to treat a gentleman by allowing him to be "gallant and chivalrous," boys, in Brown's estimation, were culturally handicapped in their knowledge of how to interact with young women. "Imagine her anxiety to the point of tears as his right hand guest at the formal dinner when he blows into his soup to cool it, dips it toward him and makes a noise swallowing it."[113]

Seeking to calm girls' anxieties about boys' shortcomings in gentlemanly etiquette, Brown revealed to the "men and boys who care" her standards of manly behavior. They included suggestions for boys' appearance and deportment. Boys were encouraged to dress neatly and in a manner that evoked a spirit of character and poise. During summer, dark coats and light flannel pants were considered in good taste while full evening dress was expected for formal occasions. Proper deportment for boys included maintaining a "genuine respect" for women by resisting bodily contact except when aiding her ascent or descent from a certain position, refraining from smoking in her presence, and standing when she entered the room. Additionally, she advised boys to avoid profane language, shun dirty jokes, and be respectful and sympathetic to the beliefs of others.[114] Though her instructions to youth clearly conformed to the gender expectations of the dominant society, Brown's stress on appropriate behavior for boys was also likely shaped by motivations within the black community. Brown and other women like her lived in a racially charged atmosphere where the dignity of black womanhood was under assault, even by members of her own race. For example, William Hannibal Thomas's turn-of-the century book on the challenges to black morality, *American Negro*, blamed black women for lewd behavior, from prostitution to abortion. Thomas felt it was impossible for black men to "respect chaste womanhood." Correlations between lasciviousness and black womanhood helped rationalize legal segregation and sexual violence. These kinds of attitudes from black male writers put women's bodies at risk and denied them respectability. Brown's exacting tutorials ensured that women and men in North Carolina's black community diffused such threats to their persons and racial character by according one another the respect whites routinely denied them.[115]

As part of her lessons to male youth, Brown challenged dichotomous characterizations of gentlemen that saw them as either "effeminate, spineless" or "crude and rough." "A real gentleman," she wrote, "avoids both of these extremes." She advised black boys to maintain a balance between emasculating and primitive behavior. In summing up her conception of a gentleman, the "finest type of man," Brown spoke plainly. "He is neither cave man nor fop."[116]

An examination of the Young Men's Institute (YMI) in Asheville provides additional insight into the issue of gender identity for male youth. The YMI's internal dynamics illuminate not only the existence and importance of the social and professional bonds among black men but also how black men used community space to mark black women's subordination within the organization. While North Carolina's black Baptists pinpointed environment as the source of bad boys, the reconfiguring of environment within the YMI ushered in and reinforced a gender climate that empowered black men. For the YMI's black men, solving the "boy problem" entailed establishing themselves as role models for male youth and distinguishing themselves from boys and women by displaying bold gender leadership.

Negotiating Community: Gender, Manhood, and Public Space
in the YMI

The invitation in the March 1904 edition of the *Asheville Citizen* was blunt
and unequivocal. "We want 500 men to hear Dr. Swopes at the Y.M.I.
tomorrow afternoon." Another announced, "Dr. R. R. Swopes will speak
at the Y.M.I. tomorrow afternoon. We want 500 men and boys to hear
him." The straightforward, urgent appeals repositioned the Young Men's
Institute from a democratic and gender-inclusive space to a sex-segregated,
male-centered space. At the men's event, which was well attended and "rich
in thought," Dr. Rodney Rush Swopes discussed the "Making and Unmak-
ing of a Man."[117]

Swopes served as rector of All Souls Church in Biltmore Village in
Asheville, North Carolina, part of the Biltmore Estate financed by George
Vanderbilt. He also supervised the YMI in Asheville during its early years.
While newspapers like the *Asheville Citizen* failed to report Swopes's
speech, the *Citizen-Times* noted that the YMI's "monthly meetings, especially for men," proved "very helpful to the young men of the city and have
been the means of turning many lives in the right direction."[118]

The YMI has been characterized as broad based and inclusive. Male
members remember the YMI as the "center for Negro culture in Asheville"
and a place where "the people . . . flocked."[119] Descendants of early YMI
members see it as a unifying force for the black community. Written accounts assess the institute as the "cornerstone for civic, business, recreational, and social life of Blacks in Western North Carolina," "the epitome
of a black self-help organization," the "cultural cornerstone of Asheville's
black community," and a "meeting place and true community center."[120]
Contemporary newspaper articles proudly point to the YMI as a long-
standing cultural, economic, and social resource for Asheville's black
population. While initially founded as an organization for black men
and boys, the YMI "eventually served everyone in the African-American
community."[121] Men and women, young and old were invited to hold
church/song services and group meetings, hear renowned speakers such
as W. E. B. Du Bois discuss race relations, and be entertained at banquets
and concerts, most notably one featuring a violin performance by the
grandson of Frederick Douglass. In short, the black community's desires
for self-development, culture, and the assertion of race pride were met at
the YMI.

Histories of the YMI also point to the innumerable ways black women contributed to the institution, blurring its distinction as a masculine enterprise.[122] Former YMI member Ernest McKissick, for example, stressed the importance of contributions by women such as Maggie Jones, charter member of the North Carolina Federation of Negro Women's Clubs and organizer of its first chapter in Asheville, in building the YMI. "The women of Asheville helped to make a YMI, buy that building," he recalled. "Because the men alone couldn't have bought it." YMI secretary William Trent also noted the "fine service" rendered by Maggie Jones, Mrs. Anna George, and Friddie Abernathy (members of a ladies' auxiliary group) in raising money to buy the YMI building. The initial organizational meeting of the YMI, moreover, included both women and men. In fact, the group's first officers featured Hattie High, who served as the YMI's musical director.[123]

Gender analysis has been largely absent in histories of the YMI. The dynamics between YMI members and the black women involved in the institute's activities have failed to garner the same attention as the group's reputation as an independent community-based institution. (This is partly explained by the relatively small amount of scholarship devoted to blacks in western North Carolina.) Both scholars and the public have emphasized that the YMI was a racial self-help organization and have overlooked the gendered aspects of its history. A deeper look, however, reveals an institution that consciously incorporated gender ideals within its structure as a means of affirming and asserting the gender and leadership status of its male members.

The YMI is a two-story, 18,000-square-foot, Tudor-style brick-and-pebbledash edifice on the corner of Eagle and Market Streets in downtown Asheville. It was commissioned in 1892 by Biltmore Estate owner and philanthropist George Washington Vanderbilt.[124] British West Indian Edward L. Stephens, a Cambridge University graduate who worked for Vanderbilt, "persuaded him to build a Black YMCA."[125] In its early years, the YMI was referred to as the YMCA. Vanderbilt consented to the idea for the "convenience and service of colored men and boys," as he found no social outlet for the hundreds of black male artisans, bricklayers, and other laborers who were constructing the Biltmore Estate, a project that involved a workforce of 1,000 men and took almost five years to complete. It is regarded as one of the first integrated construction projects in the South.[126]

Black community leader Isaac Dickson held the group's first organizational meeting in his home. Dickson, the son of a slave mother and Dutch father, had established the first public high school for blacks on Beaumont Street. The school opened in 1888 with three teachers and focused on reading and writing skills through grade five. The popularity of the school, which accommodated 300 students, was such that 800 potential applicants were denied admission. Dickson had also founded Catholic Hill School in 1891, the city's first black high school.[127]

Edward Stephens, then principal of Catholic Hill School, along with local pastors and approximately thirty young men and women representing the city's various religious denominations met in Dickson's home in the fall of 1890 to discuss the formation of a "colored YMCA." At the meeting, Stephens suggested that the association focus on the "moral, intellectual, and social improvement of its members." Meetings would be held each Sunday afternoon at a designated church site until the group could find its own building. Encouraging remarks were then offered by pastors and some of the young men assembled. The officers of the association were listed as Edward Stephens (president), H. B. Brown (secretary), Isaac Dickson (treasurer), and Hattie High (musical director).[128]

Three years later, the YMI building had largely been completed, at a cost of $32,000. The third anniversary of the YMI drew an overflowing crowd to the institute's auditorium on a wintry evening in 1893. Some seventy black men braved the weather to hear Rev. J. S. Morrow and Edward Stephens, the group's first general secretary.[129] Charles McNamee, business manager of the Biltmore Estate and trustee of the YMI property, also attended. Though the occasion offered refreshments, music, and a sense of gaiety, it proved less a testament to the institute's strengths than a reminder of its shortcomings. Rev. J. S. Morrow began by speaking about "Man's Right." Man, Morrow, contended, had a "right to go where he pleased and do what he pleased—so long as he pleased to do right." Invoking the politics of respectability in his construction of manhood, Morrow stressed that YMI men should strive for the "virtuous and upright life" that the institute represented. The YMI's Rev. C. S. Dusenbury also chastened the men, saying he "regretted that they had not shown a more unanimous spirit to make of the institute what its founder intended."[130]

The two-story YMI building fulfilled numerous communal purposes. It provided space for schools that needed a place for play rehearsals and graduation ceremonies.[131] The second story housed a boarding house, a school of domestic science for girls, a bathing department, a Bible school, a gymnasium, and a kindergarten. The YMI also housed a night school and the city's first black library. It offered meeting spaces for civic organizations, clubs, schools, and churches. Businesses housed in the YMI included a realty company, cabinet shop, beauty shop, barber, shoe shop, drugstore, and undertaker. The YMI had an auditorium for concerts, dances, banquets.[132]

The YMI's annual report, delivered by General Secretary C. H. Baker of Washington, D.C., said that eighty men were members in good standing and reported that more than 1,500 baths had been taken and 82 "entertainments" given at the institute. An institute band had also been organized and a kindergarten housed in the building was doing "splendid work." The number of visitors to the institute had reached 10,000. Yet in a further challenge and test of the group's effectiveness as leaders and men, Baker revealed that a deficit of $1,200 had accrued. The debt, which had been "met by Mr. Vanderbilt," was nonetheless discouraging, for Vanderbilt had "given the building to the people to see what sort of stuff they were made of."[133]

As YMI members worked to better fulfill the group's mission and fortify their identity as men, institute leaders and supporters soon found themselves in a struggle to save the building "for the race." Frustrated by the inability of Biltmore Estate's black laborers to carry the expense for the property, Vanderbilt and institute trustees considered abandoning the YMI in 1900. That year, William J. Trent, a graduate of Livingstone College who in 1898 had served as YMCA secretary for the Third North Carolina Regiment during the Spanish-American War, "took charge" of the YMI, becoming its general secretary.[134] Perhaps inspired by Trent's bold declaration of leadership, Asheville's black community rallied to save the YMI. In the fall of 1905, Vanderbilt proposed selling the building to the black community if they could raise $10,000 in cash within six months. If not, the institute would go on the market at a price of $15,000.[135] With that announcement, the people were "stirred as never before." By the deadline of 31 May 1906, community members had netted $2,500 in cash. Of that amount, YMI member George Greenlee had raised $1,000 from white citizens. Based on individual and church donations and a loan of $6,500 from white businessman Kelly Miller, the amount was raised and the building was officially incorporated as the Young Men's Institute on 14 May 1906.

A month later, YMI officers paid $10,000 to Vanderbilt for the title to the building.

Given the YMI's varied functions and offerings, all black organizations—religious, civic, recreational, business—seemed to lose their distinctive markings once they were absorbed within the structural framework of the institute. The YMI seemed almost to supplant the role of the black church as the hub of the black community when a number of churches began worshiping at the institute. When churches of any denomination sought worship space, the YMI gladly consented. Brown Temple, Asheville's only Christian Methodist Episcopal Church, had its initial services in the YMI auditorium. Hopkins Chapel A.M.E. Zion Church also sought refuge in the YMI after it burned down in 1907. Church members rented out the YMI's basement for three years until Hopkins was rebuilt.[136] Hopkins Chapel member Ernest McKissick found God not in a church but at the YMI. "That's where, to tell you the truth, I confessed religion," he said. "I was baptized in that building."[137]

Alongside the YMI's identity as a comprehensive economic, religious, and cultural center for Asheville's black community, however, was a gendered imperative to portray YMI leaders as proud, respected, and self-sufficient men. The YMI's architecture contributed to this goal. Business and commercial properties were located on the building's first floor and its church, social, and recreation departments were located on the upper level. YMI members seemed to give pride of place to the manly world of business.[138] Some of the city's most prominent professionals belonged to the YMI. Among them were James V. Miller of Miller's Construction Company. Born a slave in Rutherford County in 1858, Miller built homes, churches, and office buildings through his company, which was established in the 1910s and flourished until his death in 1940. Miller built St. Matthias, Hopkins Chapel, and Ebenezer and Mount Zion Missionary churches. His son, physician Leotus O. Miller, built a successful practice in Asheville. The younger Miller, who pioneered an innovative blood pressure treatment, was also credited with founding the Blue Ridge Hospital and Training School for blacks in 1922. Miller served as chief of staff for the hospital, which not only treated black patients but also trained doctors and nurses. The hospital also educated the black community about proper hygiene and sanitation.[139]

Other professionals located at the YMI included George Hamilton, a café owner; Fenton Harris, operator of a printing shop and an owner of the

YMI drugstore; Max Baxter, another former slave, who served as the city's first black building contractor, realtor, and banking consultant. Benjamin James Jackson, owner of a fruit and vegetable market in Asheville, was widely considered Asheville's most prominent businessman. In 1887, he became the first black to own a stall in the Asheville City Market located on City-County Plaza. Considered the best in the marketplace, Jackson's vegetable and fruit produce sold to patrons at the Battery Park Hotel and other hotels, cafes, restaurants, and boarding houses. In his novel, *Look Homeward Angel*, Asheville native Thomas Wolfe paid tribute to Jackson's entrepreneurial acumen. As he wrote,

> The self-respecting Negro, J. H. Jackson, stood in his square veg-etable stall, attended by his two grave-faced sons, and his spectacled businesslike daughter. He was surrounded by wide slanting shelves of fruit and vegetables, smelling of the earth and morning—great crinkled lettuces, fat radishes still clotted damply with black loam, quill-stemmed young onions newly wrenched from gardens, late cel-ery, spring potatoes, and the thin rinded citrus fruits of Florida.[140]

Wolfe's language spoke respectfully about Jackson's enterprise and initia-tive. This admiration extended to his family as well. His sons' and daugh-ter's deportment was characterized as serious, responsible, and business-like. Jackson, too, was a member of the YMI. Among his more noted contributions, Jackson served as chorister for that group's popular Sunday evening song services.[141]

Alongside the impulse of YMI's leaders to exude a manly professional profile was a commitment to mentor and shape boys into manhood. Reflecting to a degree the program of the YMCA, the YMI sought to promote brotherhood among men in its interactions with black male youth. The institute's curricula featured sports such as baseball, lessons in hygiene, music and debating clubs (in the form of mock trials), guest lecturers, and a night school. While many programs the YMI offered were similar to those black YMCA organizations provided, the YMI was exceptional in that its operations were completely autonomous from a white-led national organization. While they were undoubtedly influ-enced by the workings of the YMCA, it was Asheville's black business and professional men who shaped the functions and purposes of the YMI.

One of the YMI's goals in mentoring black male youth was to affirm the importance of male bonding and networking to their identity as men. The professional and personal obligations of adult members to the YMI overlapped as many chose to integrate their work and/or home lives at the institute. For example, pharmacist Henry E. Jones lived at the YMI and operated his pharmacy business in the building. John Nipson Jr. also called the YMI home.[142] Other YMI men located their residences along College, Eagle, Valley and Cherry Streets, all within vicinity of the Institute's headquarters. Still others used the YMI to strengthen father/son bonds, such as James V. Miller and his son Leotus Miller, both of whom were members of the institute.

The partnership between YMI leaders James Walker and William Trent was emblematic of the power and endurance of networking among black men. Both men were educated at Livingstone College, a coeducational religious facility in Salisbury, graduating together in the class of 1898. In college, Trent and Walker had sung in Livingstone's traveling music group, including a performance at the Atlanta Exposition in 1895, where Booker T. Washington gave his famous address that encouraged blacks to remain in the South and earn livelihoods through industrial and agricultural labor and focus on securing economic opportunities instead of demanding civil rights.[143] Trent would later replicate Washington's racial doctrine of self-help and promote his work at the YMI. Yet he also adapted tenets of W. E. B. Du Bois's "talented tenth" philosophy as he believed that the privileged educated few should assume responsibility for elevating the masses and promoting racial opportunity. Trent's dedication to the racial ethos of socially responsible individualism was particularly visible in his college work with black male youth. In his recollections of Livingstone, William Fonvielle described Trent as one who "has great love for young men, and he is doing everything possible to help them, both by precept and example."[144] Realizing that the key to racial advancement and respectability lay in a good education, Trent, Walker, and other YMI men supported the educational pursuits of deserving boys. As one writer described it, Trent "took it upon himself to open the doors and impart the vision."[145]

In college, Trent and Walker had organized and played in the country's first black intercollegiate football contest.[146] The mutual regard between the two men persisted well after graduation. After Trent's service in the Third North Carolina Regiment in 1898 and a year's stint working at Greenville College in Tennessee, Trent and Walker were reunited at the YMI, where they continued to work closely together until Trent's departure for Atlanta's YMCA in 1911. The two men, who often posed in pictures together and attended the same church, appeared to exhibit a genuine sense of camaraderie and mutual respect toward each other throughout their partnership. Trent noted the crucial role his friend had played in negotiations for sale of the YMI property. "I have always said that it was providential that Dr. Walker was the spokesman, for if I had . . . spoken . . . I am sure we would not have saved the building."[147]

The nurturing networks that YMI men cultivated among themselves were passed on to younger generations of members. Ernest McKissick joined the YMI as a boy in 1907 or 1908, when he paid a yearly membership fee of 50 cents. McKissick's later remembrances of the activities he engaged in as a YMI member illustrate the playful tenor of his youth. "We had downstairs shower baths and tub baths. We'd box and wrestle in the basement. Upstairs in the gym we played volleyball and basketball. . . . I'm eighty some years old, and that's part of me."[148]

McKissick's more than 50-year bond to the institute was determined by more than the aesthetic attractions at the YMI. Having arrived in Asheville from South Carolina in 1900 at age 5, McKissick began his education at the Hill Street School under Principal Walter S. Lee. He later attended Catholic Hill School through the second grade. Subsequently finding himself adrift, he took comfort in the moral and educational support proffered by several YMI leaders, who he recalls "saw something in me and . . . wanted to take me in."[149] The men who took him in as a boarder and household helper at the YMI were Dr. James Walker, Professor Trent, and pharmacist Henry Jones. However, his "mainstay" and "idol" was Dr. Walker, "because he put me on my feet and started me out." For his first job, Walker had McKissick drive him via horse and buggy to see his patients. McKissick described the job: "He would go and make visits; I would stay out and hold the horse. My horse's name was George; a pretty buggy and black horse." After a short while, Walker judged it best for McKissick to work at the YMI drugstore. When not working at the drugstore, he worked as a bellhop at Asheville's Battery Park hotel and did other odd jobs around town.[150]

Yet most of his energy was spent at the institute. McKissick gained a reputation as a fine tenor soloist for a YMI choral group that performed for churches and at civic and social events. Some called his voice "the mocking bird of the Land of the Sky." His affinity for the YMI and industrious behavior were not lost on the group's leadership, which sought to reward him. Alonzo McCoy, Walker, Walter S. Lee, and Trent agreed to help fund McKissick's college education. "We have decided to give you, each one of us, ten dollars apiece. We are going to raise some more money for you," they advised him. "You work this summer and save all you can, and we are going to send you to Livingstone College. That's what we want to do." McKissick enrolled in the fall of 1913. At college, his singing talent blossomed as he contributed to Livingstone's concert company, choir, and choral union. In April 1918 he was drafted into World War I, where he served in the country's first black artillery unit, Battery F of the 349th Infantry Division. While overseas, McKissick became conscious of the troublesome meaning that calls for democracy abroad held for black Americans. He recognized that "democracy wasn't working at all at home" due to the pervasiveness of Jim Crow laws in the South. And yet McKissick felt obligated to serve his community nonetheless. "I wanted to come back home to Asheville," he said. "I wanted to come back home to be with my people and see them and see what I could do. And I wanted to try to help young people, young boys, and all."[151] After all he had accomplished through his interactions with the YMI's leaders, McKissick had reason to feel that the YMI was "part of me" and that because of his training there, he was poised to contribute something beneficial to his race and gender.

Other YMI activities designed to increase the pride and manly vigor of young men were athletic and intellectual contests such as baseball games and mock trial competitions. C. C. Lipscombe managed the boys' baseball team, which played against local and regional teams, and hosted an annual Easter baseball game. Moreover, echoing the feeling of Baptist Sunday School Convention leaders that boys required "live" bait to keep them interested, the YMI offered "rare" treats to boys at the institute.[152]

Cultural and social programs were generally open to everyone, as were some meetings convened to address the institute's financial debt. When Richard B. Harrison of Chicago came to the YMI in 1912 to speak about true friendship through a reading of the poem "Damon and Pythias" at a special joint Sunday meeting, Trent invited "every man and woman in the city . . . [to] attend."[153] The public was also invited to the First Baptist Sabbath School's presentation of its Christmas cantata at the YMI in 1903.[154] Additionally, an "urgent call" went out for men and women who were interesting in joining a choral club. The eighteen men and women invited to the organizational meeting included the YMI's B. J. Jackson, J. W. Walker, Fred Fowler, J. H. Hamilton and Asheville residents Eloise Orner, Emma Davis, Hattie Earl, and Daisy Fowler.[155] Trent emphasized unity and cooperation at the first meeting. "In order to make this undertaking a success, we must realize the importance of united effort," he said. "We must expect to make some sacrifice of time and a little money." Trent hoped to raise money to hire a pianist and purchase music compositions and predicted in 1904 that the collective effort would raise "the standard among the musical talents of Asheville and the state."[156]

Charity events to benefit the institute were also presented as community affairs. Institute leaders widely advertised a three-day glass and china fair held in December 1903 in the local press. The community also gathered at the YMI in April of that year for an Easter carnival. A gold watch, silver umbrella, and bracelet were among items auctioned off at the 1904 event, which also featured a life-sized gold-framed pastel portrait of a local pastor, which was given to the "most popular lady" attending the festivities. Meetings addressing the YMI's financial standing were also gender inclusive. A 1904 board of directors meeting at the YMI was open to all, as was one held in 1912. YMI fund-raising rallies typically featured overflowing crowds. At one such rally, held in the summer of 1907, the YMI netted $826.10 from the estimated 500 people who crowded into the building. These and other events were designed to include the entire community.[157]

And yet, at other times, only men were welcome at the YMI. An invitation to attend the "grand Pentecostal service" on Sunday, 9 January 1904, at 4:45 p.m. was "for men only." The ladies' Woman's Christian Temperance Union (WCTU), which normally met at the YMI, was requested to hold its regular monthly service at Mt. Zion Baptist Church. Another Sunday YMI meeting on 10 March 1904 was also advertised as "for men only"; women were invited to hold their organization's meeting at St. James A.M.E. Church. Moreover, the YMI's popular song services, which featured guest lecturers as well as music and spirituality, became "men's day" one Sabbath day in January 1904. The ladies were politely asked to meet at Mt. Zion. And it was men who were invited to attend a Bible class one afternoon in August 1912.[158]

Evelyn Brooks Higginbotham has observed that in the early decades of the twentieth century, black urban areas became increasingly sex-segregated male domains. Not unlike race segregation, in which laws restricted black movement in "white physical space," in black communities middle-class gender conventions distinguished male from female spaces. While "male turf" included streets and pool halls, churches and households were designated as female locales. Due to the limitations imposed by Jim Crow, many black women were expected to adopt mainstream gender roles to assert their morality and a respectable identity. This included adopting favorable forms of public behavior. Pool halls and barbershops equated to a male subculture that was at odds with domestic or "respectable" values. Within the gendered geography of urban communities, then, black women who transgressed or sought to blur these gender boundaries risked censure from black middle-class men and women. In a study focused on Durham, N.C., scholar Dolores Janiewski noted that "respectable women hurried through the streets between their public and private workplaces." YMI leaders allocated public space at the institute in ways that mirrored the street culture they so roundly condemned because it subordinated women.[159] In this respect, street culture and black-middle class culture converged, complicating black middle-class men's work to distinguish themselves as respectable.[160]

Men were poised to become racial and gender leaders during and after World War I. Several YMI leaders met on 17 November 1916 to organize the Colored Betterment League. Inspired by the patriotic response of western North Carolina's black men to the war effort, which included service from second lieutenant James Bryant Dickson, grandson of the YMI's Isaac Dickson; First Lieutenant George B. Greenlee, also of the YMI; and McKissick, the league sought the "general uplift and promotion of the best interest of the colored people of Asheville and to foster the law and order of the colored community." As YMI men took satisfaction in the bravery exhibited by their compatriots who campaigned for democracy abroad, they aimed to set a manly standard of leadership at home. In the words of some men attending the meeting, they wished to "accomplish things which encouraged peace and prosperity of the city."[161]

It was new for men to take leadership roles in community-building efforts. Before the war, women and men had worked together. When the black community rallied at the YMI in 1913 for a new hospital to replace the segregated ward reserved for them at the white Memorial Mission Hospital, two canvassing teams, comprised of five teams of men and five teams of women, spearheaded the campaign. Prominent clubwoman Maggie Jones was among the canvassers. In the 1920s, however, it was the YMI's men who spearheaded the movement. Leotus Miller, rather than the community, was largely credited with securing Blue Ridge Hospital for the exclusive use of black residents. Miller was described as "unwavering in the founding, the building and the maintaining of Blue Ridge Hospital here." Likewise, he was praised as "putting ideals into effect."[162]

Despite what churchman Nicholas Roberts described as a "bad atmosphere" that obstructed the manly exercise of first-class citizenship at the turn of the century, North Carolina's black male leaders did not waver in their collective determination to usher into manhood the next generation of race leaders.[163] Working in religious, educational, and community-based institutions such as the Baptist Sunday School Convention, the Mary Potter Institute, and YMI, black men endeavored to groom black boys into respectable, industrious, useful citizens who embraced both their racial and gendered selves.

North Carolina churchmen's attempts to solve the "boy problem" included providing wholesome alternatives to urban youth culture, encouraging a softer church discipline for boys, stressing traditional gender roles in the home, and improving the structure and quality of Sunday school instruction. Devising innocent amusements proved to be taxing work for churchmen as they sought an accommodation between their religious beliefs and boys' increasingly secular pursuits.

Educators George Clayton Shaw and Charlotte Hawkins Brown, conscious of their role in cultivating the race's morals and manners, sought in similar style to create respectable race men who valued industry, home life, and the merits of domesticity. Brown, aware of the need for proper training for boys, insisted that the way boys conducted themselves should complement rather than compromise the behavior and reputations of black women. She counseled boys to covet a masculine middle ground somewhere between brash and effeminate behavior. Shaw, who chronicled his many rescues of boys from broken environments with dramatic flair, also expected boys to behave respectfully and fit themselves for both leadership and domestic life. Shaw's wife also figured in this manly pursuit, as she too promoted boys' welfare. Her reminiscences of the Mary Potter School and her husband's work in it illustrate her empathy for boys' proper development.

The YMI, on the other hand, demonstrated the limits of cooperation between the genders in efforts to address the boy problem. YMI's black men shaped their gender interests around the institute's prominent identity as a community organization. Thus, sometimes the YMI presented itself as a pillar of racial solidarity by embracing an array of local black institutions, public speakers, social gatherings, and activists, male and female alike. Yet YMI men were also careful to fortify and demonstrate their manhood through exhibitions of business and professional prowess, male networking, and the mentoring of young boys. Moreover, though mindful that "the women of Asheville helped to make a YMI," the institute's message of united effort was tempered by a competing motivation to assert an image of manly dominance. When they felt it was necessary, YMI leaders excluded black women from the institute. While women retained a place within the YMI, their activism was circumscribed so that the organization's primary, or authentic, identification as a black male institution remained intact.

North Carolina's black middle-class men, working through prominent community institutions, steered young men into manhood while addressing their own needs for a healthy masculine identity. At the same time, several men determined that saving black youth, preserving ideal male and female identities, and cultivating a dignified manhood ultimately lay in private all-male spaces.

Figure 1. Charles Dusenbury, courtesy of Heritage of Black Highlanders Collection, D.H. Ramsey Library Special Collections, University of North Carolina at Asheville.

Figure 2. J. A. Whitted, used with permission of Documenting the
American South, The University of North Carolina at Chapel Hill
Libraries.

Figure 3. Calvin Scott Brown and G. W. Bullock, used with permission of Documenting the American South, The University of North Carolina at Chapel Hill Libraries.

Figure 4. YMI Orchestra (1908), courtesy of Heritage of Black Highlanders Collection, D.H. Ramsey Library Special Collections, University of North Carolina at Asheville. Seated on floor: *left*, Dr. William J. Trent; *right*, Charles Thomas Howell.

Figure 5. YMI drugstore, interior (1910), courtesy of Heritage of Black Highlanders Collection, D.H. Ramsey Library Special Collections, University of North Carolina at Asheville. *Left to right*: Thomas Moore; Dr. Ed Jones; Dr. William Torrence.

Figure 6. YMI drugstore, courtesy of Heritage of Black Highlanders Collection, D.H. Ramsey Library Special Collections, University of North Carolina at Asheville. *Left to right*: 1) Mrs. Maggie Jones; 4) E.W. Pearson; 5) Dr. L. O. Miller; 6) behind 5, Stanley McDowell; 11) Jim Miller (Dr. Miller's father).

Figure 7. Maggie Jones, courtesy of Heritage of Black Highlanders
Collection, D.H. Ramsey Library Special Collections, University of
North Carolina at Asheville.

Figure 8. Ernest B. McKissick, courtesy of Heritage of Black Highlanders Collection, D.H. Ramsey Library Special Collections, University of North Carolina at Asheville.

Testimonial Dinner

for

DOCTOR WILLIAM JOHNSON TRENT

in recognition of twenty-seven years of
unselfish service
as President of Livingstone College
Salisbury, N. C.

FEBRUARY 12, 1952

GIVEN BY
The Board of Bishops of the A.M.E. Zion Church
The Trustees of Livingstone College
The Committee and Faculty of Livingstone College

Figure 9. W. J. Trent tribute program, courtesy of Heritage of Black Highlanders Collection, D.H. Ramsey Library Special Collections, University of North
Carolina at Asheville.

3

"Badge of a man"

Gender and Fraternity in North Carolina's Black Secret Society

At the appointed hour, Robert McRary ordered his grand marshal to assume command of the street parade. The dignified procession wearing Masonic regalia wound its way through Raleigh's principal streets, ending the public ritual at St. Paul's A. M. E. church. There, grand orator J. E. Dellinger shared with his audience an issue that was typically discussed only in private—what the nature and characteristics of a good Mason were. Proclaiming that "the craft" had a "definite place in human history" and had influenced "the current of history for good in a very decided manner," he lauded the Prince Hall Masons because their order was based on the "science of human brotherhood, and the philosophy of human kindness."[1] "The craft," a colloquialism for freemasonry, is a ritualistic order that emphasizes the noble principles of charity, brotherhood, and love for all members. Working to "make the burdens of men and women lighter," Masonic men strengthened the black race by erecting and bolstering community institutions and by aiding the indigent. Masonry's mandate also extended to the household. Dellinger stressed the duty of masons to safeguard and nurture the home and its inhabitants, maintaining that "ours is an institution for the making and the keeping of the home, and home life. . . . The home, we take it, is first of all for the children and for the benefit of the children. And that man is less than a man, out of which you can not make a decent mason, who does not feel and take a kindly interest in children." He added, "everything that can be done must be done to give the child life of to-day every opportunity to be able to make the most of that manhood life, and womanhood life that must come to them to-morrow."[2]

Other characteristics Dellinger cited as uniting "all good men in the bonds of fraternal unity" included tolerance and patience. A good Mason avoided confrontations and quarrelsome behavior. "He would avoid strife, as if it were an infection," Dellinger stated, adding, "the good mason is ready to 'give in' rather than continue a useless wrangle." Good Masons also refrained from political partisanship. The "good man and mason is not moved by any consideration of partisan politics, or any question of sectarianism or schisms of doctrine or dogmas of faith," according to Dellinger. Finally, good Masons knew how "to labor and to wait." Dellinger asserted that despite pervasive racial discrimination that was "obnoxious to any mason's sense of fairness and justice," a man with a grievance and a "grouchy scold" did more harm than good. Duty to oneself, one's family, one's fellow man, and one's country were paramount obligations. As he explained,

> To be called into court, and tried and punished, without judicial representation therein is trying and exasperating in the extreme. To be required to support a government by taxation wherein any representation is denied us, would tend toward desperation, but the good mason is admonished by patience, that political conditions some times move backward, and that social revolutions move most slowly, and that the best way to better living conditions is to live best under the conditions that obtain.[3]

Within the private spaces of North Carolina's black secret societies, black men engaged in the task of constructing manhood. Not unlike white male fraternities, black Masonic groups emphasized benevolence, mutual aid, and adherence to a strict moral code.[4] Within the contexts of disfranchisement and Jim Crow, however, the participation of southern black men in freemasonry took on added and significant meaning. Fraternal societies such as North Carolina's Prince Hall Masons were safe sites where men temporarily eluded the indignities of racism by participating in communal activities and self-affirming rituals that satisfied racial goals. Prince Hall Masons also worked to craft a respectable, virile, and chivalric male image. The minutes of lodge meetings reveal the importance of gender and how conceptions of gender were reshaped over time to craft uplifting images of black manhood and black womanhood. Fraternal work thus reinforced the capacity of black men to mold new racial and gender identities that were not distorted by the indignities of Jim Crow.

Historically, the black fraternal order has rivaled the black church as a benefit society and a social, recreational, and economic institution. Luminaries such as W. E. B. Du Bois and Booker T. Washington affirmed the status of the black secret society as a formidable racial institution. Du Bois remarked that secret societies advanced the race through their "mastery of the art of social organized life."[5] Washington lauded the fraternal organization as the place where businessmen learned how to accumulate capital and where the black masses learned "habits of saving."[6] Historian John Hope Franklin argued that antebellum fraternal organizations founded in northern black communities were crucial to the ability of blacks to achieve status and respectability in American society. Sociologist Howard W. Odum said that the number of members of black fraternal orders equaled or exceeded the number of members of black churches. Thus, scholars who have examined black freemasonry generally have emphasized its economic, religious, political, and communal functions.[7]

Given the significance of black fraternal organizations to African-American men, the dearth of scholarship on these institutions is striking, especially for the early-twentieth-century South. Statistics illustrate the popularity of black freemasonry in a region rife with white racism. For example, in 1909, 2,600 of 3,336 Prince Hall lodges were located in the South. By the 1920s, more than 150,000 masons were members of southern lodges. Several studies suggest that Prince Hall freemasonry ebbed after 1900 as a result of increased competition from urban entertainment and new black institutions, but actually the fraternity grew rapidly well beyond the turn of the century. Prince Hall membership exploded from 1900 to 1930, dropping off only after the Great Depression.[8]

Almost none of the literature on black freemasonry explores the connection between African-American fraternal beliefs and gender identity.[9] A recent exception to this is Martin Summers's study, which demonstrates how Prince Hall Masons used freemasonry to propagate ideals of manliness and respectability among its members. He also scrutinizes the ties between fraternity, gender identity, and Prince Hall's female auxiliary—the Order of the Eastern Star—by showing how black men maneuvered their identification with patriarchy by alternatively quashing, affirming, or containing black women's authority. However, his analysis does not extend to the South.[10] In an age when southern black men were deemed powerless or at the very least compromised in their attempts to protect black women, the secret society accorded black men fundamental manhood rights, those of provider (or producer) and protector. The gender identity of black men and women, not surprisingly, played critical roles in Masonic enterprises. Unlike many white Masonic orders, which discouraged white women's participation, black Prince Hall men such as North Carolina A.M.E. Zion minister James Walker Hood encouraged women to form auxiliaries to assist in the men's work. Late in life he reflected that "there are three important organizations in this State which I have taken special interest, namely: The A.M.E. Zion Church, the Masonic Fraternity, and the Eastern Star."[11] Scholars have acknowledged the interaction between black male Masonic orders and black women's secret societies; one Prince Hall historian has asserted that blacks did not appreciate the "great line of demarcation between the two [orders]."[12] Within the all-male secret world of masonry, black women, like their brethren in the church, carved out niches of authority, finding purpose in Prince Hall's larger humanitarian mission. Women's active participation in a racial (albeit male-dominated) institution seemed on the surface to indicate gender accord. Yet this co-operation did not eliminate gender conflict between Masonic men and women.[13]

The Eastern Star auxiliary to the fraternal order placed black women under the authority and protection of black Masonic men. While affirming patriarchal ideals, the notion of protection had complex meaning for race relations in the South due to the stigma attached to black womanhood. Within the racial and gendered essentialism inherent in white supremacy, black women's bodies and morality were deemed wanton and ill deserving of respect. Buttressed with a legacy of slavery in which black men were compromised in their ability to shield black women from sexual assault by white men, many African-American men and women committed themselves in slavery's aftermath to protect, and thereby elevate, the respectability and nobility of black women. Within black fraternal movements, men's valuing of domestic ideals—provider and protector—provided the framework in which they attempted to realize a nobler manhood and womanhood. The need for men to provide for their wives, daughters, mothers, and sisters proved a powerful moral calling and served to cement familial, community, and racial bonds.

At the same time, there were limits to how much patriarchal authority Eastern Star women tolerated. The presence of Prince Hall leaders signaled women's subordination to men, a position that Eastern Star women at times resented and challenged, for it subverted their community-building efforts. Nevertheless, the work of women of the Order of Eastern Star to uplift the black community ultimately gained significance only through the women's relationships to Masonic men. Indeed, the legitimacy of the auxiliary depended on including men as members.

Prince Hall leaders also scrutinized the manly tenets of tolerance, patience, and a unified brotherhood. Though manhood as constructed within the black Prince Hall Masons was nurtured and affirmed within private all-male spaces, its ideals were contested. Fraternity men were challenged to define a respectable manhood in the context of the threat of rival factions in their ranks, the aspirations of Eastern Star women to claim ownership over their own work, and growing calls from black Masons for the black fraternity to engage more directly in politics.

"Whence Came We"

The roots of African-American freemasonry reach to the post–Revolutionary War era. Not unlike the country's earliest black social institutions, the fraternity was established by a combination of initiative and responses to racial discrimination.[14] In 1775, Prince Hall, a Barbados-born artisan, and fourteen other black Bostonians was inducted into an English army lodge after being denied admission by the Grand Lodge of Massachusetts. After the Revolution, black lodges, which had consolidated into the Prince Hall Grand Lodge, claimed their independence from the Grand Lodge of England. In doing so, they stressed a Masonic history of democratic and egalitarian ideals. The objectives of freemasonry paralleled those of African-American mutual aid societies, which assisted the needy, particularly widows and their children, in exchange for dues. These groups also provided information about employment and cultivated social bonds. By 1791, the Prince Hall order had spread to Philadelphia and Rhode Island, where the membership acquired an elitist caste. Many of the first Masons in these states were wealthy men. They included Philadelphia's Absalom Jones, founder and first bishop of the African Methodist Episcopal Church, and abolitionist James Forten.

The structure of the Prince Hall Masonic order mirrored that of its white counterparts. Each fraternal lodge had at least seven ranking members: worshipful master, senior warden, junior warden, senior deacon, junior deacon, secretary, and treasurer. To meet as a constituted lodge of freemasons, a new lodge had to obtain a charter from an authorized Grand

Lodge that had jurisdiction over the geographic area where the lodge was situated. The grand master presided over the Grand Lodge.

Masonry is organized around degrees of membership: Entered Apprentice, Fellow Craft, Mark Master, Past Master, Most Excellent Master, and Royal Arch. A prospective member had to undergo a particular set of steps. If his petition was accepted by lodge members, an applicant underwent rituals for each of the first three levels of membership to initiate him into the "mysteries" of freemasonry.[15] Once he attained the rank of Master Mason, the applicant became a full member of the lodge and of freemasonry. The new member was subject to Masonic governance, which established guidelines for instruction, organization, discipline, and membership. The rituals for the first three degrees of membership, which were performed by both black and white Masons, were drawn from a hodgepodge of medieval, esoteric, and early Christian sources. Both races devoted at least two monthly meetings on weekday evenings to the complex initiation rituals.

Despite these similarities, white freemasonry's habitual designation of black fraternal orders as "clandestine" and illegitimate led blacks to construct alternative representations that challenged depictions of their race as degraded and undignified. Prince Hall leader Martin Delaney stressed the African origins of masonry. Black and white Masons attributed the mythic origins of the fraternity to King Solomon, who synthesized all previous wisdom, manifesting it through the building of the temple of Jerusalem.[16] The rites of initiation for the first three Masonic degrees symbolically depicted a deepening understanding of the wisdom of the temple. Delaney expanded on this basic theme, reworking Masonic history to the advantage of his race. He credited "the Africans" as creators of "this mysterious and beautiful Order."[17] Prince Hall leaders also appropriated aspects of the Masonic moral code of Euro-Americans, again adapting such beliefs to suit the race's needs. For example, self-discipline, education, and industry proved especially important to black Masons in the South, where freemasonry helped meet the high demand for black institutions after emancipation.

The rise of black freemasonry in the South began during the Civil War. Before 1860, black lodges existed only in Maryland, Virginia, and Louisiana, centers of populations of free blacks. Three years after the war's end, however, black masonry touched every southern state. The expansion of masonry in the region coincided with the growth of black churches.[18]

North Carolina's Grand Lodge was founded in 1870 by A.M.E. bishop Joseph W. Hood. Raised in Pennsylvania and ordained in New England, Hood pastored a congregation in Bridgeport, Connecticut, before his denomination sent him south as a missionary to freedmen. Arriving in the coastal city of New Bern, North Carolina, in 1864, Hood held the positions of assistant superintendent of public instruction for the North Carolina Freedmen's Bureau, superintendent of missions for the A.M.E. Zion Church, and superintendent of the Southern Jurisdiction of the Masonic Grand Lodge of New York. In these capacities, he helped found A.M.E. churches and numerous Masonic lodges. In 1872, Hood became bishop of the church, subsequently rising to senior bishop. Two years later, he was the steward of 366 churches with a combined membership of over 20,000. Shortly after coming to New Bern, Hood established King Solomon Lodge No. 1. Lodges in Wilmington, Fayetteville, and Raleigh soon followed. In 1870, the four lodges formed the North Carolina Grand Lodge and unanimously elected Hood as their grand master, a position he held until 1883. By 1874, the state had eighteen Prince Hall lodges with a combined membership of 478.[19]

Hood's ease in moving from church to lodge work is evidence of how religion and masonry intersected. Several members of the Prince Hall lodge were also active in church circles, among them James Whitted and Calvin Scott Brown, officers in North Carolina's Baptist Missionary and Educational Convention. Both the church and the lodge held annual meetings lasting several days; the conferences were organized hierarchically with by-laws and central committees. The conferences of the two organizations also shared similar programmatic features; both had worship, business, and recreation components. Both the church and lodge were important sites where black leadership was expressed and validated.

Yet while church and lodge had many structural similarities, masonry remained distinct from religious work. Addressing North Carolina's Grand Lodge in 1897, Grand Master James Young expressed this difference as rooted in gender. "I would not have you think that Masonry is identical with, or assumes to do the work of the Church," he said. "The one deals with natural, the other with spiritual. Masonry makes the man, religion redeems the soul."[20] Women's status in the church, as accorded them under traditional gender norms and as interpreted under liberal feminist theology, helped justify their role as race workers and religious workers in that public body.[21] But in the privatized space of the lodge, the psychological and ideological aspects of masculinity created an all-male space.

In the first decades of black masonry in North Carolina, lodge members were primarily the elite. Their rosters included politicians George H. White and Henry Cheatham, educators James B. Dudley and James Shepard, educator and businessman Berry O'Kelly, physician Leotus Miller, and military heroes Ezekiel Ezra Smith and James Young (both of whom served with the Third North Carolina volunteer unit in the Spanish-American War). As more blacks began to accumulate property at the turn of the century, lodges became less elitist, incorporating more members from the black middle and working classes. Prince Hall's reputation for attracting community leaders persisted despite its changing demography. "Our doors are being alarmed, as never before, by the representative men in all our communities," remarked Robert McRary at the group's 1909 conference in Wilmington, "and while masonry regards no man for his wealth or worldly honors, the accession to her ranks of the best men of all the ages and races has been one of her proudest distinctions."[22] R. Kelly Bryant, a local historian and former executive with North Carolina Mutual Insurance Company in Durham, also observed a shift in Prince Hall's membership ranks. A lodge organized in Durham in 1878, Bryant recalled, was comprised mainly of ministers and teachers. Over time, that list expanded to "include workers and all other kinds of people."[23]

As Prince Hall's class base expanded, so too did its gender composition. Shortly after assuming leadership of North Carolina's Grand Lodge in 1870, Hood ordered the creation of an auxiliary Eastern Star branch for the female relatives of masons. The women's primary responsibility, in Hood's mind, was to maintain and support the Masonic order.

The Order of the Eastern Star was formed in France in 1730, founded by Dr. Robert Morris, an attorney and educator from Boston, Massachusetts. Morris, a Master Mason and former Grand Master of Kentucky, wanted to create a female branch of freemasonry to promote fraternal unity. Morris's suggestion prompted widespread opposition from male Masons, who perceived women as too inferior to merit their own organization. Faced with such fierce resistance, Morris developed another strategy for incorporating women in Masonic institutions. He created the Eastern Star degree, the rights of which were conferred upon female relatives by Mason men. This adoptive rite grew to incorporate five degrees derived from Biblical women—Adah, Ruth, Esther, Martha, and Electa.[24] Together, the degrees symbolized the highest and purest principles of morality and religion and embodied the tenets of the Eastern Star—fidelity, constancy, loyalty, faith, and love. The degrees represented the five stages of a woman's life—daughter, sister, wife, mother, and widow and cemented the place of women in freemasonry as symbols of domestic virtue.[25]

Hood's decision to include the Order of the Eastern Star as auxiliaries to Prince Hall Freemasonry proved unique to black masonry; white fraternal orders largely opposed women's auxiliaries. White men apparently feared that women's participation would violate their manly domain and erode the group's masculine character. In the late nineteenth century, white masons were sometimes threatened with punishment should they "tell their wife the concerns of the order."[26] In contrast, Hood's liberal attitude toward women can likely be attributed to masonry's connections to the black church and black mutual aid societies, both of which depended on the active (if not wholly equal) participation of black women. As bishop in the state's A.M.E. church, Hood supported women as ministers within his denomination. He ordained Julia A. J. Foote as deacon at the group's New York annual conference in 1894 and supported women's struggles for ordination at the turn of the century.[27]

In 1880, North Carolina's J. W. Hood founded the first black Grand Chapter of the Order of the Eastern Star in Washington, D.C. Its goals were charitable and benevolent and its teachings were based on the Bible. In 1881, another grand chapter formed in Raleigh, North Carolina. The creation of additional grand chapters and local chapters continued apace in the country, and by 1924 the order claimed thirty-five grand chapters, 3,500 local chapters, and more than 100,000 members. After the organization of each chapter, it was "adopted" by a Masonic lodge. It thus served as an adjunct or auxiliary to Prince Hall masonry.[28]

Organized hierarchically with by-laws and a constitution, the structure of the Eastern Star complemented the men's group in all but one aspect: for a women's auxiliary to exist, it had to have some male members in positions of leadership. Thus, the Eastern Star's standing as a female organization was compromised because the group gained and retained its legitimacy only in relation to the presence of men. Eastern Star members were aged eighteen years and older. The male members were Master Masons in good standing and the female members had to be related to a

Master Mason in good standing. Eligible relatives included wives, widows, sisters, daughters, mothers, granddaughters, step-mothers, step-daughters, step-sisters, and half-sisters.[29] Each Eastern Star chapter also had some eighteen officers who were either elected or appointed. Two offices were reserved for men—Patron and Associate Patron—and nine offices were reserved for women. These positions included Matron and Associate Matron. Pharmacist York Garrett of Tarboro, whose father was a member of several secret societies, recalled that his father told him that "all Eastern Star organizations had to have a man of it, at least two men to make it legal to protect the women."[30] But women "couldn't be a member of the men's organization."[31]

Though Eastern Star meetings required the attendance of male Masons, the women retained independence over the operation of their order, at least in theory. While a presiding "brother" in good standing conferred the five degrees of the order on its female members, the Eastern Star's Worthy Matron was the presiding and executive officer of the chapter. This organizational structure over time shaped black women's expectations concerning their duties and the opportunities available to them.

In her history of the Eastern Star among "colored people," member Sue Brown recounted the founding meeting of the Supreme Grand Chapter of the Order of Eastern Star, later known as the International Conference of Grand Chapters of the OES in 1907. The meeting, which was held in Boston, had been called by future North Carolina OES leader Letitia L. Foy. Representatives of various grand chapters hoped to forge a "closer fraternal relationship, whereby there might be brought about a better interpretation of and more uniformity in the ritualistic work."[32] The women wanted to "cooperate" in the labors of masonry by assisting the men. Yet they also coveted opportunities for independent growth.

Women's work to aid the men included "directing the charities and other work in the cause of human progress."[33] Several local chapters owned property, and Grand Lodges of the Order of the Eastern Star aided Masonic temples, which were valued at from $7,000 to $650,000, by providing funds to build and maintain them. Women bought bonds to help purchase Masonic properties and decorated the buildings after they were built. The growing public presence of American women, as evidenced by the post–Civil War rise of women's religious and moral reform societies, including national groups such as the Women's Christian Temperance

Union, supported the order's effort to become an instrument for women's advancement. The "spirit of the age," observed a white Eastern Star grand matron in Connecticut, "demanded an extension of women's influence and usefulness."[34] Brown noted the diverse activities Eastern Star women spearheaded, which included operating burial funds and endowment departments. Others ran their own printing presses or organized youth departments.[35] At the same time, the Order of the Eastern Star valued its ties to the Prince Hall Lodge and sought to strengthen them. The parallel impulses of Eastern Star women to lead and assist, which were both rooted in their familial relationships to men, foreshadowed conflict with black masonry, which though it included women, perpetuated a sexual division of labor in which male authority dominated.

"Badge of a man"

Toward the dawn of the twentieth century, Grand Master James Young issued a challenge to his Masonic brethren. In an 1897 address, he encouraged his men to "arise and put on our armor, re-consecrate ourselves in the work, and in the closing years of the nineteenth century, inaugurate an era of prosperity for the Order in this Jurisdiction."[36] Young's exhortation sought an alignment between the fighting spirit endemic in warfare and the internal battle to reconstitute institutional strongholds within the black community. His forum for militancy lay within, not outside, this communal infrastructure. Yet racial unrest in North Carolina, culminating in a race riot in Wilmington in 1898, temporarily shattered the state's Prince Hall lodges.

The Wilmington Riot of 1898 was the culmination of attempts by white Democrats to illegally oust North Carolina Fusionists (white populists and black Republicans) from power. Across the state, black men responsible for retaining the power of the Republican Party, whose accomplishments included gubernatorial and other electoral victories in 1896, were rewarded with governmental positions. Hundreds of blacks were appointed to political office in North Carolina. Congressmen George White appointed twenty black postmasters in the Second District, soon dubbed the "Black Second" congressional district. This surge in black office-holding signaled to many white men the dangers of black power. These men, which included state Democratic Party chair Furnifold Simmons and Democratic

Speaker Charles B. Aycock, feared not only black political power but also social equality. In particular, black postmasters were singled out as threats to the racial order because their work encouraged interracial contact between blacks and white women.

The campaign against "negro domination" came to a head when black newspaper editor Alex Manly published an editorial asserting white women's sexual desire for black men. A white mob burned Manly's office. It is estimated that more than 10,000 whites participated in the riot that ensued. After four days and nights, about twenty-five blacks and one white had been killed. More than 200 people, mostly blacks, had been injured. Local black leaders, fearing additional bloodshed, resigned their offices. More than a thousand blacks left Wilmington. North Carolina politics had reached a turning point. White Democrats quickly regained control of Wilmington's city government and North Carolina Democrats seized state and local offices in the 1898 election. By 1899, the first of several Jim Crow laws had passed the state legislature. The "white man's government" had been restored.[37]

In the aftermath of the riot and its consequences, district deputy grand masters reported that "Masonry among colored men has undergone a severe test." The district leaders noted that "many of the brethren have been thrown out of work and many had to flee for their lives to parts unknown, and the brethren more favored were unable to give them assistance in the hour of need." One deputy grand master observed that "in consequence of the recent excitements and unrest of the citizens of this State, Masonry like other institutions has suffered in my district."[38]

Despite the political and social upheavals created by the Wilmington race riot and the Jim Crow legislation that followed, Masonic men heeded Young's call. The increase in fraternity membership in the face of escalating race oppression and exclusionist policies suggest the essential function of freemasonry for black men, both practically and psychologically. While Jim Crow held that black men were politically, socially, and economically impotent, masonry provided a cultural space where black men could assert a virile manhood in opposition to white male privilege. Black men's exercise of patriarchal leadership, good character, and fidelity to traditional domestic ideals (provider and protector of family life) were, in their view, proof of manliness. Though the fraternity's growth slowed in the 1880s and 1890s, likely due to economic depression and the exodus of blacks from the state, the first decade of the new century proved much more promising for the order. In 1900, there were 90 lodges and 2,037 members in North Carolina. By 1910, 358 state lodges listed more than 10,000 members. In that year, at least 300 communities in North Carolina had a Masonic lodge. Grand Lecturer J. W. Perry justly noted that "we have a great deal to be thankful for."[39]

As the membership of the lodge continued to expand, including laborers and farmers, the lodge remained focused on cultivating leaders. Membership requirements stressed intelligence, clean habits, Christian learning, and "good citizenship." While Grand Lodge rhetoric embraced universal brotherhood, the rhetoric emanating from Prince Hall lodges was classist. According to Grand Master McRary, "individually and collectively, the men who compose the fraternity in this Jurisdiction include in their number the most intelligent, the most temperate, the most industrious and frugal, the most moral and upright of the Race in the State." Another Mason boasted that the fraternity elected "recruits only from among the better class, those distinguished in their community for soundness of body and moral excellence." He noted that "through these we aim to improve the Race."[40]

A humanitarian ethos rather than political considerations guided the men in their work. Such membership requirements stressed not just the class dimensions of freemasonry for North Carolina's black men but also an unwillingness to engage in the political sphere. Fidelity to "soundness of body and moral excellence" superseded political considerations and formed the core of black men's Masonic activity. Grand Master James Young described the Mason's duties as first to "God, next, to his neighbor, then to himself." Young stressed that while "politics should never be discussed in a Masonic Lodge, it is demanded of every Mason that he carry his Masonry, its truths and principles—into politics, as well as into business and society."[41] Aware of the increasing race hostility around them, Prince Hall turned their energies inward and away from the newly segregated society around them. Yet they did not retreat completely. Using freemasonry as a protective shield, Prince Hall members devised another avenue for advancement by cultivating leadership within the race and forging a dignified manhood.

Prince Hall freemasons occupied a vital part of black America's communal infrastructure. Schools, churches, and lodges formed the core of black communities. Raleigh resident James E. Williams recalled that the race's "real history" existed in educational institutions such as Shaw University, churches, and fraternal groups. "Because these were the institutions where the majority of our people assembled and, with their meager earnings, placed their monies together to at least hold and develop the land."[42] North Carolina's Grand Lodge regularly dispensed benevolence and charity to its members and the broader community. Lodges often provided short-term financial aid to those who faced illness or other misfortunes. For example, W. H. Haddock, who had lost his crop due to water damage, received $5 from his fellow lodge members in 1908. That same year, the Prince Hall Lodge in Henderson provided assistance to R. D. Harrison, who needed funds to purchase an artificial foot. Masonic financial aid continued after a member's death. In 1880, the state lodge created a benevolence plan to provide death benefits to the widows of deceased members. The fund was centralized across the state at the turn of the century, and the grand treasurer began to manage the money. In 1908, he dispersed $22,925 to widows. That same year, widows' benefits increased from $175 to $225. By 1910, the death benefit had been elevated to $300. Prince Hall Masons also assisted the children of deceased members. They made large donations to the state's black orphanage in Oxford, which had been established in the 1880s. By the second decade of the twentieth century, the orphanage was receiving 10 percent of the Grand Lodge's annual revenue. A black orphanage in Winston also began receiving financial assistance in 1910.[43]

As the exclusive preserve of deserving men, Masonic lodges held their members to a high standard of moral ethics. In his address "The Mission of Masonry to Man," J. Y. Eaton equated masonry with no less than the "development of man himself." The word "Mason" embodied ideas of growth and improvement. Masons were builders, constructors, and creators. A dignified manhood could not be purchased (indeed, monetary pursuits only "corrupt[ed] national ideas and lower[ed] the standard of manhood") but rather was obtained through the pursuit of a "broad humanitarianism." The true meaning of masonry was found in men "whom the lust of office does not kill. Men whom the spoils of office cannot buy. Men who have honor. Men who will not lie. Tall men, sun-crowned, who live above the fog in public duty and in private thinking."[44]

The reputation of masonry depended upon expelling every individual who violated fraternal principles. Grand Master McRary argued that the order could not include "men whose mouths are the funnels of whiskey barrels, and the fount of obscenity and profanity." He argued that when "gamblers, libertines and violators of civil and moral law are tolerated ... the pure stream of Masonry [is] sullied." Only morally correct behavior could protect the order from censure by the Grand Lodge. McRary called upon "husbands of noble women . . . fathers of manly boys and virtuous girls . . . men and brethren, one and all, pioneers of what will one day be a great Race to pledge anew your sacred honor to wear the proud name of a true Mason as the emblem of innocence and the badge of a man."[45] Prince Hall freemasonry's preoccupation with race, community, and masculinity were thus inextricably bound.

Obedience to a "Rightful Authority"

As a hierarchal rational order guided by bylaws and central committees that stressed moral and communal responsibility, the Grand Lodge devoted considerable time at annual meetings to inspecting its work. Masonic leaders believed that these ritualistic procedures, which included an airing and (in the best-case scenario) resolution of internal grievances, advanced the goal of brotherhood both within and outside the race. In the "Significance of Brotherhood," writer John E. Bruce claimed that fraternalism was "the medium through which to give the right direction to the thought and policy which is to govern and control the race." Such unity transcended religious or political differences, he said. Yet internal hostility that Masonic leaders characterized as envy, malice, and revenge continued to plague the order. Despite repeated pleas for a universal brotherhood and sisterhood, black Masons and Eastern Star women, not unlike white followers of freemasonry, ascribed to their respective orders a "multiplicity of uses" that invariably created friction with Grand Lodge leadership.[46]

Aware of the potential for dissension among members, North Carolina's Grand Lodge leaders repeatedly implored their fellow Masons to pay attention to their duties and the tenets of masonry. "Every lodge should be a protection to the community in which it is situated," Grand Master McRary reminded the men. "Duty to self, one's family, one's church, and obedience to rightful authority are conspicuous among the teachings of Masonry."[47]

Conflict about what constituted "rightful authority" of Prince Hall lodges informed much of the dissension among Masons and their Eastern

Star counterparts. North Carolina's Prince Hall Grand Lodge regularly struggled with the threats "illegitimate" or clandestine lodges posed to the order. The recurring phrase "Guard well your outer threshold" became commonplace in Grand Lodge proceedings as leaders sought to repel the incursion of potentially subversive forces in their ranks. Grand Master McRary warned his brethren in 1912 "against the encroachments of the hawkers of unauthentic Masonic degrees." He especially counseled young Masons against falling prey to "cheap Masonry," which defiled the institution's purity and nobility. McRary issued a decree against clandestine Masonry in order to "[put] a quietus on the efforts of those blood-sucking vampires."[48]

Currents of dissension also ran between freemasons and Eastern Star women, despite Masons' routine praise of the women's order. Readily acknowledging the women's "claim" on them by virtue of familial relation, Grand Lodge leaders called the order an "excellent organization" and encouraged subordinate lodges to give their "unstinted support." In this context, OES members sought to protect the "great labors of Masonry" through their charitable and other benevolent work. Yet Eastern Star members' "great labors" have been reduced in this instance to the purely domestic: babysitting the female relatives of Masons and decorating lodges. Yet the women benefited their male counterparts in more significant ways. In some instances, the creation of Eastern Star chapters resulted in increased male attendance at Masonic lodge meetings. In addition, the moral influence of women benefited members of Masonic lodges. Grand Master Robert McRary was "thoroughly convinced that the softening and ennobling influence of the lady member ... tend to make us all better and purer men." Grand Lodge masons, in another proceeding, even went so far as to elevate the Eastern Star's organizational status above men's. In what may be regarded as another strained attempt to convince his male brethren to embrace Eastern Star women, McRary claimed that the Eastern Star order "antedates us." The biblical woman Ruth, whom the Eastern Star pointed to with pride, was the grandmother of King Solomon, who freemasons looked to as an important antecedent to their beliefs. He urged Masonic men to "encourage and afford every reasonable facility to the spread of the benefits of this most excellent society."[49] McRary's numerous remarks to mason men about the merits of Eastern Star women and their work is indicative of the seeming lack of respect Prince Hall members accorded them. His statements, when read collectively, reveal discord and tension between the sexes that would manifest itself repeatedly in lodge proceedings.

Despite McRary's pleas that Masonic men respect OES women, Prince Hall members exerted control over the supposedly independent order. A revealing exchange between the leaders of the two organizations demonstrates this recurring gender tension. In 1908, in the only Eastern Star correspondence recorded in Grand Lodge proceedings, Supreme Grand Matron Fannie Badham relayed a grievance to the Masons. The brief letter, addressed to "the Most Worshipful Grand Lodge of Masons," rang with confidence and assertiveness. Proclaiming herself a "devoted sister in the work," Badham first wished the men well in their proceedings, which on this occasion was marked by sorrow. (The Grand Lodge recently lost its Grand Master, L. R. Randolph, who had died of a stroke.) Masonic men thus assembled in a "lodge of sorrow," paying tribute to Randolph and reflecting upon the "irreparable loss" sustained by his death.

Having dispensed with her conciliatory remarks, Badham revealed a troublesome issue. The "progress of the Order," she argued, had been "somewhat hindered in some parts of the state because some of the brothers seem not to know anything of us or realize our relation to them and are charging the Sisters rent for use of halls that belong to them." Badham likely interpreted men's usurpation of women's access to the halls as a violation of Masonic code that emphasized familial unity and communal bonds. Badham's deliberate use of "sisters" and "brothers" in her letter were reminders of the rightful relation of Prince Hall men to Eastern Star women and their obligation to them in that regard. One of these duties was to respect the close ties that bound them together as Masonic laborers. Invoking the manly attribute of protector, she concluded her communication by beseeching the intervention of Grand Lodge officials in the matter. Acknowledging the position of the Grand Lodge as masonry's highest authority, she pointed out that it had the power to discipline the subordinate chapters. "I know that the Grand Lodge is the only true place to reach them and ask that it be spoken of or impressed in some way and you will do great good." Records do not reveal whether any debate occurred regarding Badham's grievance nor do they identify those who supported her position. But the Grand Lodge decided by a motion that "no Lodge should hereafter charge the Eastern Star rent for the use of their halls."[50]

Male Masons' actions to allow Eastern Star women access to Masonic resources proved only temporary. A year later, Prince Hall Mason W. S.

Simmons proposed that a commission be appointed whose duty would be to "inquire into and examine the workings of the Order of the Eastern Star." Simmons stated that since the Eastern Star Order received its legitimacy from Masons, its "workings should and ought to be according to Masonic principles and usages," suggesting that perhaps the women's activities had failed to meet such principles. Eastern Star women's reaction to Simmons proposal is not recorded in Grand Lodge minutes. But Grand Master Robert McRary dismissed the resolution, making it clear that "within this Jurisdiction, the Order of the Eastern Star is not under the legal supervision of the Most Worshipful Grand Lodge."[51]

Conflict surfaced in 1910, again regarding women's access to Masonic halls. The Worshipful Master of Wilmington's Giblem Lodge issued a complaint for the "abrupt exclusion" of Eastern Star Chapter, No.4 from the hall belonging to Giblem Lodge. Grand Lodge officials ordered the Grand Master of the district to visit the lodge to "investigate the complaint, and settle, if possible, the disturbance."

That same year, Supreme Grand Patron W. George Avant rose to defend himself in lodge proceedings, having been implicated by a fellow Mason in a controversial situation involving Eastern Star chapters in Wilmington. Avant disclosed "certain facts" so that his position would not be "misunderstood." The matter surfaced again in 1911, having acquired an added dimension. Past Grand Masters J. H. Young and J. J. Worlds formed a committee to investigate the Eastern Star "controversy" at Wilmington as it related to Past Grand Master J. W. Telfair.[52]

The nature of the Eastern Star controversy in Wilmington remains a mystery. The exact nature of the disagreement between Avant and the order was never disclosed in minutes of the proceedings. But given past entanglements between Prince Hall men and the Eastern Star, it can be surmised the issue centered on questions of institutional authority.

Perhaps not surprisingly, at the 1911 annual meeting, the Masons discussed whether the Grand Lodge should scrutinize the labors of the Eastern Star further. Grand Master Robert McRary pondered whether the lodge had been "derelict in the matter of fostering the Order . . . in our Jurisdiction." While not going so far as to assume "absolute authority over the policy and fortunes of the Order," McRary reasoned the Masonic body could afford to "concern ourselves more about the Order and the proper conduct of its affairs, than we have hitherto done."[53]

"They must be saved": A Call for Masonic Rehabilitation

By the 1920s, many Masons had determined that they no longer wanted to "labor and wait," and had tired of making the best of a bad situation. The specter of race prejudice remained uncomfortably in force for North Carolina's black population. They confronted segregated and cramped Jim Crow railroad cars, residential segregation laws (Winston-Salem passed one in 1914) that often placed blacks in areas that lacked sufficient sewer and water and featured lingering racial violence. Lynchings in Rolesville and Lewiston claimed the lives of two North Carolina blacks, and a race riot occurred in Winston-Salem. With such conditions, black masonry in North Carolina provided members the fellowship they needed to weather the racial storms swirling about them. Participation in masonry enabled black men to work collectively for the members of their lodge and the black community. The power and respectability conferred upon black men by their Masonic affiliation gave them hope that such positive imagery might resonate within white society."[54]

However, some members began rejecting the Masonic values of tolerance and patience and talk of politics, specifically the use of the ballot, began appearing in the minutes of Grand Lodge proceedings. Disregarding past admonitions that "politics should never be discussed in a Masonic lodge," fraternal leaders now argued that loyalty to the nation meant the just pursuit of all manhood rights, including the right to vote. "The day when a man's privilege to cast the ballot is determined by the color of his skin is fast passing away in North Carolina," observed Grand Master Capehart.[55]

Loyal patriotism, as endorsed by some North Carolina black men, called for a tenuous mix of patriotism (love of country) and acquiescence to white authority. These men, though seeking to improve race relations, nonetheless counseled temperance and patience with race segregation. Having blacks speak out against Jim Crow facilities, racial violence, legal and political injustices signaled to some whites a breach in cooperative race relations. Patriotic black leaders, claimed white powerbrokers, were those who didn't demand political and civil rights. As president of Durham's North Carolina College for Negroes (now North Carolina Central University), Grand Master James Shepard successfully used the concept of patriotic loyalty to elicit educational patronage from white officials.[56]

In the context of the secret lodge, however, the meaning and uses of black loyalty had changed. North Carolina's Grand Lodge proceedings and policies had stressed black patriotism by exhorting political and hence racial passivity in the face of segregation and, during wartime, by encouraging people to buy war bonds. Yet World War I had prompted revised understandings of loyalty and its relationship to a respectable black manhood. Liberty and freedom, Grand Master Capehart now claimed, was the birthright of every American citizen, whether black or white, bond or free. He urged his Masonic brethren to resolve that "here and forever more that the hand that wields the sword in defense of the Stars and Stripes, should wield the ballot in the battle for civil rights." Loyalty meant more than fidelity to one's country (and, in the context of the South, adherence to Jim Crow laws). It also meant the vigorous pursuit of racial and gender interests—that is, the acquisition of racial justice and Masonic men's use of their prerogative to protect, hence control, black women.[57]

Judging the race's previous handling of the franchise as "somewhat a failure," Grand Master Capehart surmised that the "political pendulum seems now to be swinging back toward us."[58] The 1928 election of Oscar DePriest to Congress, at that time the only black representative in that national body, had given the race its "voice again." The Republican De Priest, of Chicago, served Congress for three terms before he was defeated in 1934. Closer to home, North Carolina could boast of the election of former resident Dr. F. S. Hargrove to the New Jersey legislature. Defining the pursuit of racial justice in activist terms, Capehart urged his people to "exercise their right of citizenship by availing themselves of every opportunity to register and vote. Remember that the ballot is the priceless heritage of American Liberty, bought by the patriotic blood shed upon the battle fields of the world." This heritage and blood drew no distinctions along lines of race, class, or creed, he maintained. "On Bunker Hill, Valley Forge, San Juan, and No Man's Land the Negroe's blood has richly paid the price of the ballot, the price of American citizenship."[59]

In an expansion of the gendered meanings of citizenship, the Eastern Star's Sue Brown pushed for black women's use of the franchise. While she did not "suggest the taking of our Order into politics, yet in this new day our women everywhere should be urged to make use of their right of suffrage, where they are permitted to do so and that when they vote not to fail to place in office men and women who will safeguard the interest of our

group as well as the public in general in both State and National Legisla-
tures." Brown urged black men and women to urge the U.S. Senate to pass
the federal Dyer Anti-Lynching bill. Toward that end, the International
Conference of Grand Chapters of OES donated $200 to the NAACP's
anti-lynching fund.[60]

The nagging fear of factions, however, continued to destroy the confidence and purpose of Masonic men. Internal strife among masons and
other fraternal organizations centered on financial mismanagement and
were reported with regularity in black and white presses, contributing
to public perception that corruption and greed rather than cooperation,
brotherhood, and charity was the true meaning of freemasonry.[61] For example, the Knights of Pythias of North Carolina had a sizable deficit in
1928 that was attributed to "excessive salaries, large expense accounts, big
office rents, huge traveling expenses, purchase of worthless bank stocks
and other forms of bad management."[62]

The Great Depression sapped the fraternity of its economic strength.
Nationally, black secret societies lost both members and property. In the
South, many lodges devoted most of their activities to protecting mort-
gaged buildings. Although North Carolina's Grand Lodge was burdened
by the economic downturn, it managed to survive. Morale among members, however, remained low.[63]

In response to these developments, Prince Hall leaders engaged in the
"rehabilitation" of freemasonry. At the meeting of the Prince Hall lodge
in Burlington, North Carolina, Grand Master C. S. Brown described the
state's grand lodge as at a "low-water mark."[64] He lamented that many
lodge members had refused to hold meetings and pay dues. Other Masons
had been accused of stealing money. The fraternal order had been torn
apart by "contending factions that were deadly desperate in their inten-
tions." The result was that "confidence had been destroyed . . . [and] the
endowment department was bankrupt and destroyed." In Prince Hall's
treasury, "there was not a penny to be had, and debts had accumulated."
Brown's survey of subordinate lodges found twenty that had made but a
"faint-hearted" attempt to pay Grand Lodge dues. The general policy of
the masons had become to get by "without paying any more money." In
sum, there was "chaos and discouragement on every hand."[65]

When he was elevated to Grand Master at the end of the 1920s to "rehabilitate" freemasonry in North Carolina, Brown outlined his plan. In
the interest of unifying the body, Brown urged that officers, deputies, and

committee men be individuals who had stood "high" in previous admin-
istrations. He issued a proclamation urging all lodges who had not paid
their dues and dormant lodges to meet and reorganize and get in "working harmony" with the Grand Lodge concerning payment of dues ($1 per
man). He allowed all "non-financial" Master Masons (those who had not
paid their dues) to be restored to any lodge in the jurisdiction if they paid
their dollar. Brown traveled 5,656 miles through "sunshine, storm and rain"
to meet with the Masonic brethren about his proposed rehabilitation plan.
The plan seemed to meet general approval from Masons as he "witnessed
the survival of fraternity and hospitality."[66] Yet his talks with members also
revealed that many were "discouraged and indignant." The men "poured out
scathing invectives against our ex-Grand Officers, accusing them of stealing and high-handed robbery, fit only to be put behind prison bars. Many
seemed distrustful of everybody; they had lost faith."[67]

This Masonic crisis also touched the women of the Eastern Star. One of
the more notable proposals in the rehabilitation plan concerned a change
in policy regarding the Eastern Star. Prince Hall men manipulated the
meaning of "protection" to assert their dominance over women. At issue
was the order's alleged mishandling of its finances. Careful study of the
Eastern Star's 1927 financial reports revealed a disturbing trend. Even
though Eastern Star's leadership had levied a special assessment of a dollar per member that year, resulting in revenues of $9,000, the additional
income had not been enough to reverse the poor financial condition of the
order's Grand Chapter. The OES had levied another special assessment in
1928, but Capehart reasoned that if the second assessment was not more
successful, the order would lose more members. Sensing the growing unrest among Eastern Star members about their unstable financial situation,
Capehart felt certain that things would only "go from bad to worse unless
there is some change in policy."[68]

Finding the women "helpless in their attempt to improve their condition," the Grand Master determined that it was time for Prince Hall's
Grand Lodge to act by exercising its authority and supervision over the
group to prevent it from going bankrupt. Acknowledging the women's resistance to male interference, Capehart said that "it seems that the officers
of the G. Chapter do not wish to recognize the authority of the Grand
Lodge of Masons as expressed in the Code." He admitted that he had
come to a crossroads in his dealings with the auxiliary. He could enforce
the Grand Lodge's authority over the women as expressed in the Masonic

code or allow the order to "sit idly by as it did years ago until the Chapter is hopelessly lost." On the one hand, he believed it proper that the "wives and daughters expressly under the immediate supervision of the M. W. G. Lodge, should be delivered and saved." At the same time, Masonic tradition allowed the Eastern Star "free expression" regarding the management of the order. Ultimately, Capehart sided with the interests of the Grand Lodge, determining that it should enforce its authority over the chapter. Despite this decision, Capehart tried to placate the Eastern Star's women officials. He stressed that the Grand Lodge had "no selfish purpose in the matter," but that it only "wishes to be helpful, by advice and council [sic] to the end that the business of the Chapter shall be conducted according to approved business methods for the good of the Chapter and the benefit of the members." Yet clearly gender relations between the two fraternal bodies had shifted, with supervisory and decision-making power now vested in the Grand Lodge. Though no explicit record of women's reaction to the Lodge's decision exists, it is likely they indeed perceived themselves helpless in contesting male directives.[69]

In addition to steering its women's auxiliary to financial safety, North Carolina's Grand Lodge also reasoned that the time had come for men to "manfully measure up" by committing their labors toward the resurrection of the fraternal order. This included improving benefit plans for widows and daughters of Master Masons. "They must be allowed to feel the strong arm of Masonic protection." Brown also aimed to reform the motivations of Masonic male leaders, who seemed to place their own financial gain above the community-centered ideals of freemasonry. Within Masonic rituals, the importance of dutiful and responsible labor is manifest. For example, the initiation of fraternal members into the first three degrees prompted the presentation of "working tools." After a refreshment break, it was not uncommon for the Grand Master to call members back to "labor." To be industrious and maintain sound business practices was especially important during a time when black men had limited opportunities to acquire land, be proprietors, and engage in skilled labor. As important, the success of Masons in their financial dealings lent credence to a nineteenth-century construct of manliness built upon men's ability to compete in the business marketplace.

However, the contradiction between economic gain and freemasonry ideals was repeatedly recorded in Prince Hall proceedings.[70] While Masonic leaders expected that fraternity brothers would engage in business enterprises, like Grand Master C. S. Brown they abhorred the notion of Masonry as a means of acquisition rather than benevolence. Conflicts over money with both Eastern Star women and Prince Hall members suggest the difficulty North Carolina's Grand Lodge leaders experienced as they sought to maintain the values of freemasonry. Having grown tired of "begging men to be Masons," Brown stated in 1933 that whereas heretofore men had sought Masonic office largely for monetary benefits, "hereafter the love of Masonry must be the dominant imperative." He encouraged black men to do the right thing and let Masonry "live or die" on its own merits. "We have been on our knees now for a year. Let us get up like men, lock the door, and open it only when real men knock."[71]

Just what constituted "real men" for North Carolina's Prince Hall masons was a question that was discussed in private spaces. The Prince Hall order functioned as a vehicle of acculturation to white middle-class values, demonstrating to European-American lodges the authenticity of the fraternal order and that they were dutiful citizens through their support of their families and communities. But the larger purpose of Prince Hall masonry involved the fashioning of an iconic black masculine image. During the worst of the Jim Crow years, black men wielded the secret tool of freemasonry to realize black empowerment and secure race solidarity. The challenges imposed by legalized segregation in the South made Prince Hall masonry a physical, social, and intellectual refuge for its male members. The lodge provided "mutual protection and helpfulness" to those in need or those to whom services were denied in white society. And its members relished inhabiting a world "where for a day they are knights and nobles, kings and courtiers."[72]

But this indulgence in self-representation and reinvention spawned internal threats that damaged Prince Hall claims of a united brotherhood. Conflict surfaced within the Grand Lodge over the merits of accommodation versus the more strident use of politics as a response to segregation. Prince Hall men also grappled with how best to reconcile their fraternal and gender roles, their responsibility to protect the community and black women.

Prince Hall leaders realized that Eastern Star women were valuable and essential co-laborers in Masonic work. Yet they felt compelled to assume leadership and financial control over the women's order. Permitting the

Eastern Star to function autonomously threatened the important roles of provider and protector. These two markers of manhood, routinely denied to black men under Jim Crow laws, assumed greater importance as masons struggled with divisions in their ranks. The desire of Masonic men for internal cooperation and order within their organization rippled through the women's auxiliary in subtle and (by the end of the 1920s) intrusive ways.

From the women's perspective, male dominance within the order devalued black women by undermining their confidence and depriving them of opportunities to exercise and cultivate independent leadership and power. Though Eastern Star women are largely silent in North Carolina's Grand Lodge proceedings, instances of their resistance are clearly evident. Fraternity men's private discussions and actions concerning the order were not conducted in a vacuum. Rather, black masons consciously reacted to women's ongoing activities. Thus, when Prince Hall men engaged in dialogue about the auxiliary's status and relationship to freemasonry, women were participants in the debate through their actions.

The legacy of black women's institutional activity provided Eastern Star women with an alternate means of engaging in race work. For all the duties assumed by OES chapters, auxiliary members were also prominent in community work outside fraternal circles. Notably, many OES members participated in the black women's club movement, including Mary Talbert, sixth president of the National Association of Colored Women. This foundation of established, separate, and independently led women's organizations meant OES members could divorce themselves from regulation and control by Masonic men. Yet it is clear that by virtue of their participation in masonry, OES women also wished to belong to a fraternal "family" led by ostensibly dependable, honorable, and industrious men. Women's quest for work independence and domestic security, however, did not mean wholly succumbing to patriarchy. Because OES members had a history of organized, community-based activism to draw on, Prince Hall members were especially compelled to hold on to their female counterparts or sacrifice a constitutive element (providing for and protecting their families) of both freemasonry and their manhood.

Because the presence of men within women's organizations inhibited women's free exercise of authority, the question arises as to why Eastern Star leaders, committed as they were to their individual empowerment, continued to pursue their partnership with Prince Hall men. A likely explanation is that leaders of the Order of the Eastern Star sought a compromise between autonomy and dependence. Because membership in the Eastern Star was predicated on familial roles, women were not entirely independent and coequal in the Grand Lodge. By virtue of their relationship to men, Eastern Star women were symbolically and practically subject to male authority. At the same time, Eastern Star leaders relished the idea of a separate yet closely linked association with men. Through the auxiliary, they were able to perpetuate a distinct work identity. The gradual eroding of this understanding by Prince Hall men upset this delicate balance. Eastern Star women thus likely interpreted fraternal men's actions not as chivalric but as intrusive, disrespectful, and indeed unmanly.

As North Carolina's Prince Hall masons struggled to quell their fraternity's inner demons and affirm their gender identity, they remained sensitive to the importance of forging connections with the white world. Professing a universal "brotherhood of men," black masons, through their benevolence and emphasis on moral behavior and traditional gender roles, emphasized common values held by the "best" of both races. Grand Master Robert McRary gently reminded his brethren of the utility in engaging a community besides their own. "I recommend that we solicit wherever and whenever possible the good offices of our white friends in securing to us fair and righteous treatment in all our relations to the community and the State."[73] Other local black men expressed a similar objective; openly courting white men's support in their quest for racial justice, they also aimed to satisfy the black community's internal needs without compromising their identity as respectable men.

4

"Let the white man put himself in the negro's place"

Black Men Navigate the Terrain of Race Ambassador

In March 1904, an overflowing crowd of Asheville's black men and women gathered at the YMI assembly hall to attend a meeting that was billed with the title "Solve the Problem." There they received advice that the Asheville *Citizen-Times* described as "practical, timely, beneficial." Using blunt and gendered language, YMI secretary William J. Trent pleaded "most manfully for racial integrity, purity, manliness and moral force, leaving the result with God."[1] Miss. L. T. Jackson, principal of the Hill Street School, similarly counseled self-help, or the "social regeneration" of the black race, as the way to hasten better race relations. Rev. C. B. Dusenbury's address "What Really Is the Problem" recommended that black people exercise more economy and morality, again "with an implicit confidence in God." Rev. Samuel Orner took the discussion in a new direction. Really solving the problem, in his estimation, required the active engagement and imagination of both races. In particular, he stressed that white and black men needed to envision themselves as their racial opposites to grasp and feel the reality of racial inequality. "Put yourself in the white man's stead," he said pointedly.

> See him exalted in a day to the legislative hall, the senate . . . and the bar with a citizen's power in his hand, then you can realize the white man's position. . . . Let the white man put himself in the negro's place, liberated yet not free, privileged yet no right to exercise those privileges; rights that no man is bound to respect, a titled citizen without legal protection; then the white man can get an idea of the things that trouble the negro's inner soul and stir his manhood.[2]

Orner hoped that this role-playing exercise would elicit from white men a mix of sympathy, understanding, and acknowledgment of a shared vision of manhood and citizenship.

The gendered rhetoric of interracial outreach and collective problem-solving continued at the YMI's annual Emancipation Day ceremonies that year. As part of the 1904 commemoration in Asheville, celebrants filled the assembly hall to capacity. The program began with music sung by a chorus of 100 schoolchildren followed by speeches from residents Ida Briggs (a domestic science teacher) and Ada Young. In the principal address, "Thirty-Nine Years a Freedman: The Status of Affairs in this Country as It Affects the Negro," Rev. Orner traced the black man's hardships, loyalty, patriotism, and progress up to the current day. The speech, observers noted, showcased Orner's talents as an orator and scholar, skills illustrative of his value not only to the race but to Asheville as well. Commenting in the *Citizen-Times*, an Emancipation Day participant lamented that Orner's speech was not reprinted in the white press "so that our friends of the other race may know what men we have and are producing and the progress we have made." At the close of the ceremony, in keeping with the event's stress on racial progress and uplift, a New Year's offering was taken up and given to the city's Colored Orphans Home.[3]

This chapter focuses on black male leadership roles and its transition within the context of North Carolina's state fair and Emancipation Day ceremonies. These community events, which drew black and white audiences, became forums wherein the merits or shortcomings of race strategies were debated.

Emancipation Day ceremonies and the "colored" state fair (the latter organized by Raleigh educator Charles Norfleet Hunter) were central sites for stimulating interracial dialogue, intraracial unity, and debate in the early Jim Crow South. In these settings, North Carolina's black community put on performances that showcased the industriousness, citizenship, and cultural heritage of African Americans. Through exhibits and rhetoric, black North Carolinians aspired to advance pride and progress within the race and interracial dialogue outside of it. The state's leading black men were prominent on these occasions; they were the primary organizers, they wrote the Emancipation Day resolutions, and they delivered the keynote addresses. In part, this gendered structure advanced the race's claim that it had evolved into the highest state of "civilization." This discourse emphasized sexual differentiation among men and women of civilized races. According to scholar Gail Bederman, while the behavior of savage (nonwhite) men and women was almost identical, civilized women were "womanly," delicate creatures and their men the most "manly." These men had firm characters, controlled themselves, and protected women and children.[4]

The location of Emancipation Day and state fair ceremonies in public spaces meant that the whole black community took ownership in their meanings. Well attended and inclusive, the commemorations and fairs typically hosted thousands of black men, women, and children. Men and women alike voted on Emancipation Day resolutions. The annual fairs and Emancipation Day ceremonies, while affording black North Carolinians opportunities to develop professional networks and assess the present and future of the advancement of the race, also functioned as places of amusement and pleasure. Capitalizing on their traditional roles as kin keepers and culture carriers, black women participants in the fairs and Emancipation Day events did their part to forward the communal interests of the race. Though a gender hierarchy clearly guided the overt workings of the public ceremonies, black women were active participants in the racial dramas that unfolded in their midst.[5]

Whether as spectators or participants, white elite southerners also performed specific roles in the Emancipation Day and state fair gatherings. Though Emancipation Day was principally an African-American holiday, white Americans shared in the freedom celebrations either by invitation or on their own volition. Prominent white citizens observed and participated in the celebrations, and Emancipation Day and state fair events were attended by both blacks and whites. This fact and its implications for interracial cooperation in the twentieth-century South have been overlooked in most studies of Emancipation Day ceremonies, which portray whites as outsiders who, if they were present at all, reacted to the proceedings from a distance. Historians have read such commemorations primarily as vehicles for black self-expression, self-determination, and agitation. They have sought to learn how blacks shaped their own version of the American past. Scholarship has also revealed the dynamic of community cohesion and discord at Emancipation Day ceremonies, observing how the process of black community-building precipitated internal and external conflicts. Scholars who have dissected the uniquely African-American occasion of

Black Men Navigate the Terrain of Race Ambassador

Emancipation Day have not typically located it within the interracial co-operation movement of the early twentieth century.[6]

As interracial gatherings, the ceremonies impacted black and white audiences, producing multiple and conflicting messages about the meaning of racial progress, equality, and leadership. Statements about the progress of the race offered by the North Carolina governors and other white elites who addressed Emancipation Day and state fair gatherings were tempered with calls to maintain the racial status quo. Some scholars have asserted that because whites supported Emancipation Day ceremonies, the events were somehow "emptied of their former significance." Some have claimed that increased racial violence in the South "divested them of their full meaning," transforming many celebrations into low-key occasions.[7]

While powerful white southerners indeed perceived such events as opportunities to ensure that blacks knew and kept their "place," this interpretation understates the numerous instances of black agency that occurred in these forums. At the same time that whites instructed blacks on the enduring politics of white supremacy, black leaders of Emancipation Day and state fair events preached positive messages of uplift to the black masses; these men never limited their racial vision to accommodationist strategies.[8] Rather, they navigated between three competing ambitions—to effect a revised "authentic" American history that incorporated and legitimized a legacy of black autonomy, self-determination, and heroism and transmitted that heritage to future generations; to develop and invigorate the internal life of the black community; and to court white benevolence.

Performing myriad functions and inspiring numerous interpretations, the Emancipation Day ceremonies and state fairs were discursive landscapes in which competing arguments about racial pride and progress were aired and reworked, within and across generations. In the wake of World War I and in the context of New Negro ideology, black men found themselves in the center of renewed debate within the black community about the meaning of freedom, progress, and a dignified manhood.

The origins of African-American freedom celebrations lie in the antebellum period. In 1808, celebrants commemorated the banning of the foreign slave trade. On 4 July 1827, African-Americans celebrated New York State Abolition Day. West Indian Emancipation Day, begun on 1 August 1834, was another popular pre–Civil War black freedom holiday.[9]

The institutionalization of black freedom celebrations and exhibitions in the South began during the Civil War. In 1862, emancipation ceremonies were held in the Sea Islands of South Carolina and parts of Tennessee. Three years later, black Tennesseans celebrated emancipation at the state capitol. A Nashville newspaper reported that the event was "attended by several white persons . . . besides a very large number of civil, well dressed and orderly colored people." While some celebrations were "solemn," others could be festive. Celebration sometimes featured "a procession, a barbecue, speaking and music."[10] Although Emancipation Day ceremonies statewide shared certain features, such as singing, speechmaking, and voting on resolutions, there were differences as well. The commemorations, held in city streets, churches, or other community venues, could be less somber in tone. They also were not necessarily timed to the anniversary of the second Emancipation Proclamation in January 1863. Some jubilee celebrations were held in months other than January, such as March or April.

By the 1880s, black state fairs had formed in several southern states. Tennessee led this development. The Davidson County and Middle Tennessee Colored Agricultural and Mechanical Association secured a fair site in 1870. Race leader Frederick Douglass delivered the Nashville fair's oration in 1873. The emergence of black fairs in the South coincided with a push by white America to demonstrate its embrace of modernity. But such efforts were marred by racism. The nation's world fairs for the period 1876 to 1916 provided fairgoers with forums to "reaffirm their collective national identity in an updated synthesis of progress and white supremacy."[11] The 1893 World's Columbian Exposition in Chicago, for example, stressed not only artistic, scientific and technological advancements but also white supremacy. Although the Chicago exposition was hailed by Congress as "an exhibition of the progress of civilization in the New World," it kept African Americans out of its treasured White City and confined "uncivilized" dark races to its Midway Plaisance.[12] After repeated exposure to ridicule and exclusion within America's mainstream expositions and world's fairs, national black expositions gradually migrated South toward the latter half of the nineteenth century.[13]

Black fair supporters, co-opting the "progressive" rhetoric of their white counterparts, claimed that separate exhibitions benefited race relations by positioning black progress in respectable places apart from white displays, which often denigrated and insulted the race. In a time of hardening race relations, when whites believed that blacks had regressed to a savage state and the image of the "black beast rapist" had eclipsed the dialectic of the dutiful master/faithful slave in the white mind, a new race paradigm gained favor among the black elite. To counter assertions of black deviance and predictions of the race's inevitable genocide, blacks such as Booker T. Washington preached an accommodationist program centered on emphasizing racial progress. Determined to shape "New Negroes for a New Century," he encouraged the black masses to display their moral and industrial progress to skeptical whites. As "modern engines of propaganda, advertising, and salesmanship," southern black fairs and commemorative ceremonies symbolized the creed of the black New South, which aimed to prove how compatible the race was with the modern age.[14] In his chronicle of forty years of black progress, essayist R. R. Wright included among his roster of accomplishments the black fair. Wright wrote of the convening of the first Georgia State Fair held in 1908. The event, occurring in the aftermath of the Atlanta race riot of 1906, "did much to bring to the foreground the intelligent, industrious Negro, and thus to raise the race in the estimation of the whites."[15] The speeches and parades of Emancipation Day commemorations were additional opportunities for the black race to recast itself as heroic and stress its worthiness within the modern world.

*   *   *

North Carolina's black fairs date to Reconstruction. The North Carolina Industrial Association (NCIA), established in 1879 by Charles N. Hunter and his brother Osborne, began the first black state fair in North Carolina that year with what would become an annual appropriation of $500 from the state legislature. Supported primarily through state funds, the Negro State fair helped fulfill the NCIA's main objectives, which were "to encourage and promote the development of the industrial and Educational resources of the Colored people of North Carolina," "to gather statistics respecting their progress in the various pursuits and customs peculiar to civilized and enlightened nations; to hold annually . . . an exhibition of the progress of their industry and education."[16]

Exhibits for North Carolina's black state fair were diverse; they included farm products, poultry, cattle, home economics, educational displays, art, mechanical work, and inventions. The first black fair was held on the Old Camp Russell campground in Raleigh before that site was converted into a home for Confederate soldiers. After that, fair organizers used the grounds of the State Agricultural Society. Initially, state officials did not charge fair sponsors to use the grounds. In subsequent years, however, the black fair was charged a $50 fee that later increased to $100. Fair speakers included nearly all of North Carolina's governors and race leaders such as Booker T. Washington, Frederick Douglass, and Marcus Garvey.

Hunter also played a pivotal role in the staging of Raleigh's Emancipation Day commemorations, which were some of the state's largest and grandest gatherings. Besides selecting many of the speakers, Hunter drafted resolutions, which Emancipation Day attendees voted on. These resolutions contained calls for black equality, racial self-help and friendly relations between the races.

Raleigh's first Emancipation Day ceremony was held in 1872. Hunter invited Charles Sumner of Massachusetts and white supremacist Bartholomew F. Moore, an author of North Carolina's Black Codes, to speak, but both of them declined. The pairing of such ideological opposites was consistent with Hunter's race relations philosophy, which placed faith in the ability of powerful whites to see the black race as its equal once given opportunities to witness its accomplishments.

North Carolina's Emancipation Day and state fair gatherings during the early decades of the Jim Crow period served a variety of purposes. Whether in churches, on city streets, or at fairgrounds to celebrate the end of slavery, the commemorations were well organized and orderly, contributing to an image of a race that had evolved to the highest state of civilization. Organizers believed that the ritual aspects of such events, which typically featured parades, speeches, prayers, and patriotic songs, would persuade whites of blacks' capacity for self-controlled and dignified behavior.

Collectively, the fair and Emancipation Day commemorations placed blacks and whites within the same physical space in order to advance whites' knowledge of black civility. They addressed the race question through rhetorical and visual performances. The exhibition of African-American progress publicized the race's moral and material value—literary, musical, artistic, and historical achievements of the race; the amount of taxable property, church property, fraternal, and lodge property black organizations owned; and the number of enterprises black businesspeople acquired. Such progress affirmed the status of African Americans as citizens.

North Carolina governor Charles Aycock, a frequent speaker at Emancipation Day ceremonies, however, illustrated the limitations of elite whites. Although they might consider themselves to be "progressive" because they reached out to the black community at such events, their attitudes regarding social customs and laws governing southern race relations were deeply entrenched. Aycock was known as the "education governor" and the "apostle of race relations" for his staunch advocacy of public education for blacks and whites. He was heralded as one who "first represented the spirit of the new South following the Civil War." And yet it was Aycock's support of white supremacy that elected him to the governor's seat in 1900. The same year that Booker T. Washington spoke at the state's black fair, calling for blacks to abstain from politics and instead focus on their economic and moral welfare, Aycock boasted that the state had "solved the negro problem." Addressing the North Carolina Society in Baltimore in 1903, Aycock outlined the solution to the race problem, which included disfranchisement and blacks' adoption of "industry, thrift, obedience to law, and uprightness." He especially cautioned against black militancy, claiming that "violence may gratify his passions but it cannot accomplish his ambitions; that he may eat rarely of the cooking of equality, but he will always find when he does that 'there is death in the pot.' Let the negro learn once for all that there is unending separation of the races, that the two peoples may develop side by side to the fullest but that they cannot intermingle."[17] For many southern white elites, progressivism and the subordination of blacks went hand in hand.

In his heralded treatise on the "New South," southern industrial booster Henry Grady argued that in the new regime not much would be new for the black race. "The whites shall have clear and unmistakable control of public affairs," he wrote. "They are the superior race, and will not and cannot submit to the domination of an inferior race." Wade Hampton, governor of South Carolina, agreed. In 1890, he argued that the constitution had been violated when "the negro was allowed to vote, and no greater crime against civilization, humanity, constitutional rights and Christianity was ever perpetuated under the guise of philanthropy."[18]

Yet Aycock also acknowledged the "duty" of whites toward blacks, saying that while it was every man's duty to develop himself, "he shall take pains to see that in his own development he does no injustice to those beneath him. This is true of races as well as of individuals."[19] This duty, he said, included ensuring that blacks had educational opportunities. Aycock regarded the "negro," who constituted a third of North Carolina's population, as his "personal friend." As a lawyer and governor he had defended and protected blacks, but yet "there flows in my veins the blood of the dominant race.... When the negro recognizes this fact we shall have peace and good will."[20] Obliged to govern by virtue of whites' superior evolution to that of other races, Aycock's loyalties would remain with white men. But he and other powerful whites also felt obligated to elevate those inferior to them. This gentleman's agreement struck in the wake of segregationist legislation thus necessitated reciprocal responsibilities and duties.

North Carolina's boast of having "led all southern states in race relation advancement" and of promoting "good feeling" between the races hinged on blacks' obedience to a racial etiquette that precluded aggressive acts to stamp out racial injustice.[21] The myth that race relations in the state were progressive "worked" so long as blacks did not seek restoration of the vote, clamor for social equality (a somewhat nebulous term that in some white minds signaled interracial marriage), or aspire to other changes that undermined the state's New South creed, an ideology that embraced modernity and industry on one hand and southern tradition on the other.[22]

Advocates of the New South creed looked both forward and backward as they took refuge in a racial ideology that ostensibly advanced the interests of both blacks and whites. In their patronage of black institutions, the state's powerful white leaders could, for example, indulge in a bit of self-congratulation, taking pride in the part, albeit limited, they played in the accomplishments of the black race. Black leaders, conversely, by playing on the myth, could demonstrate their ability to realize a tolerable, if not wholly equitable, racial environment. In theory, the myth that southern race relations were progressive also functioned to retard extreme forms of racial violence such as lynching.[23] (Obviously, this was true in theory only.)

Yet the balance between civil behavior (accentuated by displays of white paternalism) and racial discord (characterized by militant claims for equality) proved an increasingly delicate one to maintain. Any breaches (perceived or actual) of blacks' place elicited anxiety, especially among white southerners. In an editorial to Raleigh's *News & Observer*, John Hall of Warrenton (who was white) wrote that while whites "are, and always have been the friends of the negro," they should beware of the "danger line." The barrier to voting and political power for blacks, as cemented in the disfranchisement amendment, must be maintained, he said. For the "patience and forbearance of the white race cannot last forever. Unless stopped, your continued challenges will be answered." White columnist Thomas M. Hufham echoed this sentiment. He contended it was in the best interest of blacks to remain out of politics because the race possessed the "moral obtuseness which exists regardless of education." He ended by reminding his white brethren of their responsibility to keep blacks away from voting booths: "The white man, however honest, who induces him to vote at any kind of an election is sowing dragon's teeth."[24]

The die of racial accommodation had been cast most publicly, if not resolutely, at the convening of North Carolina's black fair in 1903. The guest of honor, Booker T. Washington, implored the race to remain rooted in the South, to pursue vocational education, and to content itself with an agrarian life. Washington had been advocating this strategy since 1895, when he first articulated his solution to the "Negro Problem" at the Cotton Exposition at Atlanta. Seated behind Washington at North Carolina's fair were some of the state's most influential black men. These included James H. Young, the first black colonel in the Spanish-American War and a leading member of the Fusionist Party, which, in the 1890s, had temporarily boosted the political power of Republicans and blacks statewide. Also present were respected educators Simon G. Atkins of Winston Salem State University, James B. Dudley of Greensboro's Agricultural and Technical College, and James E. Shepard of Durham's North Carolina College for Negroes.[25] The presence of these men silently endorsed Washington's template for racial progress.

At a time when southern whites were firmly opposed to black citizenship rights yet receptive to the ideology of progress, black leaders such as Hunter orchestrated public displays that showcased the industrial, intellectual, and moral evolution of the race. These men staked their claim to racial dignity and respectable manhood outside the manly realm of politics. This avenue for race relations, premised on interracial appeals, has often faltered. Several historians have documented blacks' vulnerability in this regard, noting the persistence of racial constructions that conflate progress and morality as ultimately the preserve of white males.[26]

And yet, as part of his public race relations campaign, Hunter had determined that the rights, privileges, and opportunities for which blacks contended would not be attained by "rancorous appeals," hostile demonstrations, or other methods of force. In a letter to North Carolina's superintendent of instruction, Dr. E. C. Brooks, Hunter reiterated his position, which he had first articulated in 1879, that "the negro should turn his attention and devote his chief energies to moral, educational and material foundations. . . . His blind pursuit of political will-o'-the-wisps would end only in disastrous disappointment. We urged that we must grow from within and not from without." Hunter's claims, which he routinely articulated in addresses to state fair and Emancipation Day audiences, assumed that the relationship between the races was interdependent and beneficial. "The white race in the south cannot ascend without drawing the black race up with it," he said. Conversely, "the black race cannot rise without lifting the white race which is the upper strata." Though accused by some race leaders of committing "political heresy" and being a race traitor, Hunter confidently proclaimed that "I stand today where I have always stood."[27]

Hunter's benevolent appeals to whites rested largely on faith and his personal history, wherein he had been first exposed to the liberating potential of white patronage. Born in Raleigh in 1851 to artisan slave parents, Hunter belonged to the William Dallas Haywood family, which allowed his father Osborne, Sr., to work in the city as a carpenter-wheelwright. After his mother died when he was age four, the young Hunter was principally reared by the Haywoods, toward whom he maintained a "tender affection" throughout his life. As a child, Hunter had determined that the race problem had nothing to do with skin color. Hunter's approach to race relations was also shaped by his indulgence in a racial imagination premised less on how things were than on how they could be over time. Despite the confluence of an expanded southern economy, an intensification of racism, and the diminishment of black political power, men like Hunter subscribed to a millennialist outlook. They fashioned what Walter Weare has termed a "psycho-cultural response" to the race problem. Translating the worst of times into the best, black middle-class architects of expositions and fairs latched onto the belief that grand displays of racial progress combined with appeals to white men's Christian conscience and a romanticized racial past would engender black self-esteem and catapult the race beyond white prejudice. Hunter placed great stock on moral and economic rather than political acumen as the building blocks of the race's manhood and salvation.[28]

Hunter, like black exposition supporter R. R. Wright, felt that North Carolina's segregated fairs uplifted the race. He maintained that the fair was a mechanism for black self-expression and for "awakening new life, energizing new forces, inciting to better things." Logistics also played a part in Hunter's rationale for continuing the segregated event. Describing the fair as a "great social gathering," he noted that the crowds that assembled on Raleigh's Hillsborough Street a week after the white fair were very large, some in excess of 20,000. Hunter projected both overcrowding and an overtaxed transportation system if both races converged at the same location.[29]

Hunter's arguments against an integrated fair, while they reflected the sentiment of leading blacks such as Booker T. Washington, were also meant to undercut local black opposition to a "colored" fair. Describing his effort to obtain legislative support for a black exhibit at the Jamestown Exposition in Virginia in 1907, Hunter recalled that his "progressive" movement was opposed by "one or two negroes in Raleigh." Hunter's critics would later claim more vigorously that separate fairs disproved claims of black achievement and exacerbated rather than lessened friction between the races.[30]

Despite the segregated status of the fairs and Emancipation Day ceremonies, Hunter believed that if blacks could discover "the good side of whites and if they will find our good side then the era of estrangement and bitterness will pass."[31] As a former slave, Hunter wanted to foster paternalistic goodwill among politically powerful whites by preaching a politics of racial etiquette that included the virtues of patience, forbearance, and self-reliance to blacks. This deferential positioning of his racial and gendered self, he hoped, would remind whites of the "good relations" that had existed between the races during slavery and of the ability of blacks to conduct themselves in a respectable manner outside that institution. At the same time, he hoped to nurture black empowerment by emphasizing the character of the race and its shared historical memory.

At Raleigh's Emancipation Day ceremony in 1907, Hunter exhorted blacks to "seek honorable employment and render faithful and efficient service." He further counseled that the race should "keep out of [the] courthouse" and "frown upon idleness."[32] Though tinged with the accommodationist language of self-help and character-building, Hunter's oratory encouraged the race in matters that were essential to the well-being of the black community. He advised blacks to attend Sunday school and church and urged parents to be attentive to the home training of children. Hunter's messages of internal uplift and external cooperation with whites were given equal weight on the stage of Emancipation Day commemorations, reflecting the complexity and fluidity inherent in accommodationist strategies. Hunter was a product of his time and place who shifted his racial positioning as needed. He adeptly invoked multiple racial identities, demonstrating what historian Earl Lewis has termed the "multipositionality" of the self.[33]

Other black speakers at Emancipation Day celebrations exhibited this tendency to both praise and condemn their black audiences. At the Emancipation Day ceremonies in Raleigh in 1906, Charles N. Williams, superintendent of the city's Deaf, Dumb and Blind institute, spoke about the steps necessary to realize the "black man's progress." The road to "true citizenship," he claimed, lay in improvements in the race's moral, educational, and material abilities. This entailed paying greater attention to children's home training and the exercise of politeness and honesty. Besides cultivating friendly relations with other whites and cooperating with them, Williams urged the race "to accept the circumstances and conditions and make the best of them that we can."[34] A year earlier, Raleigh's Emancipation Day audience was admonished to live "Godly lives, both in the home and elsewhere, to see to it that we ourselves and our children, when not in school, are regularly employed upon some labor, to be quiet and peaceable citizens, not to disturb our neighbors, but each attend to his own business, to stand unqualifiedly for a righteous life, a pure manhood and a protected womanhood."[35]

Professor J. H. Branch, principal of Raleigh's Washington Graded School, gave similar advice to the black community in a 1917 address. He took pains to define an African-American citizenship based, in part, on attitudes and behaviors consistent with the expectations of white southerners. Good citizenship, he said, consisted primarily of property ownership, a stable home life, and the cessation of crime by "the young element of our race."

Opening the black state fair ceremony in 1915, educator Berry O'Kelly remarked that despite numerous setbacks, the race continued to progress by seeing to its own advancement. "Our people are beginning to realize the importance of self-help and are putting forth efforts in behalf of their own uplift," he informed his audience. "In this, they are finding helping hands extended by our white people." In an essay entitled "Signs of Growing Co-operation," Robert R. Moton, Washington's successor at Tuskegee, sup-ported these views, applauding the fact that blacks were "becoming better organized" and were "willing to accept the advice and leadership of their own race for racial betterment and civic improvement." Moton argued that the adoption of self-help strategies to advance the race eased the attempts of black leaders to "throw the weight of their influence on the side of sane co-operation with the best element of our Southern white people."[36]

In his address, J. H. Branch encouraged black men to have "more respect for the women of the race, the same respect and honor that the white man shows to his womanhood." His remarks were partly aimed at satisfying white requests that the race "respect and honor virtue wherever you see it, especially in your own womankind," a statement that implied that black men were wanting in this manly and "civilized" virtue.[37] Branch's words gave credence to black men's role as protectors of black women, thus refut-ing white supremacist logic that sanctioned racial violence against black men for their presumed moral and sexual depravity. Branch's oration of womanly protection likely resonated with those black women in the audience in the context of broader institutional efforts to protect black women's bodies and morality. These included Garveyism and the efforts of the National Association of Colored Women (NACW) and the Ur-ban League. Both the NACW and the Urban League worked to shield female migrants from rural areas from the dangers of city life such as prostitution.[38]

While speeches at North Carolina's Emancipation Day ceremonies and state fairs stressed black self-improvement in order to placate powerful whites and solicit their support, they also contained subversive elements. Conscious of the fact that whites were more likely to participate in co-operative endeavors when they perceived that blacks were pursuing self-help, Marcus Garvey told his predominately black audience at the 1922 fair that lazy behavior and lack of initiative were the reasons for blacks' misery. Garvey also berated the audience for depending too much on whites and God to determine their fate and salvation. White supremacists and the white press approved of Garvey's speech; the *Greensboro Daily News* called it "quite the cleverest speech ever heard."[39] But the speech also illustrated Garvey's skill at verbal deception. In his message of black self-reliance and economic independence, Garvey critiqued African Americans for being ineffective organizers and producers.[40] His messages about black self-sufficiency and entrepreneurial innovation were what appealed to Raleigh's black audience, which received the speech enthusiastically.

In other ways, spectators refashioned the occasions to meet their communal and recreational needs. The annual state fair and Emancipation Day gatherings typically drew large crowds, ranging from 3,000 to 4,000 people. Surely the routine pilgrimages to these events were dependent on more than the repetitious orations by leading race men, speeches whose themes blacks undoubtedly had heard many times already in their local churches and schools. Rather, the men, women, and children who endured chilly campgrounds, cramped churches, and lengthy programs (which could last up to four hours) found comfort and pleasure in other ways. Indeed, the men and women who crowded the YMI assembly hall well before the 1903 Emancipation Day ceremonies began at 3 p.m. prepared themselves for "a feast of reason and flow of soul." The program, called "one of the best ever given in our town," was praised not only for its many addresses on the race question but also for its entertainment offerings, which included an elaborate musical performance.[41] The musical performances at Greensboro's Emancipation Day ceremony one year were so popular that they nearly overshadowed the program's principal feature, the Emancipation Day address delivered by Principal E. D. Nickle of Durham's East End Graded School. The ceremony included an instrumental selection by E. H. Dixon of the Lutheran College; a hymn. "All Hail the Power of Jesus Name," sung by the audience; music by a college quartet from North Carolina's Agricultural and Technical College; selections from glee clubs of Bennett College and the Agricultural and Technical College; and music by the Guilford County quartet. Only then did Nickle's address begin. Post-speech activities included a solo by Harry Smith, music from the Premier Quartet, and a choral performance by Bennett College students. One newspaper editor wrote that "the singing was splendid and the address an able one."[42] The musical program at Charlotte's celebration was also described as a prominent feature of the meeting. There, a 125-person chorus from the Second Ward School and the Biddle University quintet entertained attendees.

Other Emancipation Day ceremonies featured picnics, tennis tournaments, potato races, horseshoe tournaments, and baseball and volleyball games. North Carolina's state fairs served up the traditional agricultural, mechanical, and handicraft exhibits and speeches, but they also featured concert bands, parades, horse races, musicals, Pentecostal revivals, and midways that featured merry-go-rounds, photo galleries, target shooting galleries, and spectacles such as "Aunt Betsy and her famous ox."[43]

Outside the spotlight reserved for black spokesmen, black women played important and public roles in Emancipation Day and fair events. As members of planning committees, participants in programs, or as "culture carriers," their actions affirmed race progress, racial kinship, and communal ties. Women performed musical selections and arranged the social activities—the barbecues, the picnics, and the pie-eating contests—that so many looked forward to. In addition, exhibits of the domestic arts at state fairs demonstrated black women's primary role in fostering communal values and a respectable home life.[44] At the 1904 state fair in Raleigh, for example, Mrs. C. N. Hunter was responsible for installing a "beautiful exhibit of household supplies." That same year, Mrs. E. H. Lipscomb of Wadesboro encouraged fair attendees to "send some literature and I will do all I can to awaken interest in our people in this section. Our school will have an exhibit." Several women also took responsibility for promoting the fair, spreading news of the cultural event in their communities. On the eve of the 1904 state fair, Mrs. Bettie Harris-Johnson of Raleigh said: "I hope you [have] abundant success and will do all in my power to bring this to pass." Sylvia V. Blake of Cary said she would "do all I can to have others come." Lossie B. Roberts of Goldsboro likewise asserted that she was "ready for any work I can do. I am coming; a large crowd from this section."[45]

Women's contributions were sometimes more conspicuous. When Charlotte Hawkins Brown spoke at an Emancipation Day celebration in Raleigh in 1926, she boldly asserted that "it remained for the Negro woman to do for the Negro race what the men had failed to do."[46] A number of scholars have documented women's critique of black men as ineffectual race leaders during this time period. Deborah Gray White argues that in the midst of disfranchisement, racial violence, and Jim Crow laws, black women began publicly denouncing black men's shortcomings in racial matters. They argued that black men had squandered the citizenship rights of the race, in part by abusing their voting privileges. It is true that both men and women had grievances against each other that arose during their community work. Yet black men's grassroots activity equaled in gravity the many community-building activities of black women during this time. How then, to explain Brown's perspective? Brown's comment that it remained for black women to do what their men had "failed to do" is a bit curious.[47]

Brown's blunt rhetoric about black men might have been a response to the reaction within the black community to black women's campaigns for the franchise. Men such as James Dudley of the Agricultural and Technical College of North Carolina aroused outrage among black men and women alike for his negative response to women's suffrage activism. Concerned that (white) women's advancement in the political public sphere would effectively push black men further from the ballot box, he urged black women not to replicate the activities of white suffragists. "I do not believe the white women who are going to become politicians and partisans are setting the best example for you to follow," he said. Dudley's words spurred protests from across the country, including from W. E. B. Du Bois, who dubbed him the "last of a pitiable group." Brown, who identified women's suffrage as the key to blacks' reentry into politics, beseeched Dudley "for the sake of the emancipation of the race from this political thralldom . . . to espouse woman suffrage, our only hope."[48]

Brown's criticism of black men also should be understood in the context of interracial and gender politics in the South. At Raleigh's 1926 Emancipation Day celebration, Brown, whose appearance was sponsored by the city's Women's Club, tailored her rhetoric to satisfy her mostly white female audience. In her address "The Negro Woman and the New Freedom," Brown highlighted the common bonds of womanhood. She positioned black women as authorities in dealing effectively with the race issue, but she told white women that they also "held the key to the situation" in their work for the race. Brown applauded Mrs. Bickett, the widow of former North Carolina governor Thomas Bickett, for sensing the "need of the Negro" and doing what she could to advance understanding between blacks and whites.

Brown also paid "high tribute" to the "Old Black Mammies." In her 1919 novel *Mammy*, she spun a tale of a doting black woman who nursed a white family and raised its children. As the woman aged and became ill, the white family provided little assistance beyond sporadic visits to the woman's log cabin. Brown used the Mammy figure to inspire guilt and a renewed sense of the duty of white women to black women. Invoking this gendered symbol of the South's racial past, Brown made it clear that she wanted white women to reflect on their neglect of African Americans as she agitated for the full implementation of black civil rights. Skillfully maneuvering within the powerful discourse of southern memory, Brown argued that it was the duty of southern white women to alter the racist power structure of the South. "If our black mammy was all that our white kind friends have said she was, they should see to it that her children possess all the rights of American citizenship," she argued. Well aware that the ballot represented the "great fundamental" in American life, Brown urged black women to register and vote intelligently to advance the social and political freedom of the race.[49]

Brown's rhetoric suggests that the grievances of black women against black men should be viewed more expansively. While such utterances illuminated intraracial conflict, they also had the potential to sow race unity. Given her Emancipation Day audience, she elevated the position of black women as a means of reaching out to white women. To do this, she castigated black men's ineffectiveness in advancing race relations. At the same time, Brown urged black women to exercise the franchise, not just for women's elevation but for "the race." This speaks to the diversity of rhetorical strategies inherent in Emancipation Day ceremonies. These interracial settings allowed Brown space to relay one position to white audiences but quite another to black ones.

Though both individual black achievement and collective striving contributed to the overall prosperity of the race, the notion that cooperation with the white power structure was instrumental to blacks' procurement of their citizenship rights was a common theme of speeches by both blacks and whites at North Carolina's Emancipation Day and state fairs. At the Emancipation Day ceremonies in Durham in 1907, resolutions lauded the "friendly feelings" that existed between the races. "There has never been much friction," the resolution read. "The honest, progressive black man has always secured the sympathy and assistance of his white friend."[50] At an Emancipation Day ceremony in Raleigh, Colonel James Young told of the "friendly feeling of the white people" of Raleigh toward blacks and of the "harmony between the races" there. He cited a recent example of this goodwill after St. Paul's Church, a landmark in the black community, burned down. The rebuilding campaign enlisted the support of white leaders Josephus Daniels and N. B. Broughton, who gave "active aid and assistance."[51]

Sometimes white reformers worked with African-American men to promote the moral environment that the black middle class felt was essential to racial uplift. It was often the case in urban centers that houses of prostitution were clustered on the edges of the black community. In some cities, the term "red-light district" was virtually synonymous with black neighborhoods. In 1914, for example, white physician R. F. Campbell documented the locations of Asheville's brothels. Campbell reported the results in the local press, which was engaged in an anti-vice campaign. He found three brothels located near a black public school that served 1,200 children. Black and white ministers worked with Campbell to successfully pressure the city's police and courts, and "within a week, the brothels were driven out of the Negro district."[52]

These examples of successful interracial cooperation buoyed Hunter's sponsorship of master/slave reunion dinners at the state fair in 1913, 1916, and later years. These events were very controversial in the black community. Hunter rationalized them as part of ongoing attempts to foster kindly sentiments between the races, or "clearer views of each other." They raised conflicts within the black community about the meaning and appropriation of slavery to forward the race's self-representation. While some African Americans urged that their triumph over slavery necessitated its remembrance, others, who had never been enslaved, rejected memories of slavery as a route to interracial cooperation.[53]

The orations of white speakers were stark reminders of the limits of the strategy of invoking slavery when advancing racial equality. Advocates of a benign segregation, such as Governor Bickett, extolled blacks' moral and industrial advancement yet cautioned them to eschew political ambitions, especially attempts to reclaim the franchise. Bickett made it clear that if blacks chose not to adopt this plan, whites would withdraw financial support of black enterprises (such as schools or black state fairs). Legitimate race progress, in the view of these powerful men, should complement rather than challenge white supremacist doctrine. Blacks' use of separate forums to exhibit evidence of racial progress and identity seemed to affirm segregationist politics and practices.

Hunter's organization of a state exhibit in the Negro Building at the tercentennial celebration of the founding of Jamestown in 1907 (which featured 9,000 exhibits covering 60,000 square feet) was designed to test white sentiment by illustrating the race's mastery of the modern age.[54] Among the 2,000 exhibits provided by Hunter's North Carolina Negro Development and Exposition Company were displays noting the achievements of blacks in the fields of science, technology, and business. In his numerous petitions to the North Carolina legislature to provide financial support for the black display at the Jamestown Exposition, Hunter played upon the racial mentality of southern whites as well as their sense of regional pride and duty toward blacks. "Any advancement shown by the Negroes of North Carolina in the arts and refinements of enlightened civilization must reflect honor upon the white people of the State under whose fostering care such results have been rendered possible," Hunter said. White support for the fair, he continued, would also encourage black patriotism and loyalty toward North Carolina and its leaders.[55] Hunter's flattering appeals to whites garnered $5,000 in appropriations from North Carolina's legislature, the only state in the country to provide financial support for black fairs.[56] This victory proved to Hunter not only the depth of whites' benevolence but how to obtain it. He had found a successful fund-raising strategy by stressing black loyalty and patriotism and the paternalistic language of the "fostering care" of whites. Hunter hoped that providing physical proof of the "enlightened civilization" of blacks would yield additional benefits.

Hunter's exhibit at Jamestown elicited praise from the white press and leading white men and seemed to supply the interracial payoff he sought. Governor Swanson of Virginia and the governor of New York, both of whom attended, praised the exhibit. Moved by a demonstration given by blind children enrolled in North Carolina's Deaf, Dumb and Blind Institute, Governor Swanson told Hunter of his interest in establishing a similar school for blacks in his native state. Swanson's $25,000 appropriations bill later passed the Virginia legislature and a school was organized at Newport News. North Carolina governor Glenn spoke to blacks at the Negro Building, where he said that the state was confronting the race problem just fine and added that well-behaved and lawful blacks knew that white people were their best friends. Addressing North Carolina's General Assembly after the Jamestown Exposition, Glenn voiced his satisfaction about the funds appropriated for the black exhibit, saying it was "one of the best investments the state had ever made."[57]

Yet despite the positive reaction from some whites, the participation of blacks in Jamestown attracted criticism from white and black patrons alike. Reports circulated stating that black visitors to the exposition had been discriminated against, both in their journey to and experience at Jamestown. Such reports noted blacks being subject to "unjust, unreasonable, and humiliating discrimination on trolley cars." At Jamestown, black visitors did not receive equal access to exposition facilities. Undaunted, Hunter, along with Exposition president Henry St. George Tucker and Director of Publicity J. W. Bolles, initiated a publicity campaign to dispel fears of race discrimination at the event. They assured blacks that every part of the exposition would be available to them on an equal basis with other visitors.[58]

In addition, black race leaders W. E. B. Du Bois and Dr. Nathan Mossell both disapproved of black expositions. Du Bois boycotted the fair, as did Atlanta University and other members of the Niagara movement. After the Atlanta riot and the discrimination against blacks at Jamestown and in the context of Jim Crow practices in the South generally, Mossell felt that blacks who supported the exposition had capitulated to the "usual Southern methods." Even Governor Glenn later retreated from the glowing remarks he had made to blacks at Jamestown. In subsequent speeches to black audiences, he said very little about their progress, instead choosing to speak about their inadequacies.[59] Glenn's comments were further evidence of rigidity in the attitudes of white southerners regarding the meaning of black progress and manhood. For Glenn and others, the black man's position in southern society was essentially fixed. He might well advance, but never so far as to threaten white men's claim to power and prestige.

Never completely oblivious to the robustness of racism in his state, Hunter focused on journalism that documented black contributions to the building of North Carolina.[60] (He also expressed his displeasure of the treatment of blacks at the Jamestown Exposition.) In his quest to debunk widespread opinion that the black race had "no history," Hunter launched intraracial campaigns to produce an "authentic" history of the black experience. As he put it, "If it is important for horses, mules, and cows . . . to have a history (pedigree), it is much more important for a race to have a history." The compilation of the historical contributions of blacks in a textbook to be published in conjunction with the Jamestown tercentennial, Hunter predicted, would not only foster "racial values" but would ultimately be of "service to future generations for which they will rise up and call us blessed."[61] During his lifetime, Hunter worked to craft an "intimate story of [the] Negro." He planned printed materials on black life in North Carolina that included stories of slave life in order to reveal the "beautiful relationship existing between the two races during those fateful days." He also wanted to include chronicles of the noble feats and character of (primarily) black men, including black preacher John Chavis and slave poet George Moses Horton. In an article he wrote entitled "Negro Life in North Carolina Illustrated" that described his proposed booklet, Hunter solicited information and statistics regarding the progress of the race—the homes, churches, businesses, lodges, schools of blacks—along with historical sketches of prominent race men and women. Contributors were encouraged to submit photos of themselves and a short biography for a fee of $8 a page, $4 for half a page and $2 for a quarter-page. Hunter pitched the booklet to the black community as "one of the most valuable compendiums of race literature ever issued in this state."[62] He sought to use history as a way to promote self-respect and virtue within the race. As he put it, "We should know more of ourselves, of our life and our achievements. . . . No person, no race, can attain to greatness without self-respect."[63]

Hunter's effort to retrace his people's historical roots and achievements was part of broader movements that sought to highlight blacks' interpretations of their experience. Black newspapers and magazines often published retrospectives that emphasized the historical accomplishments of black leaders and heroes. *The Colored American*, for example, ran full-page pictorials spotlighting the "Ten Greatest Negroes." In 1909, T. Thomas Fortune, editor of *New York Age*, called for a "usable" history for the race's young people. As he argued, the "Negro will get more of a race pride and self-confidence out of his own history. Let Negro students study Negro history. Let Negro schools teach Negro history."[64] Black historian Carter G. Woodson, founder of the Association for the Study of Negro Life and History, asserted in 1921 that "the Negro must learn to preserve his own records. He must learn the value of tradition. . . . We should also develop a literature. Negroes should read some things written by their own people that they may be inspired thereby."[65] Thomas L. Dabney, another commentator, observed that a race history would edify and inspire black youth and develop "proper respect and appreciation of the Negro among other races." Noting in 1929 that a survey of 497 black Virginia high school students had revealed how little black youths knew about their history, Dabney deemed the study of black history "urgently" necessary so that "our students shall have a working knowledge of American history" which was "necessary to instill manhood, courage, and ambition into colored youth. Negro history is needed to vitalize the race."[66]

Despite Hunter's repeated appeals to the black community that they "put all the hurry" into the matter of revitalizing the race, his project to craft a black history in North Carolina remained a work in progress for much of his life. Increasingly, he had difficulty sustaining mass interest in the campaign that sought to couple the old South to the new one. Hunter's 1927 publication of his "Review of Negro Life in North Carolina with My Recollections" failed to capture the black community's imagination. While it was meant to document the race's organizational and social history, Hunter's "Review" and other historical projects illustrate how narratives of black achievement could inspire pessimism about black progress and its power to improve race relations. As African-American historical texts proliferated in black communities, the range of opinions grew as to the merits of their political effectiveness.

Hunter's appeals to the black community for support of the "Review" and related publications on black history entailed rekindling slavery's past. While he did not deny the brutality of slavery, Hunter nonetheless extolled its lasting benefits. Through slavery, he observed, "the improved stock of the Negro race of today has come. The Negro absorbed, imitated, if you please—absorbed, assimilated the life and civilization of the white race with which he was in daily association. Above all, he received, adopted and imbibed from the whites the true religions.... This, perhaps, has been the sheet anchor, the heart and soul, of his splendid development." Though Hunter's supporters, including Bruce Cotten, descendant of a prominent slaveholding family, believed the "Review of Negro Life" would "save from oblivion" and "make some record of the lives and character of the many noble and splendid negros who have lived, worked and died in our old North State," such testimony furthered unease in those who came to view the race's slave heritage as more of a liability than an attribute.[67]

Hunter, not unlike other race reformers, sought to use slave memories as a political tool to usher in black equality after emancipation. By doing so, Hunter sought to accommodate white southern paternalism while asserting black history and race advancement. This balance proved difficult. The fact that Hunter was an educator speaks to the important, yet complicated, position of black teachers during Jim Crow.

As Adam Fairclough has argued, powerful southern whites increasingly turned to black educators as the preferred race representatives. Mayors and governors often appointed black teachers to advisory boards. Teachers also played prominent roles in the Commission on Interracial Cooperation (CIC), a group founded in 1919 that opposed racial violence such as lynching but supported race segregation and disfranchisement. Black teachers endured the strain of being financially dependent upon white politicians and officials, who often stressed black compliance with Jim Crow policies in return for their support. These circumstances influenced the particular responses of African Americans in the South and elsewhere. While Hunter's invocation of slavery as a training ground for the race's material and moral "progress" held currency for the state's powerful whites, such tactics met with opposition from black community members who questioned Hunter's credentials as a representative and loyal member of the race. Hunter's sponsorship of dinners for former slaves and his own memories of slavery served to further entrench white supremacy in southern communities as Hunter affirmed pro-slavery logic that sanctioned slavery and the "tender old ties" that had bound both races during that time.[68]

In other ways, however, the commemorative ceremonies that Hunter supported show the diversity of responses to Jim Crow as critics of Hunter postulated new race strategies in opposition to accommodationist ones. Though spearheaded by conservative spokesmen, North Carolina's commemorative and fair events demonstrate initiatives such as resolutions that pressed for state support of schools and the dissolution of Jim Crow legislation that were meant to promote black rights. Even Hunter, through his involvement in institution-building and professional organizations such as the North Carolina Industrial Association, strove to better the status of black America. Yet increasingly, his definition of black progress was challenged by those who favored more direct political strategies.[69]

A "New Emancipation" for a "New Order of Black Men"

While the rhetoric at early Emancipation Day and black fairs in North Carolina tended to be conservative at the turn of the century, the tone of both events grew more militant and political after World War I. The war became a pivotal topic around which black participants in North Carolina's state fair and Emancipation Day ceremonies revisited the meanings of racial progress, black leadership, and the ways in which institutional structures advanced or compromised uplift goals. North Carolina's black community used African-American institutions to explore the meanings of racial uplift and a dignified black manhood.

During World War I, President Woodrow Wilson's institutionalization of white supremacy at home while espousing democratic ideals abroad exposed paradoxes within his Progressive agenda. Part of this domestic agenda included the banning of African-American employment in federal offices. Upon assuming office in 1913, Wilson fired fifteen out of seventeen black supervisors who had been appointed to federal posts, replacing them with whites. Blacks were segregated or dismissed from federal posts throughout the nation. Moreover, although blacks had normally been appointed as ambassadors to Haiti and Santa Domingo, under Wilson these posts were filled by whites.[70] Despite these disturbing policies, black male organizers and participants at state fair and Emancipation Day ceremonies appropriated Wilson's wartime rhetoric of liberty and democracy to justify African-American citizenship rights and to bolster black manhood.

Across North Carolina, black World War I soldiers paraded in their uniforms before jubilant crowds of black citizens, who showered them with cheers and approbation of the good service they were about to render overseas. At a 1919 Emancipation Day ceremony in Wilmington, 100 parading black soldiers were flanked by local bands, a drum and bugle corps, and fraternal and church groups. Black soldiers used these communal settings to affirm their identity as respectable men. The parading of black soldiers affirmed the race's place in America's liberation struggles.[71]

Other public demonstrations of black patriotism punctuated the contention of black men that southern blacks had been and continued to be loyal citizens. Before the war, ritual performances of the "Star Spangled Banner," "America," "Yankee Doodle," "O Southland," and "My Country 'Tis of Thee" at Emancipation Day ceremonies asserted that the race contained dutiful American and southern citizens. During the war, Kate Herring, director of publicity for North Carolina's War Savings Committee, acknowledged the positive contributions of blacks to the war effort: "The colored people pledged to buy War Savings Stamps far more in keeping with their ability than the white people. Like the colored soldier at the front, [they] heard the call and responded."[72]

Although some blacks used wartime events to demonstrate their patriotism and loyalty, the war did much to catalyze growing unease in the black community about the state of race relations. Historian John Hope Franklin described the summer of 1919 as "the greatest period of interracial strife the nation had ever witnessed." Twenty-five riots broke out in urban areas. Moreover, the successful nomination of Frank A. Linney as U.S. attorney for the western district of North Carolina in 1921 prompted a growing number of blacks to rethink their allegiance to the Republican Party. As Republican candidate for governor in 1916, Linney had supported white agricultural reformer Clarence Poe's plan for apartheid-style segregation in the South.[73] In 1920, he openly supported eliminating blacks from formal politics. Like they had been the year before, outbreaks of racial violence were cause for concern in 1920; race riots were reported in Fayetteville and Winston-Salem. Lynching was also a growing problem; from 1920 to 1943, thirty-seven lynchings were recorded in the state.

In response to these developments, state branches of the National Association for the Advancement of Colored People (NAACP) began forming. In 1917, the NAACP established local groups in Raleigh, Durham, and Greensboro. Three years later, more than 1,000 black North Carolinians were members in seven NAACP chapters across the state.[74] Black political clubs also formed whose goal was to secure the franchise for black men.[75] The definition of effective race leadership became a topic of discussion in these and other public forums. In 1918, a meeting in Raleigh's city auditorium featured an address by NAACP founder W. E. B. Du Bois. Dr. L. E. McCauley, president of Raleigh's NAACP branch, demanded change in the type of "colored leadership" available to his people. Although he still supported thoughtful, deliberate, and conservative race leaders, he pointed out that "colored people no longer appreciated compromising leadership for selfish gain, but they do appreciate a leadership that is honest, clean, and non-compromising, and that always leads his people forward."[76]

After a speaking tour of North Carolina in 1924, NAACP secretary James Weldon Johnson judged North Carolina to be "a southern state in which the program of the NAACP can be carried out with great success. The leading colored men and women whom I talked want me to come down and tour all of the principal cities of the state for the purpose of stimulating anew the NAACP branch." After visiting Shaw University in Raleigh and Kittrell College in Kittrell, North Carolina, Johnson praised black youth, whom he claimed had lost "much of the supersensitiveness which Negroes have had about white people's opinion of them. The young colored youth in the colleges seem to be more concerned with what they are and intend to be than with mere approbation of their white environment." He also lauded research done by white academics at the University of North Carolina at Chapel Hill that documented the economic progress of blacks.[77]

Troubled by the South's racial tensions, some within and outside the black community began to express their impatience with segregation. Disillusioned by paradoxes in Wilson's overseas campaign that sanctioned democratic principles abroad but not at home, state fair supporter James B. Dudley, president of Agricultural and Technical College of North Carolina, referred to instances of "humiliating discrimination and injustices" and shared his horror over the scourge of lynching at a 1920 conference on race relations at Tuskegee.[78] Much to the consternation of Hunter and white "allies" such as Governor Bickett, Dudley also spoke out against the intransigence of racial discrimination after the war.[79]

Dudley's comments seemed to support Professor Robert T. Kerlin's pronouncement that the "Negro is a new man." Kerlin, of Virginia Military Institute, felt that the war had produced a racial consciousness characterized by an "insistent demand for equal civic rights."[80] Department of Labor spokesman George Haynes also concluded that the war had produced a "new order" of men. While emancipation had signaled blacks' transition from property to persons, it had not eradicated lynching and mob rule. True emancipation, Haynes contended, "must clothe [African Americans] with the full relations of manhood."

Indeed, public discourse within the black community in general had shifted toward renewed contemplation of the "New Negro." For J. A. Rogers, writing in the *Messenger*, the "New Negro" departed from the old in several respects. The "old Negro" worshiped the white man, had contempt for his own people, and was ready to make unmanly concessions in exchange for white patronage. "The Old, hat in hand, is always begging white people, a sort of glorified cripple with a can," Rogers maintained. "Because of this he always has two different messages, one which he gives to white people, the other to colored ones. He is a living lie." On the other hand, "the New [Negro] is erect, manly, bold; if necessary, defiant. He apologizes to no one for his existence, feeling deep in his inner being that he has just as much right to be on earth and in all public places as anyone else. He looks the whole world searchingly in the eye, fearing or worshipping nothing nor no one. . . . In a word, he respects himself, first of all."[81]

Rhetoric about distinctions between old and new race leadership and ideology filtered into public ceremonies in North Carolina. The language of patience and forbearance that had typified many of North Carolina's earlier Emancipation Day ceremonies and state fair events was supplanted in the postwar period by more militant expressions. Although black speakers continued to extend an olive branch to their white "protectors," they expressed growing irritation about racial discrimination and segregation. At the same time, they staked a claim to and reinforced their ownership of an American identity. In Raleigh in 1917, Emancipation Day speaker James Young ridiculed a report that maintained that former President Roosevelt had hatched a plan to deport American blacks to Africa. "That project is all poppycock," he said. "We are at peace with the people here and are going to stay. The white man has brought us to America and he must take care of us in this country." Speaker J. H. Branch concurred, adding that "I give notice to all concerned that we do not intend to leave this country unless it be of our own free will and accord."[82]

Two years later, an Emancipation Day crowd of 3,000 blacks approved militant resolutions denouncing racial inequality in all its forms. The resolutions demanded that blacks boycott segregated facilities, called for the outlawing of lynching and restoration of the ballot, and encouraged parents to teach their children that being black "was no disgrace." Dr. J. E. Samuels, editor of the *Missionary Herald* in Franklinton, inspired a thunderous round of applause from his black audience when he said that America would eventually "look not so much to the color of the skin as to the soul under it." He also dismissed as "nonsense" talk of emigration or colonization. "We are going to stay here, and we will be here when lynch law will have spent its course and when mobocracy will have become a thing of the past."[83]

In 1919 and 1920, black Emancipation Day spectators voiced their displeasure with white supremacy in multiple ways. A 1919 pageant comprised of seven episodes told of the race's accomplishments and their grievances, principally Jim Crow and lynch laws. In the episode titled "Today in Negro Life," Crime, represented by a black figure wearing overalls, a bandana handkerchief, and a slouch hat, was chased down the stage by another figure, Lynch Law. The episode concluded as Lynch Law placed a rope around Crime's neck. Emancipation Day spectators, according to reports, let their imaginations play out the scene's conclusion.[84] In 1920, as part of the resolutions it approved, the Raleigh Emancipation Day audience demanded that lynching be made a capital offense and that black children be taught the history of the race, "to have pride in the same, and that the same standard of instruction be maintained for every child in the State."[85]

The Jim Crow theatrical pageant, at least within the North Carolina setting, provides a glimpse into how class figured into such ceremonies. While Charles Hunter and others of the black middle class sought to distinguish and advance themselves as respectable men in part by distancing their moral and economic status from that of the masses, the pageant demonstrated the unjustness, indignity, and victimization accorded the black race as a whole. The bandana-clad "Negro" functioned as a unifying symbol of protest for the entire black community, regardless of class. Perhaps even more germane, the staging of the pageant marked a shift to the ideology and racial strategies of the New Negro. Black descendants of house servants and artisans (blacksmiths, carpenters) had evolved, explained a writer in the *Southern Workman*, into the "preachers, teachers, doctors, mechanics, farm owners, and business men, who, as leaders of their race, live in their own world apart from the whites. They are the new order of black men." This new image of the black race and its manhood rejected faith in a mythic racial past that based black progress largely on white paternalism and fond memories of slavery.[86] W. S. Turner, dean of Shaw University, told an Emancipation Day audience in 1922 that the "American people are facing today in the negro a developing race consciousness and an enlightening public opinion on the position of the negro in the life of the nation." At that event, Emancipation Day attendees resolved to send money to the NAACP to support the passage of the federal Dyer Anti-Lynching bill, to vote "our honest convictions on every issue," and to support equal funding for white and black high schools in Raleigh.[87]

Several Emancipation Day ceremonies in the 1920s featured recitations of the black national anthem, James Weldon Johnson's "Lift Every Voice and Sing," another indication of a heightened race consciousness.[88] When the question came up of whether blacks were satisfied, the response from the black community seemed less equivocal than it had been before. Responding to the comment of a Democratic senator from Missouri who claimed that blacks seemed to be "pretty well satisfied with things as they are," an editorialist in Charlotte's *Star of Zion* retorted that "if Senator Reed means that those Negroes expressed satisfaction with general living conditions, with opportunities for education, with the mob, with segregation, Jim-Crowism and disfranchisement, with the wanton violation of Negro womanhood, he talked with a bunch of Negroes who were mighty big liars."[89]

Even educator William Clinton Jackson's conservative behavior—he banned the *Crisis*, the organ of the NAACP, on the campus of the North Carolina College for Women—acquired a radical edge as he made another pitch to "solve the problem." Though he still castigated Du Bois as a "very dangerous man" whose writings are "bitter and clever" and insisted that the "Negro problem" needed to be worked out among southerners rather than outsiders, he implored white southern men to ease racial friction by dealing more fairly with the race. Asserting that the "Negro problem is strictly up to the southern men," Jackson spoke out against whites' customary use of the term "nigger" to describe the race, asserting that the average black "resents the word." He also appealed to the white people of Greensboro for equal treatment of blacks by the police and in the judicial system, saying that it could be proven that during the previous month blacks had been punished in Guilford County for having less whisky in their possession than white men who were set free. Jackson felt that it would be an indictment of southern men's Christianity and political institutions if the South failed to live up to its racial responsibilities. He cautioned that "the negro is here to stay, there's no chance of shoving him off the earth. So the intelligent thing to do is try to work out a system that will make him an asset instead of a liability."[90]

White leaders responded to such challenges by urging blacks to refrain from radical utterances and behavior. In 1919, Bickett addressed an Emancipation Day audience of 1,500 at Mount Lebanon A.M.E. Zion Church in New Bern, where he urged the black community to strive toward a "higher freedom." Physical freedom, if it was to be of any use, had to be "coupled with moral freedom and financial freedom," Bickett advised. He stressed that the race needed to exercise more thrift and self-control. Perhaps more important, Bickett encouraged blacks to "live in a spirit of neighborliness with your white friends and keep on good terms with them. Your worst enemy in this world, though he himself may not know it, is the man who would cause you to have hard feeling against the white people among whom you live. Such a man is your worst enemy and mine."[91]

At an Emancipation Day ceremony in 1920, Bickett warned that the "greatest blunder the Negroes of North Carolina can make at this time is to get into politics. I have seen it under both regimes, before 1900 and after . . . and the most remarkable progress of the Negro has been since 1900." Black progress, he contended, had been made possible by the race's "aptness" and good teachers and by the patronage of southern whites. Bickett endorsed a teachers' training school for blacks comparable to white schools in Greenville and Greensboro, better schools with longer terms, a reformatory for black boys and girls, and improved accommodations on segregated cars. And yet, he cautioned, "I can't go before the legislature and get these things done if the cry of the negro in the saddle in politics is once again raised in North Carolina. Do not throw away this golden opportunity of your race to stretch out your hands to the moon and claim it for your own."

While Bickett's argument that displays of black militancy hindered his effectiveness as an "apostle of racial co-operation," it also illustrated the erosion of white confidence in race matters. The power of blacks to bargain for white patronage rested on their subordination within the South's racial caste system. Events after World War I, however, had tested whites' faith in this interracial pact.

Black emigration to the North and Southwest in the first two decades of the twentieth century also fed white anxiety about race relations. During the Great Migration, approximately one million blacks left North Carolina in search of better economic and racial conditions. While white elites were initially concerned about the depletion of black labor, they were equally worried about how the experience of living in the North would radicalize blacks who later returned to the South. Thus, at Emancipation Day and state fair gatherings, white speakers took pains to praise both black progress and black loyalty to white supremacy. At the black fair in

1921, Governor Morrison lauded the black community's productivity as laborers, cited their patriotism and service during World War I, and commended the obedience of black soldiers to their white commanders. He said he had never known "a black who would not go under the leadership of the white to death if needed."[92] At the state fair in 1925, Governor Angus W. McLean insisted that a racial problem existed only to the extent that whites and blacks sought "selfish advancement; [tried] to intimidate others, and [had] no better weapon than the cowardly appeal to racial prejudice and racial antipathy."[93]

White observers agreed with this sentiment. An editorialist in the *Raleigh Times* claimed that black men were poised to usurp existing governmental authority: "Why should a race whose numbers comprise one-tenth the population of the country imagine that it is entitled to rule over the majority from whom it derives its charter of freedom?" Such imaginings on the part of blacks confirmed their regression into a slave mentality, he continued. "In the cases in which it has been tried[,] the negro in government . . . has proved an unqualified failure. It is the best proof that the negro is really free, that he has in most cases centered his attention on acquiring those things for himself which are to be had by his own efforts."[94]

The message was clear. From the perspective of white elites, race relations were best when blacks remained in positions subordinate to and separate from whites. As Governor Bickett put it, it would be best for blacks to "rest your case on the white man's sense of justice, and . . . keep it there." Men like Bickett believed that other types of justice would only lead to race wars and a revival of the Ku Klux Klan.[95]

The repeated warnings from white Emancipation Day and fair speakers that blacks needed to be submissive and self-reliant likely had serious consequences for Hunter. Though direct evidence is not apparent within fair records, it is possible that Hunter struggled to get financial support from white benefactors because of whites' increasing anxiety over black militancy and Hunter's own ongoing frustration over the intransigence of race relations. At Emancipation Day ceremonies in 1921, Hunter offered more spirited, less conservative festivities. Heeding advice from within the community that blacks needed to agitate more forcefully for their rights, Hunter recommended that the 1921 Emancipation Day ceremony not be "couched in high sounding phrases" but instead reflect a vigorous race consciousness. At that commemoration, keynote speaker Channing Tobias, secretary of the International YMCA in New York, criticized interracial movements by "so called friends of the Negro" that did not promote racial equality. He urged the people in his audience to embrace a new program of reform that included supporting the NAACP, selecting their own leaders, and securing their freedom through organizing and voting.

Hunter's own racial attitude, which fluctuated with the temperament of the "best" white men, changed in the aftermath of black participation in World War I. In March 1921, Hunter wrote that the black man had been "penalized, ostracized, and stigmatized" and remained an "outcast of our civilization." The wounds of his race, he maintained, had become festering sores, and he found it appropriate for blacks to take desperate measures to protect themselves, even if that meant supporting anarchy, socialism or atheism.[96] This rhetoric differed markedly from his 1923 Emancipation Day address in Pittsboro, where he predicted that the ultimate emancipation of the race lay in religion rather than black political or civil rights. However, it seems that his occasional use of radical language affected the viability of his beloved fair. The black fair did not take place in 1926 or 1927 because whites refused to allow blacks use of Raleigh's fairgrounds. The state subsequently denied the fair its annual appropriation of $500 (but it continued its $200,000 appropriation for the white fair), citing the inability of the North Carolina Industrial Association to hold the event. In 1929, the black fair again was not held because white officials refused to grant blacks permission to use the state fairgrounds. A year later, Hunter successfully petitioned whites to use Raleigh's fairground. However, his attempts to have the annual $500 appropriation reinstated retroactively proved futile. Hunter reported to NCIA executive members in 1931, the last year of the black fair, that the prospect of further state funds seemed bleak.[97]

Despite the pleas of white elites that blacks desist from "selfish advancement," debate about the proper avenues for racial progress persisted in the black community. At an Emancipation Day ceremony in 1923, Rev. Ormonde Walker condemned the Ku Klux Klan and American imperialism in Haiti. He further asserted that whites were dealing with a new generation of blacks, not former slaves but their offspring. At Emancipation Day ceremonies in 1928, Rev. L. W. Kyle argued for "full-fledged" access to the ballot and "a place in the government of the country."[98] That same year, Rev. W. C. Cleland told an Emancipation Day audience that blacks should learn to follow principles, not parties. "A Negro with principles in the Democratic Party is far better than a rascal in the Republican Party," he said, adding amid a burst of applause that "we will not achieve freedom until we learn to appreciate our franchise."[99]

The meaning of Emancipation Day celebrations was also scrutinized. In speeches, Rev. W. C. Cleland and educator William S. Turner of Raleigh's Shaw University insisted that the Emancipation Proclamation had not granted blacks their freedom, for as Cleland observed, "the Negro is not quite free yet. . . . To achieve his freedom the Negro must work and live and move not as an isolated people but as an integral part of this great government."[100] Turner also dismissed the historical and constitutional importance of emancipation, labeling it a strategic gesture to advance the cause of the Civil War rather than an act of humanitarianism.

Despite their growing militancy, the views of this generation of black men increasingly became passé to younger generations, who sought to rid themselves of Emancipation Day ceremonies and the stigma of racial passivity they perpetuated. In 1919, students at St. Augustine's College in Raleigh read from a list that illustrated their impatience with the slow pace of racial change and the conservatism of their elders in pursuing it. The demands included economic and political equality and suffrage for women. The students also warned government officials that should they fail to act on the issues, they were capable of seizing such rights themselves. Many young people viewed Emancipation Day commemorations as unwanted reminders of their second-class status, symbols that the race had not yet evolved enough and thus would always merit the paternalistic protection and racial guidance of whites.[101]

For men like Charles Hunter, the celebratory and progressive impulses of Emancipation Day required no defense. He remained proud of the white relationships he had cultivated during slavery, saying "I am not ashamed of it and have no apologies to offer." But in the same breath he lauded the Great Emancipator. Rallying around the symbol of Lincoln as the one who conferred not only the race's humanity but also its citizenship, Hunter exclaimed, "I do love Abraham Lincoln. I revere the Proclamation of Emancipation."[102] Some seemed partly swayed by such statements. In many quarters of North Carolina, Emancipation Day ceremonies continued uninterrupted, and many attempted to merge the old and new racial consciousnesses into their celebrations. An Emancipation Day ceremony in High Point featured not only the black national anthem but a dinner for former slaves. Reports of that ceremony noted several white people, all members of civic clubs, in the audience. Another Emancipation Day ceremony in Raleigh blended the singing of the black anthem with the honoring of more than fifty former slave men and women in Wake County.[103] An editorialist for the *Freeman* rationalized the need to find a compromise between the "New Negro" and old racial ideology. He favored public observance of the Emancipation Proclamation but in a "quiet, appropriate way," because "the new Negro does not enthuse over reminders of a past that is full of degradation." Noting that if given a preference, every man would trace his descent to kings and nobles rather than slaves, the *Freeman* writer maintained that "the spirit of gratitude should be kept up somehow. We should not develop racial traits that bespeak indifference to the spirit of philanthropy." In short, the race's claim to civilization, its progress, still hinged on a spirit of "gratefulness" to those who had paved its way to freedom.[104]

Disagreement about the limits of using the race's past to promote its progress lingered as well. Speaking to an Emancipation Day audience in 1928, Rev. Cleland surmised that "the negro has every right to be proud of his history, but he must not let history be the end. He must keep struggling, and through education, through the acquirement of wealth, through the use of the ballot . . . make his freedom a reality."[105] Hunter's stubborn appropriation of his slave past as a tool for mediating the racial present was indicative of the growing chasm between him and an evolving brand of black male leadership that began to favor more non-accommodationist strategies to realize the race's salvation and self-respect.[106] Hunter's disappointment over his failure to find support for his black history retrospective, his concern about dwindling fair attendance, and his struggle to prevent the fair's demise took a heavy toll. The dream of resurrecting the black fair died with Hunter, who became ill in the summer of 1931 and succumbed on 4 September.[107]

The state fair and Emancipation Day ceremonies were discursive sites where the meanings of freedom and a dignified manhood were publicly debated within and across the races. Over time, strategies for racial progress within African-American community institutions evolved from a philosophy that touted "good feelings" between the races to one that endorsed more militant, uncompromising approaches to "solving the problem." In contrast, the non-aggressive (or conciliatory) leadership style men such as

Charles Hunter preferred fell into disfavor after World War I and the birth of New Negro ideology.

In an era of increasing racial hostility, black proponents of Emancipation Day celebrations and segregated state fairs emphasized material and moral advances, pragmatically choosing not to challenge the racial orthodoxy of the South. In their addresses to fair and Emancipation Day audiences, black spokesmen sought to create a wedge of racial opportunity by emphasizing the race's rise to "enlightened civilization," but conservative messages by powerful whites stressed the limitations of such appeals in forwarding racial justice. For many elite southern whites, the place of the black race in society was essentially fixed. White supremacist doctrine ensured that although black achievement and rhetoric might advance African-Americans laterally, they would never surpass whites. Though blacks and whites shared a common civic vocabulary of progress, they disagreed about the racial and gendered meanings of that language. Powerful white leaders wanted to manage the color line on their own terms. Men such as Governor Thomas Bickett defined the civilizing traits of industriousness and virtue as the exclusive preserve of deserving white males. Aware of the limits of interracial outreach, black spokesmen such as Charles Hunter largely submitted themselves, in ways that sometimes frustrate contemporary scholars, to displays of racial accommodation in their appeals to white audiences. Faced with few viable options, Hunter continued to believe that his personal relationships with white elites and whites' purported adherence to Christian values would change race relations over time.

Yet even at their most conservative, the black fairs and Emancipation Day ceremonies carried uplifting meanings and sought to propel the race forward. Though often dominated by preachy messages from black middle-class men about the race's shortcomings and advice concerning its elevation, African-American participants took ownership in the events, refashioning them to meet particular needs. The agricultural and domestic exhibits at state fairs and the parades, singing, and sporting events at both Emancipation Day celebrations and state fairs showcased not just individual talents but also the communal ties that bound members of the black community—men and women, young and old, rural and city dwellers. The influence of black women was felt most acutely in this respect. Though largely silent in such proceedings, their behind-the-scenes organizing spoke volumes as they attended to nurturing the black community.

Their attention to the race's need for leisure-time activities surely sustained the record crowds at the gatherings.

Hunter's labors during and after the Jamestown Exposition of 1907 promoted an appreciation of black history and the racial solidarity and collective racial memory that are essential to the success of any black freedom campaign. By using his time and resources to support prominent institutions that fostered racial pride and debate, Hunter affirmed his commitment to an African-American civic discourse that has always embraced a wide range of opinion and ideas, even those contrary to his own. His actions demonstrated what scholars of the Jim Crow era have recognized: that black leaders were able to engage in simultaneous discourses of protest and accommodation. Yet as debate over the meaning of race progress grew, conflict over race leadership intensified. The challenge for North Carolina's black male leaders was how best to navigate a biracial terrain without unduly compromising the integrity of the race or its manhood.

Conclusion

Though black women came into their own as an autonomous force at the end of the nineteenth century, partially because black men were stripped of their formal political identities, which made women's work all the more visible, the degree to which black women exercised their autonomy has been overemphasized. Rather than being driven from the field of race activism completely, black men, likely inspired by black women's example, held firm to their community work and the validation that such labor conferred on their gender. They sought to defend, define, and explain themselves outside the context of electoral politics during disfranchisement. Their actions illustrate how the definition of manhood changed in response to a changing political, social, and economic context. This book has situated gender (analysis of black manhood and womanhood) more firmly within the discourse of race activism in the early Jim Crow South by providing insight into the flexible meanings of black manhood and the relationship between black male and female activists in that era.

For many of North Carolina's black men, the violent racial politics of the 1890s reinforced the need for the black community to work together for racial uplift. Black men generally viewed black women as their "partners" in race work. They understood that men and women shared a racial legacy that reached back to slavery that worked against the inclination to separate race and gender roles into distinctly "feminine" and "masculine" categories. As educator and clubwoman Fannie Barrier Williams observed in the *Voice of the Negro,* "In our development as a race, the colored woman and the colored man started even. The man cannot say that he is better educated and has had a wider sphere, for they both began school at the same time. They both suffered the same misfortunes. The limitations put upon their ambitions have been identical."[1]

John Moses Avery, future vice president and secretary of the North Carolina Mutual Life Insurance Company in Durham, addressed the importance of this racial and gendered legacy in a 1915 commencement speech to students at Livingstone College. In his speech "Useful Man or Woman," Avery posited that true African-American manhood depended on a black man's ability to regard black women as partners in his work, recognize their contributions, and assert himself as one committed to racial progress through a life of service. Avery's call for men to combine assertive behavior with respectful deference toward black women would prove challenging to implement.[2]

With disfranchisement, black men were denied a fundamental political tool needed for the race's upward mobility and claim to citizenship. Moreover, they found themselves saddled with a definition of self that demanded a response. Just as the symbolism of "the lady" both circumscribed and defined black women's activism, so too did the projection of the "black beast rapist" and "emasculated" male influence black men's role in racial uplift. Not unlike black race women who sought to use women's moral influence to improve the status of their race, black men manipulated the meanings of manhood toward the same goals. As black women experimented with different standards of womanhood (for instance, whether to play up their "feminine" side or to adopt identities as feminists) black men also pondered what best defined their manhood. Were they to be strictly patriarchal or were they to foster institutions that were gender inclusive?

Combining the exercise of patriarchal authority with rhetoric on manhood and cooperation within the black community posed continual challenges. North Carolina's black men struggled with the question of how and to what extent they should accept, encourage, and, at times, strive to replicate black women's activism. Key to this struggle was black men's appropriation of institutional spaces—secular and sacred, public and private—to promote personal and racial agendas. The use of institutional space in the black community and the degree of opportunities for men and women within them are central to my arguments. The type of spaces African American men appropriated determined the type of manhood they expressed within them. These expressions were often multifaceted and tenuous as black women activists, who had a distinctive work, fought to maintain their independence, even if in a spatial context that ultimately rendered them subordinate to men.

Black men and women worked assiduously to prevent young black males from going adrift, in many cases using similar methods and approaches to resolving the problem. Black middle-class men and women endorsed the politics of respectability, and both were intent on shoring up black domesticity, protecting black households and its inhabitants from what they considered modern and commercial contagions.

Men and women worked together in a variety of public venues to uplift the race. In fact, many men asserted that black women's labor helped build the Young Men's Institute in Asheville. And yet while male leaders of the Young Men's Institute accommodated black women's activity through sharing space and resources, they periodically restricted black women's access to activities within the institute in efforts to demonstrate a manly dominance. In doing so, black men sacrificed unity of purpose in order to fortify their manhood, an effort that included distancing their identity from those of both boys and women.

The cooperative and communal traits that were nurtured and ritualized within black fraternal spaces were also fragile. Prince Hall Masons conflicted with members of its women's auxiliary, the Order of the Eastern Star, over the ability of the women to engage in independent work. The contributions of women of the Eastern Star were hindered by men, who in occupying the privatized, all-male space of the fraternal lodge limited the range of autonomy and leadership women could exercise in this setting. Eastern Star women registered their dissatisfaction with Prince Hall's attempts to "save" them. They voiced disapproval when their members were mistreated and resented the prospect of the Grand Lodge intervening in their financial affairs, regardless of how dire the circumstances were.

The dynamics within the fraternal order show the limits of "protection" as pledged by Prince Hall members. Within the segregated South, the ability of black men to safeguard their women met constant challenge from popular racialist ideology that trumpeted black moral inferiority and sexual depravity. Additionally, during slavery and its aftermath black men were wanting in protecting black women from sexual assault, whether by slaveholders or predatory white males in domestic work settings. Repeated skirmishes over Eastern Star women's usage of Masonic halls and the refusal by Prince Hall leaders to assist with financial problems, preferring instead to take control of OES finances, signaled an absence of protection. All these conflicts expose the contradictions in the ideology of "protection" as members of North Carolina's Prince Hall organization aspired to legitimize a noble black manhood through control of its female auxiliary. To Prince Hall men, the concept of Masonic protection could be wielded to enforce a patriarchal authority. This understanding of the concept stood in opposition to black women's expectations that black male leadership would uplift its women by respecting their desire for autonomous work.

Black churchwomen saw themselves as having a clearly defined and public role in North Carolina's Baptist Convention. Churchmen's hierarchical control over that space, however, dictated what positions women could fulfill. But a persistent dialogue between churchmen and women regarding gendered ideals and work assignments reveals that such hierarchy was not absolute. Indeed, gender identity in that sacred space proved fluid enough for men to aspire to assume some of women's work while retaining a manly authority.

The public integrated spaces of state fairs and Emancipation Day ceremonies showcased the state's prominent black men and their efforts to improve the race's standing. Over time, these forums prompted internal debate by the black community over the future of race relations and what constituted respectable black leadership. Men like Charles Hunter floated uneasily between accommodating powerful whites who stressed the racial status quo and validating black progress through emphasizing black history, the material and moral strengths of the race, and institutional growth. The community institutions he so vigorously supported provided space for the black community to gather and be entertained, but they also provided a place where the community could come to meaningful conclusions about proper avenues for black advancement and unity.

Cultural and racial ideologies internal and external to the black community also shaped the relationship of black male and female activists. A tradition of shared public space within the black community competed with Victorian ideology, masculine rhetoric, and a belief in separate spheres for each gender. Adherence to separate spheres ideology and its stress on traditional gender roles undermined an African-American historical tradition that viewed public spaces such as the church as sites of active and necessary engagement for both women and men. In these public spaces, protected from the harsh reality of Jim Crow politics, black men and women strengthened communal bonds and engaged in communal politics. Yet this tradition of shared public space within the black community did not preclude conflict. The institution building of black men and women was influenced by dominant white discourses that stressed not just conventional gender roles but patriarchy.

World War I and the New Negro movement of the 1920s also fostered debate within the black community about the appropriate course for achieving racial uplift and creating a respectable black manhood. These two events prompted many black men to shift from strategies of racial accommodation to a more militant stance. Previous admonitions from black male leaders to "labor and wait" were now supplanted by spirited calls for the restoration of denied manhood rights, including the franchise. By the 1930s, race observers began to chronicle the demise of the fabled "race man" of the nineteenth and early twentieth centuries who had been content to embrace his "received culture" rather than black nationalism.[3]

During the period 1900–1930, the terms "partner" and "cooperation" among black men and women engaged in race reform assumed complex meanings. Cooperative race work among black men and women could and simultaneously might not mean similar work roles, depending on the context. Gender matters consistently framed the communal partnerships of black middle-class men and women. Efforts by black men to remain attentive to their racial and gendered needs led to contentious exchanges with black women activists, who at times felt that their identities and racial contributions were subsumed by those of men.

Gender, race, and the use of institutional space contributed to a dialogue within the black middle-class community that was simultaneously uplifting and divisive. As North Carolina's black men sought to reconcile themselves with the outer world of segregation through building institutions, they were equally attentive to the project of fashioning an African-American manhood characterized by dignity and authority that would prove uplifting to their manhood and to the black community overall.

Notes

Introduction

1. Marby, *The Negro in North Carolina Politics since Reconstruction*; Buggs, "The Negro in Charlotte, North Carolina as Reflected in the Charlotte Observer and Related Sources, 1900–1910."

2. "An Address by the Negroes," *Morning Post* (Raleigh), 2 January 1900.

3. Ironically, the gains in political power that blacks achieved in the late 1800s were largely the by-product of the state's white Redeemers, who in conceding the difficult task of disfranchising all black voters resorted to isolating (and thus diminishing) the extent of black political power. Redeemers thus sometimes gerrymandered black voters into racial districts (including the "Black Second"), sacrificing some political offices to blacks. See Williamson, *A Rage for Order*, 154.

4. North Carolina's disfranchisement campaign and its gendered implications have been examined in a number of works, including Gilmore, *Gender and Jim Crow*; Edmonds, *The Negro & Fusion Politics in North Carolina*; Prather, *We Have Taken a City*; Anderson, *Race and Politics in North Carolina*; and Cecelski and Tyson, *Democracy Betrayed*.

5. "Southern Negroes' Plaint," *New York Times*, 26 August 1900; Gilmore, *Gender and Jim Crow*, 130.

6. Gilmore, *Gender and Jim Crow*, 131.

7. "A Negro Exodus," *Star of Zion*, 13 March 1902.

8. See for example, Black, *Dismantling Black Manhood*; and Litwack, *Trouble in Mind*. Litwack's stress on black oppression mutes the theme of black empowerment. See also Packard, *American Nightmare*. Scholars have begun to demonstrate the varied ways blacks continued to act "in their own interests" during Jim Crow. See, for example, Lewis, *In Their Own Interests*; Chafe, Gavins, Korstad, and the Behind the Veil Project, *Remembering Jim Crow*; Wright, *Life behind a Veil*; and Leyburn, *The Way We Lived*.

9. Studies emphasizing women's activism after disfranchisement are extensive. They include Neverdon-Morton, *Afro-American Women of the South and the Advancement of the Race*; Rouse, *Lugenia Burns Hope*; Salem, *To Better Our World*;

Scott, "Most Invisible of All"; Frankel and Dye, *Gender, Class, Race, and Reform in the Progressive Era*; Shaw, "Black Club Women and the Creation of the National Association of Colored Women," 10–25; Shaw, *What a Woman Ought to Be and to Do*; White, "The Cost of Club Work, the Price of Black Feminism," 247–269. For working-class black women, see Hunter, *To 'Joy My Freedom*. For comparisons between black and white women's activism, see Gilmore, *Gender and Jim Crow*; and Johnson, *Southern Ladies, New Women*. While many studies have examined black and white women's views of each other in the early-twentieth-century South, scholars have failed to examine black men's attitudes toward and their relationships with black women in any depth for this time period. A notable early exception to this is Nimmons, "Social Reform and Moral Uplift in the Black Community," 20–23, 52–60. Nimmons argued that ministers, deacons, Masons, and other concerned citizens worked in a similar manner as women to uplift their communities.

10. Frances Ellen Watkins Harper, a nineteenth-century black suffragist, cast the late nineteenth century as "woman's era," as did one of the earliest black clubwomen, Josephine St. Pierre Ruffin. Ruffin founded the New Era Club in Boston and later became a founding member of the National Association of Colored Women. She published the first black woman's newspaper, calling it *Woman's Era*. Many black women believed that given the shared legacy of slavery and the absence of the vote for either gender, black men and women shared equally in improving the race and race relations. See White, *Too Heavy a Load*, 37–39.

11. The black women's club movement began in 1892 when Mary Church Terrell, Anna Julia Cooper, and Mary Jane Patterson formed the Colored Women's League in Washington, D.C. The league, which established branches in the South and in the West, urged black women to play a role in solving the race problem. Three years later, the first Congress of Colored Women of the United States met in Boston; it developed into the National Federation of Afro-American Women. In 1896, the National Federation and the National League of Colored Women merged to form the National Association of Colored Women in Washington, D.C. This group was a coalition of 200 clubs across the country. White, *Too Heavy a Load*, 27.

12. Several historians record that both black and white women rose out of the shadows of their men in the period 1880–1920. See Baker, "The Domestication of Politics"; Scott, *From Pedestal to Politics*; McGerr, "Political Style and Women's Power"; and Freedman, "Separatism as Strategy."

13. Gaines, *Uplifting the Race*, 129.

14. Scholarship on the post–Civil War period has noted the erection of gendered public and private spaces in black communities. Jacquelyn Jones has noted that the "vitality of the political process" provided a public forum for black men "distinct from the private sphere inhabited by their womenfolk." Subsequent literature has challenged this dichotomous interpretation; see *Labor of Love, Labor of Sorrow*, 66; and

The Black Public Sphere Collective, *The Black Public Sphere: A Public Culture Book*, 14. See also Brown, "Negotiating and Transforming the Public Sphere."

15. The field of queer studies is increasingly seen as important when considering issues of African-American manhood formation. Roderick Ferguson stresses the importance of considering multiple factors, including sexuality, when coming to terms with black male identity. To grasp the complexity of race and gender, one must account for "polymorphous gender and sexual formations that include a range of heterosexual and homosexual identities and practices." Toward that end, recent studies of black manhood suggest the various ways that black masculinity can and should be interrogated as a site where "new modes of gender and sexual freedom and expression" are fashioned. See Ferguson, "African American Masculinity and the Study of Social Formations," 214, 218.

16. See Hunter and Davis, "Constructing Gender"; Hunter and Davis, "Hidden Voices of Black Men"; Hine, *A Question of Manhood*; Shaw, "Black Club Women and the Creation of the National Association of Colored Women"; Brown, "Uncle Ned's Children"; Brown, "Womanist Consciousness"; Brown, "Negotiating and Transforming the Public Sphere"; and Brown and Kimball, "Mapping the Terrain of Black Richmond." For the political meaning of gender more generally, see Scott, *Gender and the Politics of History*.

17. Gutman, *The Black Family in Slavery and Freedom*, 369–386.

18. Deborah Gray White addresses this reinterpretation of female roles in slave literature in "Female Slaves: Sex Roles and Status in the Antebellum Plantation South," 249.

19. Gutman, *The Black Family in Slavery and Freedom*, 188–191; Fogel and Engerman, *Time on the Cross*, 141; and Blassingame, *The Slave Community*, 92. According to Deborah Gray White, these works have deemphasized women's place in the black family. See White, "Female Slaves: Sex Roles and Status in the Antebellum Plantation South," 388–401.

20. Friend and Glover, *Southern Manhood: Perspectives on Masculinity in the Old South*.

21. Summers, *Manliness and Its Discontents*, 8–14.

22. For the term "cultural fields," see Hutchinson, *The Harlem Renaissance in Black and White*, 4, 11.

23. Evelyn Brooks Higginbotham argues that black women in particular fashioned a "politics of respectability" in which they sought to conform to the posture of a "lady." By demonstrating to whites that they were just as virtuous, nurturing, and genteel as white women, that they too merited protection from insult and assault, black women hoped to erase negative stereotypes ascribed to their morality and the race as a whole. See Higginbotham, *Righteous Discontent*. I submit that black men were also invested in shows of respectability.

24. Bederman, *Manliness and Civilization*; Gaines, *Uplifting the Race*; Landry, *The New Black Middle Class*, 18–66.

25. Summers, *Manliness and Its Discontents*, 15.

26. Litwack, *Trouble in Mind*, 12, 36; White, *Rope and Faggot*; Dray, *At the Hands of Persons Unknown*. Dray estimates that between 1882 and 1944, approximately 3,417 Americans were lynched (or a little more than one per week), with the majority occurring in the Deep South and Mississippi Delta. For additional information on racial terrorism in the South, see Hall, *Revolt against Chivalry*; Raper, *The Tragedy of Lynching*; and Woodward, *Origins of the New South*.

27. See Haley, *Charles N. Hunter and Race Relations in North Carolina*, 125; and Gilmore, *Gender and Jim Crow*, 278n47.

28. Other southern states that passed laws to segregate streetcar transportation include Louisiana (1902), Mississippi (1904), Virginia (1906), and Texas and Oklahoma (1907). Cities such as Atlanta and Montgomery passed municipal ordinances in 1900. See Greenwood, *Bittersweet Legacy*; and Meier and Rudwick, "The Boycott Movement against Jim Crow Streetcars in the South."

29. For a detailed overview of Jim Crow's impact in the South, see Litwack, *Trouble in Mind*; White, *Too Heavy a Load*, 25–26; and Higginbotham, *Righteous Discontent*, 4.

30. Harris, *Two Sermons on the Race Problem Addressed to Young Colored Men*, 12.

31. Ibid., 32.

32. Henry and Speas, *The Heritage of Blacks in North Carolina*, 1:84, 456; Steelman, *North Carolina's Role in the Spanish-American War*; Mitchell, *Righteous Propagation*, 61–63; White, *Too Heavy a Load*, 114, 140.

33. Rolinson, *Grassroots Garveyism*, 18, 121–122, 135–141. For the politicization of rural southern black communities generally, see Hahn, *A Nation under Our Feet*. Mitchell has observed how blaming black women for miscegenation excused black men's subsequent actions to control and punish them. See Mitchell, *Righteous Propagation*, 224–239. See also White, *Too Heavy a Load*, 120–124.

34. Rolinson, *Grassroots Garveyism*, 18, 60–71.

35. Among those who left were Wilmington newspaperman Alexander Manly, whose incendiary editorials about white women's consensual trysts with black men (which he wrote to debunk the myth of the black rapist) precipitated that city's race riot. John C. Dancy and Congressman George White also left. In 1903, Dancy took a federal post in Washington, D.C., as recorder of deeds. Demographically, the region remained dominated by rural blacks, though migrations from farm to city and South to North affected the demographic strength of North Carolina's rural blacks. In 1900, North Carolina had eighteen counties with a black majority; by 1940, that number had dwindled to nine. In 1920, 80 percent of blacks lived in rural areas and

only 4.6 percent of blacks employed in nonagrarian occupations were of the professional class. See Crow, Escott, and Hatley, "Black Life in the Age of Jim Crow," 120.

36. Summers points out that black male gender identity was shaped through "quotidian practice: work, leisure, organizational life, interaction with families and communities, and so forth." In other words, Summers concedes that black male subjectivity is complex and occurs across a range of relationships. See Summers, *Manliness and Its Discontents*, 13.

37. "Remembering One Who Gave a Lifetime to His People," *Asheville Citizen*, 10 March 1987.

38. Ibid. The school was named after Walter S. Lee, supporter of classical and vocational education and self-help, and Edward Stephens, a West Indies native who became a prominent educator in Asheville and founder of the Young Men's Institute.

39. Frances L. Goodrich, "A Devoted Life and Its Results," Box P77.10.4, #1, Folder 1, Heritage of Black Highlanders Collection.

40. "Remembering One Who Gave a Lifetime to His People," *Asheville Citizen*, 10 March 1987; Goodrich, "A Devoted Life and Its Results," Box P77.10.4, #1, Folder 19, Heritage of Black Highlanders Collection.

41. "A History of Pride: Black Asheville a Blend of Traditions: School, Church, Community Involvement," *Asheville Citizen*, 13 February 1983.

42. One promising study documents the genesis of black social science in the early twentieth century as a counter to popular scientific thought on the character of black manhood. This small cadre of black intellectuals, the author claims, rose in response to "scientific foundations of white racial and gender supremacy." See Lindquist, "The Gender of Racial Science." While black social science was developing on a national level, African Americans also worked locally to counter disparaging images of their manhood. They believed that community-based gender reform was essential during the Jim Crow era.

43. The literature on the endangered black male is extensive. It includes Awkward, "Black Male Trouble"; Carbado, *Black Men on Race, Gender, and Sexuality*; Belton, *Speak My Name*; Gibbs, "Young Black Males in America"; Harper, *Are We Not Men?*; Watson, *Educating African American Males*; Majors and Billson, *Cool Pose*; Kunjufu, *Countering the Conspiracy to Destroy Black Boys*; and Raspberry, "Plight of the Young Black Man," *Washington Post*, 31 January 1986.

44. For the gendered implications of the Million Man March, see Smooth and Tucker, "Behind but Not Forgotten: Women and the Behind-the-Scenes Organizing of the Million Man March."

45. See Greenwood, *Bittersweet Legacy*; and Haley, *Charles N. Hunter and Race Relations in North Carolina*.

Chapter 1. What Can He Do?

1. *Proceedings of the Forty-Second Annual Session of the Baptist Educational and Missionary Convention of North Carolina, Held with the Jackson Chapel Church, Wilson, N.C., October 26–29, 1909* (Fayetteville, N.C.: Judge Printing Co., 1909), Reel 60 of *African-American Baptist Annual Reports, North Carolina, 1865–1990* (Rochester, N.Y.: American Baptist–Samuel Colgate Historical Library, 1997), hereafter *African-American Baptist Annual Reports.*

2. The rise of industrialization and urbanization in the early nineteenth century prompted the ideology of separate spheres, a gendered cultural construction by which the middle classes attempted to balance and order gender relations. Separate spheres ideology divided the world into two social realms, public and private. Women ruled the private sphere of the home and were expected to exemplify pure and pious behavior. Men occupied the competitive public sphere of business and commerce. In theory, this system promoted an interdependence between men and women; the home would be men's sanctuary against the vices and temptations of the public world. See Rotundo, *American Manhood.* This gender construction and its implications for men and women are further illuminated by Boydston, *Home & Work*; and Cott, *The Bonds of Womanhood.*

3. I am grateful for Gail Bederman's observations on how similar the gendered rhetoric of North Carolina black Baptist men was to that of their white Protestant counterparts. See Bederman, "'The Women Have Had Charge of the Church Work Long Enough.'" Other studies that have addressed the male "crisis" include Filene, *Him/Her/Self.* For the feminization of church work in general, see Welter, "The Feminization of American Religion." Modern civil rights histories also highlight the visible role black women played in religious institutions. See Payne, *I've Got the Light of Freedom.*

4. North Carolina Baptist male leaders were as drawn to the masculinized church dialogues as they were to other cultural imperatives of the day, which, among other things, called for high moral character and conduct, less individualistic material consumption, and separate spheres of activity for men and women. Proscriptive literature, such as Carl Case, *The Masculine in Religion* (Philadelphia, Pa.: American Baptist Publication Society, 1906), Henry Emerson Fosdick, *The Manhood of the Master* (Nashville, Tenn.: Abingdon Press, 1911) and Jason Pierce, *The Masculine Power of Christ* (Boston: The Pilgrim Press, 1912) abounded, as did publicity about the highly visible Men and Religion Forward Movement. Black Baptist men's frequent contact and dialogue with representatives of North Carolina's white Baptist association, part of a "cooperation" movement, likely enhanced exchange about the "men in church" rhetoric. Finally, the close scrutiny given race leader Booker T. Washington's words and actions (in this case, his appearance at a Men and Religion

Forward Movement convention in 1912) likely would not have escaped Baptists' notice.

The national Men and Religion Forward movement of Protestants supplies evidence from which to draw parallels with and distinctions between white and black male efforts to masculinize churches. The Protestant campaign, whose slogan was "More Men for Religion, More Religion for Men," is reputed to have been the largest and most widespread religious movement during the early twentieth century. The movement was sponsored by practically every national Protestant men's organization, including the International Sunday School Committee and the YMCA. Though aimed exclusively at white native middle-class Protestant men, the movement found adherents from white women such as reformer Jane Addams and black men such as national leader Booker T. Washington. See Bederman, "'The Women Have Had Charge of the Church Work Long Enough.'"

5. The question of woman's ordination began in 1902 for black Methodist churchwomen. See Frederickson, "Each One Is Dependent on the Other."

6. Toward the end of the 1920s, the Black Baptist State Convention had more than 225,000 members and claimed 1,300 churches and 1,400 ordained preachers. North Carolina Baptists frequently changed the name of their convention to meet religious objectives. These names included the Baptist Educational and Missionary Home Convention, Baptist State Convention of North Carolina, and Women's Home and Foreign Mission Convention. For consistency, I will use the names "Baptist Convention" and "Women's Baptist Convention" in the text.

7. Black Baptists made a point of chronicling their efforts to conduct their ministries independently of whites. The task proved daunting. As Baptist historian Whitted has chronicled, for thirty years the convention remained in a state of construction. See Whitted, *A History of the Negro Baptists of North Carolina*, 37. Whitted's history makes clear that before black Baptists began receiving appropriations from white southern Baptists, they realized the importance of establishing a "better and more united ministry." The creation of church boards by black Baptists laid the groundwork for future cooperation with white Baptists within the denomination. Moreover, when they needed large sums of money for church projects, North Carolina black Baptists raised most of the funds themselves. They thus sought "assistance without control." Whitted, *A History of the Negro Baptists of North Carolina*, 37. See also Higginbotham, *Righteous Discontent*, 251n63.

8. *Minutes of the Twenty-Fifth Annual Session of the Women's Baptist Home and Foreign Convention of N.C., held with the First Baptist Church, Washington, N.C., Oct. 5–8, 1909* (Raleigh, N.C.: Commercial Printing Co., 1910), Reel 62 of *African-American Baptist Annual Reports*.

9. The public sphere as a source of historical analysis has garnered much scholarly attention. Jurgen Habermas's theoretical work on the subject provided the frame-

work for studies examining the role of the public sphere in cultivating an educated citizenry and developing a middle class. Other scholars, however, have objected to Habermas's focus on the masculine and bourgeoisie in his conceptualization because it ignores competing publics, or other gendered groups and classes. See Habermas, *The Structural Transformation of the Public Sphere*; Ryan, *Civic Wars*; and Fraser, "Rethinking the Public Sphere."

10. Crow, Escott, and Hatley, "Black Life in the Age of Jim Crow," 95–98; *Minutes of the Thirty-Seventh Annual Session of the N.C. Baptist State Sunday School Convention, Held with the First African Baptist Church, Goldsboro, N.C., August 3–6, 1909* (N.p.: N.p., n.d.), Reel 61 of *African-American Baptist Annual Reports*.

11. *Proceedings of the Twenty-Eighth Annual Session of the Baptist State Sunday-School Convention of N.C., Held with the First Baptist Sunday-School, Raleigh, N.C., Sept. 18–21, 1900* (Raleigh, N.C.: Baptist Sentinel Book and Job Print, 1900), Reel 61 of *African-American Baptist Annual Reports*.

12. Ibid.

13. *Charlotte Messenger*, 6 January 1883; Annie Blackwell, "Woman as a Religious Factor in the Home," *AME Zion Quarterly Review* (October–January 1899–1900), 18.

14. Guy-Sheftall, *Daughters of Sorrow*, 38–40.

15. To many southern whites, the presence and participation of black women in public affairs was symbolic of the chaos emancipation and Reconstruction had wrought. The intermingling of both sexes in the public sphere struck them as particularly troublesome; they claimed that it promoted licentious and promiscuous behavior. See Clark, "Celebrating Freedom."

16. See Higginbotham, *Righteous Discontent*; and Brown, "Negotiating and Transforming the Public Sphere." African-American Emancipation Day ceremonies and parades, which were performed in public spaces, also reinforced these ideals. See Clark, "Celebrating Freedom."

17. "Snapshots of the General Conference from the Kodak of a Layman," *Star of Zion*, 18 October 1900.

18. "The Taint of the Bicycle," *Star of Zion*, 22 March 1900.

19. Gilkes, "The Politics of 'Silence,'" 84–85. The complex dynamics of black women, power, and church politics in the nineteenth century are also illuminated in Dodson, *Engendering Church*.

20. *Proceedings of the Eighteenth Annual Session of the Baptist State Convention of N.C., with the First Baptist Church, Goldsboro, October 22–27, 1884* (Raleigh, N.C.: Baptist Standard Print, 1884), Reel 60 of *African-American Baptist Annual Reports*.

21. Ibid. Joanna P. Moore, a white missionary who often worked among southern blacks, endorsed the black women's work plan. Addressing men at their 1898 convention, Moore said she planned to "uplift the homes. . . . I want to improve the home-

life of the people. Your churches will be like your homes, nothing more. The homes must be made the happiest and best place on earth." See *Proceedings of the Thirty-First Annual Session of the Baptist Educational and Missionary Convention of N.C., Held with the First Baptist Church, Rocky Mount, N.C., October 18–21, 1898* (Raleigh, N.C.: Capital Printing Co., Printers and Binders, 1898), Reel 60 of *African-American Baptist Annual Reports.*

22. *Proceedings of the Eighteenth Annual Session of the Baptist State Convention of N.C., with the First Baptist Church, Goldsboro, October 22–27, 1884* (Raleigh, N.C.: Baptist Standard Print, 1884), 25–26, Reel 60 of *African-American Baptist Annual Reports*; Whitted, *A History of the Negro Baptists of North Carolina*, 41.

23. The linkages between the concept of civilization and race, gender, and uplift ideology are still ripe for scholarly investigation. Informative works on the subject include Bederman, *Manliness and Civilization*; and Mitchell, "The Black Man's Burden." See also Moses, *Alexander Crummell*. The problematic aspects of the concept of civilization for black uplift have been explicated in Gaines, *Uplifting the Race*, which argues that in the aftermath of World War I and coincident with the New Negro movement, black intellectuals such as Hubert Harrison challenged the notion that western discourse about civilization was universalist or racially uplifting. Gaines notes that far from promoting racial liberation, ideologies of civilization sanctioned the slave trade and colonization. See also Gaines, "Black Americans' Racial Uplift Ideology as 'Civilizing Mission.'"

24. *Minutes of the Fifty-First Annual Session of the N.C. Baptist State Sunday-School Convention and Baptist Young People's Union, Held with the First Baptist Sunday School, Winston-Salem, N.C., August 5–7, 1924* (N.p.: N.p., n.d.), Reel 61 of *African-American Baptist Annual Reports.*

25. *Minutes of the Twenty-First Annual Session of the Women's Baptist Home Mission Convention of N.C., Held at Lumberton, N.C., Oct. 5–8, 1905* (Littleton, N.C.: True Reformer Print, 1906), Reel 61 of *African-American Baptist Annual Reports.*

26. *Proceedings of the Forty-Third Annual Session of the Women's Home and Foreign Mission Convention of N.C., Held with Mount Calvary Baptist Church, Goldsboro, N.C., July 13–15, 1927* (N.p.: N.p., n.d.), Reel 62 of *African-American Baptist Annual Reports.*

27. Ibid.

28. Ibid., 22.

29. Neverdon-Morton, "The Black Woman's Struggle for Equality in the South, 1895–1925," 44.

30. Mitchell, *Righteous Propagation*, 144.

31. Higginbotham, *Righteous Discontent*, 143–144; Mrs. Booker T. Washington, "The Tuskegee Woman's Club," *Southern Workman* (August 1920): 365–369.

32. *Minutes of the Fifty-Third Annual Session of the N.C. Baptist State Sunday*

School Convention and Baptist Young People's Union, Held with Central Baptist Sunday School, August 3–5, 1926, Wilmington, N.C (no publication info), Reel 61 of *African-American Baptist Annual Reports.*

33. Ibid.

34. Ibid.

35. *Minutes of the Twenty-First Annual Session of the Women's Baptist Home Mission Convention of N.C., Held at Lumberton, N.C., Oct. 5–8, 1905* (Littleton, N.C.: True Reformer Print, 1906), Reel 61 of *African-American Baptist Annual Reports.*

36. These included the Women's Baptist State Convention, the Baptist State Sunday School Convention, and the Baptist Young People's Union Convention.

37. Whitted, *A History of the Negro Baptists of North Carolina,* 44–45. Whitted was born on 10 March 1860, in Hillsboro, North Carolina. He was educated at Shaw University and Lincoln University. He served as principal of Shiloh Institute in Warrenton for ten years while pastoring Warrenton Baptist Church. In 1897, he served as corresponding secretary and general missionary for the state as part of joint work between the American Baptist Home Mission Society and the Southern Baptist Convention for Black Baptists. He held this position for ten years. See Caldwell, *History of the American Negro.*

38. *Proceedings of the Thirty-Fourth Annual Session of the Baptist Educational and Missionary Convention of N.C., Held with the Baptist Church, Lumberton, N.C., Nov. 12–15, 1901* (Raleigh, N.C.: Sentinel Publishing Co., 1902), Reel 60 of *African-American Baptist Annual Reports.*

39. *Proceedings of the Forty-Third Annual Session of the Baptist Educational and Missionary Convention of N.C., October 26, 1910* (N.p.: N.p., n.d..), Reel 60 of *African-American Baptist Annual Reports.*

40. Ibid.

41. *Proceedings of the Thirty-Sixth Annual Session of the Baptist Educational and Missionary Convention of N.C., Held with the White Rock Baptist Church, Durham, N.C., November 10–15, 1903* (Raleigh: The Baptist Sentinel Print, 1904); *Proceedings of the Forty-Fifth Annual Session of the Baptist State Convention of N.C., Held with the First Baptist Church, High Point, N.C., October 29–November 1, 1912* (Fayetteville, N.C.: Judge Printing Co., 1912), both Reel 60 of *African-American Baptist Annual Reports.*

42. Ibid.; Whitted, *A History of the Negro Baptists of North Carolina.*

43. *Minutes of the Twenty-Fifth Annual Session of the Women's Baptist Home & Foreign Mission Convention of N.C., Held with the First Baptist Church, Washington, N.C., Oct. 5–8, 1909* (Raleigh, N.C.: Commercial Printing Co., 1910), Reel 62 of *African-American Baptist Annual Reports.*

44. *Proceedings of the Thirty-Seventh Annual Session of the Baptist Educational and Missionary Convention of N.C.* (1904). Born in Selma, North Carolina in 1866,

"Sister" Bunn "did her college work" at Shaw University in Raleigh and began her missionary work in the state in 1886. She was a teacher for twenty-five years and converted many children to Christianity. Her contributions to the Women's Baptist Convention include serving as corresponding secretary and field missionary. Williams and Watkins, *Who's Who among North Carolina Baptists*.

45. Ibid.

46. Church historian Laurie Maffly-Kipp addresses the ways black Protestant leaders revised existing narratives of the race's past to forward evangelical and secular goals (such as race unity and equity) in "Mapping the World, Mapping the Race."

47. Higginbotham, *Righteous Discontent*, 122–123.

48. Felski, *Beyond Feminist Aesthetics*, 161–162. See also Bynum, *Gender and Religion*, 15–16; and Higginbotham, *Righteous Discontent*, 121.

49. Ruether, "Women's Leadership in the Jewish and Christian Traditions: Continuity and Change," 19.

50. Black Methodist women also assumed a posture of deference when courting the support of white Methodist men and women. At the same time, they made demands for fair treatment. They directed the same message to whites and their black brothers: "Give us a larger sphere; open the door of opportunity. . . . Give us an equal chance, that we may do more effectively the work that is justly ours." Frederickson, "Each One Is Dependent on the Other," 311–312. For other examples of black women's engagement in church politics, see Gilkes, "Something Within: Social Change and Collective Endurance in the Sacred World of Black Christian Women"; and Dodson, "Nineteenth Century A.M.E. Preaching Women."

51. *Minutes of the Twenty-First Annual Session of the Women's Baptist Home Mission Convention of N.C.* (1906).

52. *Proceedings of the Forty-First Annual Session of the Baptist Educational and Missionary Convention of N.C., Held with the First Baptist Church, Winston-Salem, N.C., October 20–23, 1908* (Fayetteville, N.C.: Judge Printing Co., 1908), Reel 60 of *African-American Baptist Annual Reports*.

53. Caldwell, *History of the American Negro*, 301.

54. Ibid., 299–305. Brown's memory is still alive in his adopted home of Winton, North Carolina. The C. S. Brown Regional Cultural Arts Center was built to preserve the multiethnic heritage of northeastern North Carolina and contribute to community life through the visual and performing arts. The center is housed in historic Brown Hall, part of the campus of Chowan Academy, which Brown founded in 1896.

55. Caldwell, *History of the American Negro*, 299–305.

56. *Proceedings of the Thirty-Sixth Annual Session of the Baptist Educational and Missionary Convention of N.C.* (1904), Reel 60 of *African-American Baptist Annual Reports*.

57. *Proceedings of the Forty-Fifth Session of the Baptist Educational and Missionary Convention of N.C., Held with the First Baptist Church, High Point, N.C., October 29–November 1, 1912* (Fayetteville, N.C.: Judge Printing Co., 1912), Reel 60 of *African-American Baptist Annual Reports*.

58. Whitted, *A History of the Negro Baptists of North Carolina*, 117–118.

59. *Proceedings of the Forty-First Annual Session of the Baptist Educational and Missionary Convention of N.C.* (1908).

60. The Holiness movement of the late nineteenth century arose in response to growing conservatism in American Protestantism. The adoption of a materialistic and bourgeois value system by church leaders had resulted in worship services that stressed controlled, dispassionate behavior. Holiness doctrine, as practiced in some areas, challenged this and other conservative tenets of mainstream denominations. See Ayers, *The Promise of the New South*; and Montgomery, *Under Their Own Vine and Fig Tree*.

61. *Proceedings of the Forty-First Annual Session of the Baptist Educational and Missionary Convention of N.C.* (1908).

62. Ibid.

63. *Proceedings of the Thirty-Second Annual Session of the Baptist Educational and Missionary Convention of N.C., Held with the St. John Baptist Church, New Bern, N.C., October 17–20, 1899* (Edwards and Broughton Presses, 1900), 32, Reel 60 of *African-American Baptist Annual Reports*.

64. Dr. Ezekial E. Smith, superintendent of Fayetteville State College, responded to Mial's remarks, but his comments were not included as part of the convention's official proceedings. See ibid. See also Brown, "Negotiating and Transforming the Public Sphere." For works that explicitly address black women's connections to racial violence, see Rosen, "The Gender of Reconstruction"; and Feimster, "'Ladies and Lynching.'" Feimster seeks to expand the rape/lynch discourse to include both black and white women, who she argues exerted personal and political power through their support for or opposition to southern lynchings.

65. *Proceedings of the Thirty-First Annual Session of the Baptist Educational and Missionary Convention of N.C.* (1898), Reel 60 of *African-American Baptist Annual Reports*.

66. *Proceedings of the Thirty-Sixth Annual Session of the Baptist Educational and Missionary Convention of N.C.* (1904), Reel 60 of *African-American Baptist Annual Reports*.

67. Ibid.

68. Bederman, "'The Women Have Had Charge of the Church Work Long Enough,'" 444.

69. Whitted, *A History of the Negro Baptists of North Carolina*, 113; *Proceedings of the Twenty-Eighth Annual Session of the Baptist State Sunday-School Convention of N.C.* (1900).

70. Whitted, *A History of the Negro Baptists of North Carolina*, 212.

71. Though North Carolina's Baptist Convention membership is not broken down by gender in convention proceedings, two-thirds of the members of the National Black Baptist Association were women. White Protestant churches were also comprised of two-thirds women. See Bederman, "'The Women Have Had Charge of the Church Work Long Enough.'"

72. *Proceedings of the Fifty-Seventh Annual Session of the Baptist State Convention of N.C., Held with the First Baptist Church, Wilson, N.C., October 31–November 2, 1922* (N.p.: N.p., n.d.), Reel 61 of *African-American Baptist Annual Reports*.

73. Ibid.

74. "Muscular Christianity" constituted a church movement aimed at making Christianity and Jesus more manly. Proponents of these concepts urged administrators of Sunday schools to build gymnasiums and hold class competitions and games to attract boys. See McMillen, *To Raise Up the South*.

75. Gilmore, *Gender and Jim Crow*, 32, 46–48.

76. Higginbotham, *Righteous Discontent*, 173–175.

77. See Mitchell, *Righteous Propagation*, 10–12.

78. Gibson and Crogman, *Progress of a Race, or the Remarkable Advancement of the American Negro*. For more about *Progress of a Race*, see Clark, *Defining Moments*, 163–164.

79. John Henry Adams, "The New Negro Man," *Voice of the Negro* 1 (October 1904): 450.

80. "Kind of Men Needed at the Present Time," *Star of Zion*, 24 December 1903.

81. Ibid.

82. *Proceedings of the Fourth Annual Session of the Union Baptist State Convention of N.C., Held at the Ahoskie Baptist Church, Ahoskie, N.C., December 3–4, 1918* (N.p.: N.p., n.d.), Reel 61 of *African-American Baptist Annual Reports*.

83. *Proceedings of the Fifty-Seventh Annual Session of the Baptist State Convention of N.C.* (1922).

84. *Proceedings of the Forty-Fourth Annual Session of the Baptist Educational and Missionary Home Convention of N. C., Held with the First Baptist Church of Fayetteville, N.C., October 24–27, 1911* (Fayetteville, N.C.: Judge Printing Co., 1911), Reel 60 of *African-American Baptist Annual Reports*.

85. Whitted, *A History of the Negro Baptists of North Carolina*, 129.

86. Neely, "Men and the Church."

87. Ibid.

88. *Proceedings of the Forty-Second Annual Session of the Baptist Educational and Missionary Convention of N.C.* (1909).

89. Ibid. Whitted penned in 1908 what is still regarded as an authoritative history

of the founding and missionary work of black Baptists in the state, *A History of the Negro Baptists of North Carolina.*

90. *Proceedings of the Thirty-Sixth Annual Session of the Baptist Educational and Missionary Convention of N.C.* (1904), 28; *Proceedings of the Thirty-Seventh Annual Session of the Baptist Educational and Missionary Convention of N.C., Held with the Baptist Church of Kinston, N.C., November 12–16, 1904* (Fayetteville, N.C.: North Carolina Baptist Publishing Co., 1905), 26, both on Reel 60 of *African-American Baptist Annual Reports.*

91. Whitted, *A History of the Negro Baptists of North Carolina,* 118.

92. *Proceedings of the Thirty-Seventh Annual Session of the Baptist Educational and Missionary Convention of N.C.* (1904).

93. *Proceedings of the Fifty-Eighth Annual Session of the Baptist State Convention of N.C., Held with the First Baptist Church, Raleigh, N.C., October 30–November 3, 1923* (N.p.: N.p., n.d.), Reel 61 of *African-American Baptist Annual Reports.*

94. *Proceedings of the Fifty-Seventh Annual Session of the Baptist State Convention of N.C.* (1922), Reel 61 of *African-American Baptist Annual Reports.*

95. Ibid.

96. Ibid. Baptist convention minutes do not disclose if the women's demands were met.

97. Ibid.

98. *Proceedings of the Fifty-Eighth Annual Session of the Baptist State Convention of N.C.* (1923).

99. Ibid.

100. As a result of the efforts of Baptist male leaders to unify male and female Christian workers, North Carolina Baptists adopted three different names for their convention between 1867 and 1930. These were "The Baptist State Convention of North Carolina," "The Baptist Educational and Missionary Convention," and the "Union Baptist State Convention." Reflecting on the name changes, corresponding secretary C. S. Brown conceded that "to our deep regret, we have learned that there is nothing in a name, that it takes the spirit to give life." See *Proceedings of the Fourth Annual Session of the Union Baptist State Convention of N.C.* (1918), 25.

101. Burrell is identified in black Baptist publications as the best-known woman in the state's Women's Home and Foreign Missionary Convention for her mission work. As corresponding secretary of the convention, she was lauded as the nucleus that sustained the organization. A graduate and trustee of Shaw University, Burrell taught many years in Raleigh's public schools. Williams and Watkins, *Who's Who among North Carolina Baptists.*

102. *Proceedings of the Fifty-Eighth Annual Baptist State Convention of N.C., Held with the First Baptist Church, Washington, N.C., October 28–29, 1924* (no pub. info); *Minutes of the State B.Y.P.U. Convention, Convened August 6, 1924, First Baptist*

Church, Weldon, N.C., November 2–5, 1926 (Raleigh: Bynum Printing Co., 1927), both on Reel 61 of *African-American Baptist Annual Reports.*

103. Ibid. In 1923, the all-male Presbyterian General Assembly decided to disband the women's church groups. Churchwomen privately groused about their lack of equal representation on the newly created mixed-sex boards. See Bederman, "'The Women Have Had Charge of the Church Work Long Enough,'" 457. Southern Methodist women were also not consulted when the General Conference moved to unify their Home Mission group with the men's group. See Hall, *Revolt against Chivalry*, 74.

104. *Proceedings of the State Baptist Convention in Its Sixty-Second Annual Session, Held with the First Baptist Church, Goldsboro, N.C., Oct. 30, 1928* (Wilmington, N.C.: R. S. Jervay's Print, 1929), Reel 61 of *African-American Baptist Annual Reports.*

105. Ibid.

106. *Proceedings of the Sixty-Fourth Annual Baptist State Convention of North Carolina, Held with the First Baptist Church, Rich Square, N.C., October 27–29, 1930* (no pub. info.), Reel 61 of *African-American Baptist Annual Reports.*

107. *Proceedings of the Forty-Third Session of the Women's Home and Foreign Mission Convention of N.C., Held with Mount Calvary Baptist Church, Goldsboro, N.C., July 13–15, 1927* (N.p.: N.p., n.d.), Reel 62 of *African-American Baptist Annual Reports.*

Chapter 2. Solving the Boy Problem

1. *Minutes of the Thirty-Seventh Annual Session of the N.C. Baptist State Sunday School Convention, Held with the First African Baptist Church, Goldsboro, N.C., Aug. 3–6, 1909* (N.p.: N.p., n.d.), Reel 61 of *African-American Baptist Annual Reports.*

2. Ibid.

3. Dancy, "How to Save Our Youth."

4. Ibid.

5. Floyd, *Floyd's Flowers.* Floyd graduated from Atlanta University in 1891, after which he served for five years as a public school principal in Augusta, Georgia. He was employed as a fieldworker for the International Sunday School Convention starting in 1896. After he published his book, he served as principal of a black school in Augusta. He also contributed to several publications, including *New York Independent, Sunday School Times,* and *The World's Work.* He edited *Voice of the Negro* and authored a biography. Floyd received honorary degrees in 1902 from Atlanta University and Morris Brown College.

6. Floyd, *Floyd's Flowers,* 9–10.

7. Ibid., 252–553, 46–48, 50.

8. Ibid., 51–53, 219–221.

9. Summers, *Manliness and Its Discontents*, 126–128; Rotundo, *American Manhood*, 255–262; Anderson, *The Education of Blacks in the South*, 148–150, 186–188.

10. Even Floyd concedes that gender differences among African-Americans could be blurred. He addressed gender-neutral topics such as "How to Be Handsome" and advised that boys and girls aged eleven through seventeen stay at home at night instead of roaming the streets. *Floyd's Flowers*, 26, 117–118.

11. *Minutes of the Twenty-Second Annual Session of the Women's Baptist Home Mission Convention of N.C., Held at St. James Church, Rocky Mount, N.C., Oct. 4–7, 1906* (Henderson, N.C.: Pryce T. Jones, Printer, 1907), Reel 61 of *African-American Baptist Annual Reports*.

12. Daniel Joseph Singal distinguishes between modernization and modernism as two distinct concepts. He defines modernization as a "process of social and economic development" commonly associated with evolutions in industry, technology, and urbanization. Modernism, in contrast, he defines as ideas, values, and beliefs that dominated American culture beginning in the twentieth century. Yet it is more accurate to say that modernism attempted to unify both Victorian and modernist impulses. Rather than submitting to a Victorian moral dichotomy that defined cultural values as either civilized or barbarous, modernists sought to "free the natural instincts and emotions that the nineteenth century had bottled up, and so restore vitality to modern life." See Singal, "Towards a Definition of American Modernism."

13. Hazel Carby discusses the fragility of black womanhood in a northern setting. See Carby, "Policing the Black Woman's Body in an Urban Context."

14. In fact, more whites left southern states than blacks. From 1890 to 1910, an estimated 1,243,000 whites migrated, compared to 537,000 blacks. See Ayers, *The Promise of the New South*; and Gregory, *Southern Diaspora*.

15. Rabinowitz, "A Comparative Perspective on Race Relations in Southern and Northern Cities"; *Southern Workman* (April 1902). For specific detail on the impact of industrialization in North Carolina, both positive and negative, see Escott, *Many Excellent People*.

16. See Greenwood, *Bittersweet Legacy*; and Watson, *Colored Charlotte*.

17. Mjagkij, "True Manhood," 145.

18. Ibid.

19. Higginbotham, *Righteous Discontent*, 200.

20. Kasson, *Amusing the Millions*. Southern whites and Progressive-era female reformers were also sensitive to the effects of urbanization and industrialization on youth culture and on race and gender norms. See, for example, Hall, "Private Eyes, Public Women"; Odem, *Delinquent Daughters*; Kunzel, *Fallen Women, Problem Girls*; and Alexander, *The "Girl Problem."*

21. Higginbotham, *Righteous Discontent*, 195.

22. In 1863, there were approximately 100 black Sunday schools in the South with less than 10,000 students. By 1913, there were an estimated 35,000 schools with more than 1,750,000 pupils. Monroe N. Work, "Fifty Years of Negro Progress," *Southern Workman* (January 1913): 9–15. Literature addressing Sunday schools and Southern Baptists' involvement therein include McMillen, *To Raise Up the South*; Harvey, *Redeeming the South*; Knoff, *The World Sunday School Movement*; Laqueur, *Religion and Respectability*; Bell, "Why Adults Attend Sunday School in Southern Baptist Churches"; and Moose, "Sunday School Work as Promoted by the Baptist State Convention of North Carolina."

23. *Minutes of the Thirty-Seventh Annual Session of the N.C. Baptist State Sunday School Convention* (1909).

24. "Gov. Aycock to Colored Sunday School Convention," *Morning Post* (Raleigh), 30 August 1903, in Charles N. Hunter Scrapbooks, Box 14, Folder 1, Charles N. Hunter Papers; *Minutes of the Thirty-Seventh Annual Session of the N.C. Baptist State Sunday School Convention* (1909); *Minutes of the Thirty-Eighth Annual Session of the N.C. Baptist State Sunday School Convention, Held with the First Baptist Sunday School, Raleigh, N.C., August 9–12, 1910* (1910), Reel 61 of *African-American Baptist Annual Reports*.

25. Whitted, "The Duty of the Church to the Young."

26. *Minutes of the Forty-Second Annual Session of the N.C. Baptist Sunday-School Convention and Baptist Young People's Union, Held with the White Rock Baptist Sunday-School, Durham, N.C., August 4–7, 1914* (High Point, N.C.: Petrie Printing Co., 1914), Reel 61 of *African-American Baptist Annual Reports*.

27. The Young People's Christian and Educational Congress, which was held in Atlanta, Georgia, on 6–11 August, focused on the spiritual, educational, moral, and sociological needs of the race. The country's "best" black men and women were in attendance, representing the fields of religion, education, business, and civic reform. Representatives from North Carolina included North Carolina College president James E. Shepard; J. A. Whitted; John C. Dancy; Rev. D. J. Sanders, president of Biddle University, Charlotte; and Baptist leader S. N. Vass. List of attendees from documents in Penn and Bowen, *The United Negro: His Problems and His Progress*. For additional discussion of how secularism impacted southern black communities, see Trotter, *Coal, Class, and Color*, esp. Chapter 7.

28. Ford, "Duty of the Church to the Young Man."

29. The Colored Men's Department of the YMCA made similar arguments in its push to raise the moral, educational, religious, and physical caliber of young black men. As W. A. Hunton, secretary for the YMCA College Department, noted, "Most boys stop attending Sunday-school before they are twelve years of age. The great majority of young men do not attend church service at all." See W. A. Hunton, "Colored Men's Department of the Young Men's Christian Association," *Voice of the Negro* 2

(June 1905): 388–396. The perception that leisure-time activities were dangerous for working-class black women and the efforts of church leaders to provide wholesome amusements are explicated by Hunter in *To 'Joy My Freedom*, 145–167.

30. J. N. Waring, "What to Do with Our Boys," *Southern Workman* (March 1906): 138–143.

31. Whitted, "The Duty of the Church to the Young."

32. Ford, "Duty of the Church to the Young Man."

33. John C. Dancy, "Address of Welcome to the Young People's Congress," *Star of Zion*, 23 August 1906.

34. McMillen, *To Raise Up the South*, 199.

35. Forbush, *The Boy Problem*; Rotundo, "Boy Culture." See "Gov. Aycock to Colored Sunday School Convention," *Morning Post* (Raleigh), 30 August 1903, Charles N. Hunter Scrapbooks, Box 14, Folder 1, Charles N. Hunter Papers.

36. "Gov. Aycock to Colored Sunday School Convention."

37. Charles H. Williams, "The Negro Church and Recreation," *Southern Workman* (December 1926) Other elements of the survey, which was conducted among eighty ministers in four states, revealed lingering disapproval of dancing, attending movies and the theater, playing pool, and bowling. Participants claimed that dancing was linked to sensuality (contributing to stereotypes about black men's and women's sexuality). Most of the respondents would not sanction dancing even if it was supervised, and they felt that playing pool encouraged gambling. Forty-seven of those surveyed said they offered young people social, athletic, and literary clubs and young people's leagues such as the BYPU as alternatives to urban amusements.

38. Other black religious denominations found themselves vexed by the youth problem. In 1903, North Carolina black church leaders from Baptist and Methodist bodies met at an interdenominational Sunday School Convention, where they discussed topics such as "How to Induce Children to Remain to Church Service," "The Religious Training of Our Children—How Best Secured," and "The Child's Place in the Church." "Sunday School Work: A Splendid Colored Convention Being Held Here," *News & Observer* (Raleigh), 29 August 1903, Charles N. Hunter Scrapbooks, Box 14, Folder 1, Charles N. Hunter Papers.

39. *Proceedings of the Forty-Sixth Annual Session of the Baptist Educational and Missionary Convention of N.C., Held with St. James Baptist Church, Rocky Mount, N.C., October 28–31, 1913* (Fayetteville, N.C.: Judge Printing Co., 1913), Reel 60 of *African-American Baptist Annual Reports*.

40. *Carolina Times*, 26 October 1929, quoted in Brinton, "The Negro in Durham."

41. *Minutes of the Fifty-Third Annual Session of the N.C. Baptist State Sunday School Convention and Baptist Young People's Union, Held with Central Baptist Sunday School, August 3–5, 1926, Wilmington, N.C* (N.p.: N.p., n.d.), Reel 61 of *African-American Baptist Annual Reports*.

42. "Our Young People Must Be Saved," in *Proceedings of the Forty-Forth Annual Session of the Baptist Educational and Missionary Convention of N.C., Held with the First Baptist Church of Fayetteville, N.C., October 24–27, 1911* (Fayetteville, N.C.: Judge Printing Co., 1911), Reel 61 of *African-American Baptist Annual Reports*.

43. "How to Save Our Youth," in Penn and Bowen, *The United Negro: His Problems and His Progress*, 475.

44. Macleod, *Building Character in the American Boy*, 10; "Colored Men's Department of the Young Men's Christian Association," *Voice of the Negro* 3 (June 1905); Mjagkij, *Light in the Darkness*; Mjagkij, "True Manhood," 138–152; Mjagkij, "Young Men's Christian Association, Colored Department."

45. Mjagkij, "True Manhood," 141, 146–149.

46. Ibid., 143–145.

47. W. H. Davenport, "The Tread of the YMCA in the South," *Living-Stone* 2, no. 3 (October 1890): 35–57, North Carolina Collection, Wilson Library, University of North Carolina-Chapel Hill. Some adherents of the colored YMCA program asserted the opposite, saying that it "does not offer, through its program of activities, to solve the Race problem, but it does offer a common ground where men and boys of all races may meet and work out together those principles of life that make for the development of the spirit, mind and body." See George R. Arthur, "The Young Men's Christian Association Movement among Negroes," *Opportunity* (March 1923): 16.

48. Davenport, "The Tread of the YMCA in the South." The YWCA movement among black women commenced after its male counterpart in North Carolina. In 1917, Charlottean clubwoman Mary Jackson McCrorey spearheaded efforts to form a YWCA chapter in Charlotte. McCrorey, who was married to Biddle University president Henry Lawrence McCrorey, founded the Phyllis Wheatley Branch of the "Y" in 1918. A Phyllis Wheatley club also operated in Asheville from 1913. Because these YWCAs were dependent bodies of the YMCA, McCrorey and other leaders often found themselves battling for autonomy. Although Charlotte's Phyllis Wheatley Branch was staffed by a black woman, it was managed by a committee of black and white women and fell under the supervision of the central YWCA's executive secretary. The Phyllis Wheatley Branch in Charlotte moved its headquarters at least three times, primarily due to inadequate space. By 1920 it had settled in part of the A.M.E. Zion Publication House. At that time 468 women were members. In general, black YWCAs instructed young women in leisure activities and the domestic arts. Black middle-class women also functioned as role models for respectable womanhood. See Gilmore, *Gender and Jim Crow*, 193–195; "Phyllis Wheatley YWCA Building Plans Approved," *Asheville Citizen*, 17 September 1959, in Asheville YWCA Archive, D. H. Ramsey Library Special Collections, University of North Carolina at Asheville, Asheville, N.C.; and Moseley-Edington, *Angels Unaware*, 19. See also "The Charlotte YWCA, 1902–1960" and "History of the Phyllis Wheatley Branch Y.W.C.A.," in Charlotte Young Women's Christian Association File, Robinson-

Spangler Carolina Room, Charlotte-Mecklenburg Public Library, Charlotte, North Carolina.

49. "Colored Men's Department of the Young Men's Christian Association," *Voice of the Negro* 3 (June 1905). Some YMCA leaders debated whether Christianity should constitute a prominent part of their activities. Secretary George F. Robinson of the Nashville branch asserted that he conducted the group on business rather than religious principles. But W. Edward Williams, secretary of the Baltimore YMCA, ultimately resigned after finding that it was not possible for him to do "the spiritual work for which I believe I am better fitted" in the YMCA structure. See Mjagkij, *Light in the Darkness*, 56.

50. Undated typescript; and "No Finer Program," n.d., both in Box 12, C. C. Spaulding Papers. An essayist writing in the *Southern Workman* also stressed that scouting was more than "a play program for boys." Rather, "it aims to prepare the boy to participate as a citizen." See "Boy Scout Program among Negro and Other Racial Groups," *Southern Workman* (November 1928): 438–439.

51. The seven-member committee included W. F. Witherspoon; North Carolina Mutual Insurance Company president W. J. Kennedy Jr.; and business, civic, and educational leader W. G. Pearson. See "Avery Boys Club" and W. F. Witherspoon to Dr. J. M. Manning, 20 October 1927, both in "Correspondence," Series 4, Folder 278, William J. Kennedy Jr. Papers.

52. W. F. Witherspoon to Dr. J. M. Manning, 15 October 1927, in "Correspondence," Series 4, Folder 278; C. A. Witherspoon to the Local Committee on Colored Older Boys' Conference, Durham, N.C., 10 November 1927, Series 4, Folder 278; and "C. A. Witherspoon to W. J. Kennedy," 12 January 1928," "Correspondence," Series 4, Folder 278, all in William J. Kennedy Jr. Papers. Apparently, the older boys' conference had some difficulty, as Durham's local committee was charged with financial wrongdoing. In correspondence addressed to the local committee, the YMCA's associate state secretary, C. A. Witherspoon, accused the local committee of reneging on an agreement in which food and lodging would be provided free to all registered delegates and leaders. Financial statements, however, indicated that meals and housing charges in the amount of $70 were paid out of program fees, "contrary to our understanding and arrangement." A check in the said amount was then requested of the local committee on 10 November. Subsequent correspondence indicated that Durham's local committee was working to send the money to the YMCA state office by year's end. Yet records indicate that, as of 12 January 1928, the money had not been received. Witherspoon responded dejectedly, "I am extremely sorry for more reasons than one."

53. "Youth's Craving" Conference, Series 4, Folder 278, in William J. Kennedy Jr. Papers.

54. *Address Delivered by Honorable R. B. McRary, A.M. at the New Auditorium,*

Raleigh, N.C., October 26, 1911 (Raleigh: Commercial Printing Co., [1911?]), North Carolina Collection microfilm, Reel 2, Item 18.

55. *Minutes of the Thirty-Fifth Annual Session of the N.C. Baptist State Sunday School Convention, with Providence Baptist Sunday School, Greensboro, N.C., August 6–10, 1907* (N.p.: N.p., n.d.), Reel 61 of *African-American Baptist Annual Reports; Minutes of the Thirty-Ninth Annual Session of the N.C. Baptist State Sunday School Convention* (1911).

56. *Minutes of the Thirty-Fifth Annual Session of the N.C. Baptist State Sunday School Convention* (1907); *Minutes of the Thirty-Ninth Annual Session of the N.C. Baptist State Sunday School Convention* (1911).

57. *Minutes of the Thirty-Fourth Annual Session of the N.C. Baptist State Sunday School Convention and the Seventh Annual Session of the Baptist Young People's Union, Held with the First Baptist Sunday School, Franklinton, N.C., September 19–23, 1906* (N.p.: N.p., n.d..), Reel 61 of *African-American Baptist Annual Reports*.

58. *Minutes of the Fifty-Third Annual Session of the N.C. Baptist State Sunday School Convention and Baptist Young People's Union* (1926).

59. *Minutes of the Thirty-Eighth Annual Session of the N.C. Baptist State Sunday School Convention* (1910).

60. Interview with Henry M. Houston, 29 August 1939. Houston and his son, Armistead M. Houston, operated the *Charlotte Post* newspaper out of their home in Charlotte. Houston's other activities in Charlotte included organizing the Negro Citizen League, which sought to encourage black voting. He also helped sponsor a seven-day recreation program for youth. Houston served as mayor and state deputy of the Elks Lodge. He was a member of the A.M.E. Zion church. See also James W. Eichelberger Jr., "The Sunday School Problem vs. the Secular School and Boy Problems," *Star of Zion*, 23 August 1906.

61. *Minutes of the Forty-Seventh Annual Session of the N.C. Baptist State Sunday School Convention, Held with the First Baptist Sunday School, High Point, N.C., August 3–5, 1920* (N.p.: N.p., n.d.), Reel 61 of *African-American Baptist Annual Reports*.

62. *Minutes of the Thirty-Fifth Annual Session of the N.C. Baptist State Sunday School Convention* (1907). Women such as Charlotte Hawkins Brown, head of the North Carolina Federation of Colored Women's Clubs, also stressed the importance of cultural training. The National Association of Colored Women sponsored hundreds of cultural clubs across the country that offered lessons in art, music, and literature. See White, *Too Heavy a Load*, 74–75.

63. Mrs. C. C. Pettey, "A Side Talk. With Our Girls—A Few Never for Their Consideration," *Star of Zion*, 31 July 1902.

64. *Minutes of the Thirty-Fifth Annual Session of the N.C. Baptist State Sunday School Convention* (1907); *Minutes of the Forty-Seventh Annual Session of the N.C. Baptist State Sunday School Convention* (1920).

65. Jerma Jackson's study of the sanctified movement reveals an alternate response. Gospel music singers sought to counteract secularization by emphasizing spiritual themes in their music. Jackson, *Singing in My Soul*.

66. Brinton, "The Negro in Durham," 323–324; J. H. N. Waring, "What to Do with Our Boys," *Southern Workman* (March 1906).

67. Black churches sometimes meted out punishments for offenses. Theologian and former Morehouse president Benjamin E. Mays recounted an incident in South Carolina in which a young unmarried couple parented a child out of wedlock. Their church minister demanded that the two marry and that the husband be a dutiful husband and father. If this wasn't done, the minister warned, "something unspeakably bad would happen to him." Higginbotham, *Righteous Discontent*, 201.

68. "Theological Quarters to Be More Attractive," *Shaw University Journal*, March 1928, in M. T. Pope Papers, in possession of Kenneth Zogry.

69. *Minutes of the Thirty-Eighth Annual Session of the N.C. Baptist State Sunday School Convention* (1910).

70. *Minutes of the Fifty-Seventh Annual Session of the N.C. Baptist State Sunday School Convention and Baptist Young People's Union, Held with Sycamore Hill Baptist Sunday School, Greenville, N.C., August 5–7, 1930* (N.p.: N.p., n.d.), Reel 61 of African-American Baptist Annual Reports.

71. *Minutes of the Fifty-Third Annual Session of the N.C. Baptist State Sunday School Convention and Baptist Young People's Union* (1926).

72. *Minutes of the Thirty-Ninth Annual Session of the N.C. Baptist State Sunday School Convention* (1911).

73. Lawrence Levine has also noted the power of black church music in promoting race consciousness and a sense of community; see Levine, *Black Culture and Black Consciousness*. However, there was disagreement about whether black spirituals and folk songs were dignified. For the multivalent meanings of African-American spiritual music in a southern context, see Campbell, *Music and the Making of a New South*.

74. Charles H. Williams, "The Negro Church and Recreation," *Southern Workman* (February 1926): 59–69; *Minutes of the Fifty-Seventh Annual Session of the N.C. Baptist State Sunday School Convention and Baptist Young People's Union* (1930).

75. Non-church bodies were also cautious about the types of amusements they offered. William Johnson Trent, former head of Asheville's YMI and of Livingstone College, was lauded by the black press for his innovative stewardship over Atlanta's YMCA building. The seven-story structure featured 100 dormitories, club rooms, and a gymnasium with swimming pool. But Trent refused to install a pool room in the facility. "Secretary Trent drew the line here and discarded the game as despiriting [*sic*] to the Christian features." "Mr. Trent and Atlanta's Y.M.C.A.," *Star of Zion*, 1 January 1920.

76. "The Negro Church," *Southern Workman* (September 1900): 501.

77. *Minutes of the Fifty-Third Annual Session of the N.C. Baptist State Sunday School Convention and Baptist Young People's Union* (1926), 23. Several religious leaders felt that women were responsible for training children at home. "The greatest need of the Negro today is the moral and spiritual training in the home," said A. M. Moore. "These mothers must be trained and the Sunday School Convention must through organized effort do what the individual cannot do." Nicholas Roberts praised black women as "having much to do with shaping the home life" and said that women "make the best teachers." Dr. N. F. Hargraves agreed that women "are especially adapted to teach little people." C. C. Spaulding said "I believe the real evangelism of Christ is preached by the life of a consecrated home-maker—the mother." The combination of better home training and consecrated Sunday school teachers was crucial to solving the boy problem, in the view of these men. As part of efforts to develop black women teachers with the proper morals, the Baptist State Sunday School Convention established a fund to help educate "deserving" girls as teachers. Supporters of the fund aspired to raise $500 each year. Ibid., 45–46.

78. *Proceedings of the Twentieth Annual Session of the N.C. Teacher's Association, Held at Kittrell College, Kittrell, N.C., June 12–17, 1901* (Elizabeth City, N.C.: E. F. Snakenberg, Printer, 1901). The North Carolina Teachers' Association proceedings are contained in the published microfilm *African-American Baptist Annual Reports, North Carolina, 1865–1990* (Rochester, N.Y.: American Baptist–Samuel Colgate Historical Library, 1997).

79. *Minutes of the Fifty-Third Annual Session of the N.C. Baptist State Sunday School Convention and Baptist Young People's Union* (1926).

80. Interview with Henry M. Houston, 29 August 1939. In his study of black communities in Philadelphia and New York, W. E. B. Du Bois observed that the need for black women to work outside the home left "children without guidance or restraint for the better part of the day—a thing disastrous to manners and morals." See Du Bois, *The Philadelphia Negro*, 194.

81. After emancipation, free persons of color debated the meaning of family and the degree of authority men and women had in African-American households. The racial and gendered politics of the southern household are explicated in such works as Edwards, *Gendered Strife and Confusion*; Bercaw, *Gendered Freedoms*; and Fox-Genovese, *Within the Plantation Household*.

82. Higginbotham, *Righteous Discontent*, 210–211.

83. "The Influence of a Home," *Minutes of the Thirty-Eighth Annual Session of the N.C. Baptist State Sunday School Convention* (1910).

84. Penn, "How Can Mothers Teach Their Daughters and Sons Social Purity?"

85. *Minutes of the Forty-Second Annual Session of the N.C. Baptist Sunday-School Convention and Baptist Young People's Union* (1914).

86. *Minutes of the Fifty-First Annual Session of the N.C. Baptist State Sunday-School Convention and Baptist Young People's Union, Held with the First Baptist Sun-*

day School, Winston-Salem, N.C., Aug. 5–7, 1924 (N.p.: N.p., n.d.), Reel 61 of *African-American Baptist Annual Reports.*

87. *Minutes of the Forty-Seventh Annual Session of the N.C. Baptist State Sunday School Convention* (1920).

88. *Minutes of the Fifty-First Annual Session of the N.C. Baptist State Sunday-School Convention and Baptist Young People's Union* (1924).

89. *Minutes of the Thirty-Ninth Annual Session of the N.C. Baptist State Sunday School Convention* (1911).

90. Ibid.; *Minutes of the Fifty-First Annual Session of the N.C. Baptist State Sunday-School Convention and Baptist Young People's Union* (1924).

91. *Minutes of the Fifty-First Annual Session of the N.C. Baptist State Sunday-School Convention and Baptist Young People's Union* (1924).

92. *Minutes of the Thirty-Fifth Annual Session of the N.C. Baptist State Sunday School Convention* (1907). Observing the failure of Sunday school teachers to make religion attractive and vital to boys ages fourteen to eighteen, who naturally craved "adventure and rousing action," author Franklin Winslow Johnson, in his *The Problems of Boyhood,* stressed the need for boys to exhibit Christian conduct in school, at home, and in the marketplace as well as at church. See W. A. A., "Book Review," *Southern Workman* (April 1915): 246–247.

93. *Minutes of the Fortieth Session of the N.C. Baptist State Sunday School Convention and Baptist Young People's Union, Held with the Sandy Grove Baptist Sunday School, Lumberton, N.C., August 6–9, 1912* (Goldsboro, N.C.: Nash Bros. Printers and Binders, 1913), Reel 61 of *African-American Baptist Annual Reports.*

94. "The Origin and Growth of Mary Potter Memorial School," Reel 1, Item 4, George Clayton Shaw Papers.

95. "1888–1932: A Glance Backward—A Present Meditation—A Forward Look," Reel 1, Item 1, George Clayton Shaw Papers.

96. "Things You Will Want to Know About," undated leaflet, Reel 1, Item 5, George Clayton Shaw Papers.

97. "Mary Potter Memorial School," undated leaflet, Reel 1, Item 5, George Clayton Shaw Papers.

98. Ibid.

99. "1888–1932: A Glance Backward—A Present Meditation—A Forward Look." George Clayton Shaw was born in Louisburg, North Carolina, on 19 June 1863. He received a B.A. degree from Lincoln University in 1886. Two years later, he received his doctor of divinity degree from Auburn Theological Seminary in New York. In 1890, he married Mary Elizabeth Lewis of Penn Valley, Pennsylvania. Shortly after leaving Auburn, Shaw settled in Oxford, North Carolina, where he founded both the Mary Potter School and the Timothy Darling Church. Shaw was active in civic

affairs. He served on the board of trustees of Johnson C. Smith University, chaired the board of trustees of Oxford Colored Orphanages, was treasurer of the State Teacher's Colored Association, and was a member of the black Masonic lodge. He was reputedly respected by both blacks and whites for his skill in developing "stalwart and efficient leaders" and for his own leadership ability. Shaw died of pneumonia on 1 January 1936. See "1888–1932: A Glance Backward—A Present Meditation—A Forward Look"; "Dr. G. C. Shaw, Head Mary Potter School, Dies Wednesday," Reel 1, item 8; "The Origin and Growth of Mary Potter Memorial School," Reel 1, item 4; and Mary E. L. Shaw, handwritten manuscript (Shaw memoirs), Reel 1, item 2, all in the George Clayton Shaw Papers. See also Caldwell *History of the American Negro*.

100. Shaw, *What a Woman Ought to Be and to Do*, 7.

101. Mary E. L. Shaw, handwritten manuscript, 9.

102. Ibid.

103. The $50,000 Pittsburg Hall was funded by the Presbytery of Pittsburgh. In its promotional materials, the hall is described as "an imposing three-story structure and modern in every sense of the word." "Things You Will Want to Know About," undated leaflet, Reel 1, Item 5, George Clayton Shaw Papers. "1888–1932: A Glance Backward—A Present Meditation—A Forward Look," 12.

104. Mary E. L. Shaw, handwritten manuscript, 10.

105. "Origin and Growth of Mary Potter Memorial School."

106. Ibid.

107. Ibid.

108. Ibid.

109. Charlotte Hawkins Brown was born in 1883 in Henderson, North Carolina, the daughter of Francis Hawkins and Edmund H. Hight. The family moved to Cambridge, Massachusetts, in the 1880s, where Brown began attending public schools. As a senior, Brown received financial support from Alice Freeman Palmer, former president of Wellesley, to attend State Normal School at Salem, Massachusetts. In 1901, Brown accepted a teaching job in rural Sedalia, North Carolina. With the help of white donors, she turned the one-room facility into an accredited school and junior college, naming it the Palmer Memorial Institute in honor of Alice Palmer. In 1911, Brown married Edward S. Brown, a teacher, but the partnership ended a few months later. Brown was nationally recognized as an educator and was active in the National Council of Negro Women, North Carolina Teacher's Association, and other groups. She was the first black woman to serve on the national board of the Young Women's Christian Association and lectured and wrote widely on black women, education, and race relations. Brown's shepherding of Palmer ended in 1952. She died in 1961 and was buried on the Palmer campus, now a state historic site. Gilmore, *Gender and Jim Crow*, 179–183; Marsha Vick, "Charlotte Hawkins Brown,"

in Smith, *Notable Black American Women*, 109–114; and Colonel Hawkins Jr., "Charlotte Eugenia Hawkins Brown Family," in *The Heritage of Blacks in North Carolina*, 1:168–170.

110. Hunter, "The Correct Thing," 40.

111. "Younger Boys' Circle," Reel 4, Frame 120; and "Small Girls' Circle," Reel 4, Frame 114, both in *Charlotte Hawkins Brown Papers*.

112. S. H. Archer, "Football in Our Colleges," *Voice of the Negro* 3 (March 1906).

113. Brown, *The Correct Thing, to Do, to Say, to Wear*, 97.

114. Ibid., 97–99, 109–111.

115. Mitchell, *Righteous Propagation*, 83–84; Thomas, *The American Negro*.

116. Brown, *The Correct Thing, to Do, to Say, to Wear*, 106–109.

117. *Asheville Citizen*, 12 and 15 March 1904.

118. All Souls Church was commissioned by Vanderbilt in 1896 to "serve as a real spiritual influence in the community." Dr. Swopes came from Wheeling, West Virginia, to serve as rector. In 1898, the church had 100 members and 66 families on its rolls. The church also sponsored a kindergarten for black children at the YMI. See Boyer, *Early Days*.

119. Interview with Mr. and Mrs. (Magnolia Thompson) Ernest McKissick, 2 August 1977.

120. Davis, *The Black Heritage of Western North Carolina*. Davis's account of the YMI is the only comprehensive scholarly account of the organization and its members. See also "YMI Cultural Center, Inc.," YMI Clipping File, Box M77.10.3, Folder 8, Heritage of Black Highlanders Collection.

121. "Vanderbilt, YMI Link Powerful: Exhibit Explores Tie, Illustrates History of Local Cultural Center," *Asheville Citizen*, 17 February 2002. The YMI was placed on the National Register of Historic Places in 1977.

122. Nina Mjagkij notes that women such as Madame C. J. Walker typically made large financial contributions to the black YMCA. Other women served as volunteers or raised money for the YMCA through their auxiliaries. See Mjagkij, *Light in the Darkness*; see also introduction to Hine, *A Question of Manhood*.

123. "Colored Y.M.C.A.: The First Meeting Well Attended and Very Promising," *Asheville Citizen*, 1 September 1890; and "Colored YMCA Meeting," *Asheville Citizen*, 30 August 1890, both in Pack Vertical File, vol. 1. "Colored Y.M.C.A." specified that the intent of the meeting was to "organize a Y.M.C.A. for colored men and women."

124. After becoming entranced with Asheville and its mountains, George Washington Vanderbilt employed hundreds of black artisans and laborers to build his Biltmore estate in the French Broad River valley. "Biltmore" was named for Bilt, the Holland town from which the Vanderbilt family originated, and "more" for an old English word meaning rolling upland country. The construction of the 125,000-acre estate, which was fashioned after a sixteenth-century French chateaux, began in 1892

and ended five years later. Richard Sharp Smith, supervising architect of the Bilt-more House, later built the YMI. See Boyer, *Early Days*, 5; and Davis, *The Black Heritage of Western North Carolina*, 66.

125. Stephens was born in an English colony in South America. When he was two, his family moved to Europe, where he attended schools in England, Paris, and Switzerland. He took postgraduate courses in Germany. He was fluent in French, German, Portuguese, Spanish, Dutch, and Italian. Stephens, who spent a year in Africa as a missionary, labored for the "upbuilding of black life in Asheville and Bun-combe County"; see "Edward Stephens," Box M77.10.4, Folder 6, Heritage of Black Highlanders Collection; and "A Well-Informed Negro: Brief History of the New Principal of the Colored Schools," *Asheville Citizen*, 30 August 1890, Pack Vertical File, vol. 1. See also Davis, *The Black Heritage of Western North Carolina*, 66; and Harris, *Short History and Report of Young Men's Institute, Inc*. Though the YMI was sometimes referred to by black and whites as Asheville's YMCA, for consistency it will be called YMI throughout the chapter.

126. "Vanderbilt, YMI Link Powerful," *Asheville Citizen*, 17 February 2002.

127. Catholic Hill School was destroyed by a tragic fire in 1917 that killed seven students. Dickson also served on Asheville's inaugural school board in 1888. Ste-phens-Lee High School replaced Catholic High; it was named for Edward Stephens and Hester Lee, the deceased wife of Walter Smith Lee, Catholic High's former principal. See "A History of Pride: Black Asheville a Blend of Traditions: School, Church, Community Involvement," *Asheville Citizen*, 13 February 1983.

Dickson, born in June 1839 in Shelby, North Carolina, moved to Asheville in 1870. Dickson's numerous community-building activities in Asheville included as-sisting in the founding of St. Mathias Episcopal Church, for which he served as treasurer for thirty-five years. St. Mathias was the first black Episcopal church estab-lished in the state. Dickson also founded the Venice Lodge, the first Masonic lodge in Asheville. His influence secured the purchase of a building on Market Street that housed additional black Masonic lodges. Dickson served as treasurer to Venice Lodge for twenty-five years. He was member of the YMI and contributed his ser-vices to A&M College in Greensboro. See "The Late Isaac Dickson," Box M77.10.10, Folder 4; "A 'First' in Asheville," Box M77.10.4, Folder 9; and "Asheville's First School Election," Box M77.10.4, Folder 9, all in Heritage of Black Highlanders Collection.

128. No women are recorded as attending the meeting. See "Colored Y.M.C.A.: The First Meeting Well Attended and Very Promising."

129. Succeeding Stephens were Professor John Love, a native of Asheville and a graduate of Oberlin College; C. H. Baker of Washington, D.C.; and T. Edward Owens, a graduate of Brown University, where he was a classmate of John D. Rock-efeller Jr. See [W. J. Trent], "The Young Men's Institute," Box M77.10.3, Folder 8; and "Young Men's Institute: A Well Attended Meeting Held There Yesterday," *Asheville Citizen*, 13 February 1896, both in Pack Vertical File, vol. 1.

130. "Three Years in the Institute: Anniversary Reunion of the Y.M.I.," 1896, Pack Vertical File, vol. 1.

131. Interview with Mr. and Mrs. (Magnolia Thompson) Ernest McKissick, 2 August 1977.

132. Davis, *The Black Heritage of Western North Carolina*, 67.

133. "Three Years in the Institute: Anniversary Reunion of the Y.M.I." In 1896, Baker began directing a 26-voice choir and a twelve-piece orchestra. The YMI Orchestra performed at several civic and religious events, including the first church services of St. Matthias Episcopal Church in 1896. See Davis, *The Black Heritage of Western North Carolina*.

134. While Vanderbilt's benevolence to the black community concerning the YMI is noteworthy, such a gesture can also be viewed as self-serving. White philanthropists sometimes predicated support for black uplift initiatives on the expectation that such efforts would promote race segregation. See Macleod, *Building Character in the American Boy*, 214; and [W. J. Trent], "The Young Men's Institute."

135. According to published accounts, Vanderbilt agreed to a $22,000 "discount" price for the black community to "encourage the colored people of the city in their efforts to provide an institution which would be to the negroes what the Y. M. C. A. is to the white people." See Boyer, *Early Days*, 20.

136. Several prominent black men called Hopkins home, including J. W. Walker, W. J. Trent, Congress of Racial Equality director Floyd B. McKissick (son of Ernest McKissick), and Albert Manley, former president of Spelman College in Atlanta. See "The Hopkins Chapel African Methodist Episcopal Church Centennial Journal, 1968," Box M77.10.1, Folder 4, Heritage of Black Highlanders Collection.

137. Interview with Mr. and Mrs. (Magnolia Thompson) Ernest McKissick, 2 August 1977.

138. Black women's youth associations such as the Phyllis Wheatley Center in Greenville, North Carolina, also created gendered physical spaces. That building's second floor (the center's main entrance) hosted primarily women, girls, and the library. Its lower floor was reserved for men and boys. Thomas F. Parker, "The Phyllis Wheatley Center in Greenville, North Carolina," *Southern Workman* (November 1925): 497–504.

139. See Davis, *The Black Heritage of Western North Carolina*, 30–31; and "Dr. L. O. Miller, M. D.," *The Church Advocate*, 24 February 1945, Box M77.10.3.12.19.1, Heritage of Black Highlanders Collection; and "Dr. L. O. Miller Dies: Prominent Negro Doctor," *Asheville Citizen*, 1 October 1960, Pack Vertical File, vol. 1.

140. "Black Highlander's Role . . . Highland Center to Preserve Contributions by Asheville Blacks," *Asheville Citizen*, 10 July 1977; "Black-Owned Businesses Have Long History Here," *Asheville Citizen*, 22 August 1977, both in Heritage of Black Highlanders Collection; Wolfe, *Look Homeward Angel*, 171.

141. See "The Life Story of a Successful Black Man, Benjamin James Jackson, Sr.," Box P77.10.4, Folder 5, Heritage of Black Highlanders Collection.

142. In addition to housing male members, the YMI also housed African Americans traveling through the area who would not be admitted into Asheville's hotels due to segregation. This implies that perhaps black women took advantage of the YMI. The Asheville City directory, however, includes only male YMI members as residents of the building. See "Vanderbilt, YMI Link Powerful," *Asheville Citizen*, 17 February 2002; and *Asheville City Directory*.

143. Critics of Washington believed the speech legitimized race segregation in the South. See Gilmore, *Gender and Jim Crow*, 25–26; and Rydell, Findling, and Pelle, *Fair America: World's Fairs in the United States*, 29–30.

144. Fonvielle, "Reminiscences of College Days," North Carolina Collection Microfilm, Reel 112, Item 6.

145. Ibid.; "Dr. William J. Trent," *Salisbury Sunday Post*, 16 June 1963, Box M77.10.3, Folder 12, Heritage of Black Highlanders Collection. See also "Livingstone College Ex-President Dies," *News and Observer* (Raleigh), 13 June 1963, North Carolina Collection Biographical Clipping File through 1975, vol. 147, 734.

146. The Central Intercollegiate Athletic Association (CIAA) was organized in 1912 with black universities Hampton, Howard, Shaw, Lincoln, and Virginia Union as charter members. Parker and Callison, *The Biddle-Johnson C. Smith University Story*, 59–60.

147. W. J. Trent, "Young Men's Institute: A History," 2, in Heritage of Black Highlanders Collection.

148. Interview with Mr. and Mrs. (Magnolia Thompson) Ernest McKissick, 2 August 1977.

149. Ibid.

150. Ibid.

151. Ibid.; "Black Highlanders in World War I, Jean M. McNeill," Box M77.10.3, Folder 2, Heritage of Black Highlanders Collection.

152. "YMI Ball Players Beat Spartanburgers," *Asheville Citizen*, 25 July 1918.

153. "YMI Notes" *Asheville Citizen*, 25 July 1912.

154. "Local Dots," *Asheville Citizen*, 24 December 1903.

155. "An Urgent Call," *Asheville Citizen*, 8 January 1904.

156. Ibid.

157. "Great Union Services YMI," *Asheville Citizen*, 24 December 1903; "Glass and China Fair," *Asheville Citizen*, 30 December 1903; *Asheville Citizen*, "An Urgent Call," 8 January 1904; "Local Dots," *Asheville Citizen*, 14 January 1904; "Local Dots," *Asheville Citizen*, 10 March 1904; "Local Dots," *Asheville Citizen*, 16 March 1904; *Asheville Citizen*, "Local Dots," 7 July 1907; "YMI Rally Was a Notable Success," *Asheville Citizen*, 17 July 1914; "YMI Notes," *Asheville Citizen*, 25 July 1912.

158. "Local Dots," *Asheville Citizen*, 7 January 1904; "Local Dots," *Asheville Citizen*, 9 January 1904; "Local Dots," *Asheville Citizen*, 10 March 1904; "YMI Notes," *Asheville Citizen*, 25 August 1912.

159. Street culture, according to historian Evelyn Brooks Higginbotham, "became the metaphor for all that was unwholesome and dangerous—for the 'demoralizing habit of hanging out, for 'perpetual promenading,' and for 'gamblers and criminals.'" *Righteous Discontent*, 199.

160. See Higginbotham, "Beyond the Sound of Silence," 58–59; and Janiewski, "Seeking 'a New Day and a New Way,'" 167.

161. See Davis, *The Black Heritage of Western North Carolina*. At the organizational meeting, C. B. Dusenbury was selected chairperson and N. M. Martin was chosen as secretary. The committee members appointed to draft the organization's bylaws included Dr. Ruben Bryant and W. S. Lee. Also in attendance were the YMI's J. W. Walker, H. E. Jones, Thomas Kay Palmer, J. W. Nipson Jr. and B. J. Jackson.

162. Ibid.; *Asheville Citizen*, 10 July 1913; "Dr. L. O. Miller, M. D." and "Dr. L. O. Miller Dies; Prominent Negro Doctor," *Asheville Citizen*, 1 October 1960, Pack Vertical File, vol. 1.

163. *Minutes of the Thirty-Seventh Annual Session of the N.C. Baptist State Sunday School Convention* (1909), 20.

Chapter 3. "Badge of a man"

1. *Proceedings of the Forty-First Annual Communication of the Most Worshipful Grand Lodge of North Carolina, Free and Accepted Ancient Masons* (Goldsboro, N.C.: Nash Bros., Printers and Binders, 1910). McRary shepherded the state's Masonic lodge for twelve years, from 1908 to 1920. I am immensely grateful to Marvin D. Chambers, Most Worshipful Grand Master of the Prince Hall Grand Lodge of North Carolina, for allowing me unrestricted access to Masonic records at the headquarters of the Prince Hall Grand Lodge of North Carolina in Durham.

The "craft," or freemasonry, first appeared in the lodges and grand lodges of London in 1717. It gradually spread throughout the globe, touching many regions and cultures. For more on the origins of freemasonry, see Bullock, *Revolutionary Brotherhood*.

2. Ibid.

3. Ibid.

4. Historian David M. Fahey challenges the perception of fraternal organizations as secret, correctly asserting that such groups in some cases printed and copyrighted their rituals and that Masonic men did not conceal their membership in freemasonry. However, for many men, the private spaces offered a male counterculture separate from home or church and thus attained the aura of a protected secret preserve. Fahey, *Black Lodge in White America*.

5. Du Bois, *The Philadelphia Negro*, 221–224.

6. Palmer, "Negro Secret Societies," 210.

7. Franklin, *From Slavery to Freedom*, 165; Odum, *Social and Mental Traits of the Negro*, 267; and Palmer, "Negro Secret Societies." Several works on black freemasonry have stressed these dimensions. They include Work, "Secret Societies as Factors in the Social and Economical Life of the Negro"; Kenzer, *Enterprising Southerners*, 67–106; Fahey, *The Black Lodge in White America*; Williams, *Black Freemasonry and Middle-Class Realities*; Muraskin, *Middle-Class Blacks in a White Society*; and Grimshaw, *Official History of Freemasonry among the Colored People of North America*.

8. See Muraskin, *Middle-Class Blacks in a White Society*, 29.

9. Much of this no doubt is explained by the scarcity of available records. David Hackett, who analyzes the linkages between North Carolina Prince Hall Masons and religion, cites the difficulty in obtaining comprehensive state records of Masonic proceedings. More than once he was told that "the lodge building and whatever records were there were not available to me because they were 'secret.'" Hackett, "The Prince Hall Masons and the African American Church," 772n9. Scholars of freemasonry have encountered the dearth of available data. Hackett noted the frustration of Joseph A. Walkes Jr., president emeritus and founder of the Prince Hall research journal *Phylaxis*, who had difficulty accessing the records. And John Bruce, in his brief chronicle of Prince Hall's founder, remarked, "In these respects many Negro organizations are woefully lacking in system and detail. Records of importance in many instances have been loosely kept on scraps of paper, which have not infrequently been lost or mislaid, and as a result nothing definite could be stated when the accuracy of any happening was questioned or disputed"; see Bruce, *Prince Hall, the Pioneer of Negro Masonry*, 2. Documenting African-American branches of the Order of the Eastern Star has proven even more difficult. In many respects, the proceedings of these orders were more secretive than Prince Hall proceedings. The most comprehensive source is Brown, *The History of the Order of the Eastern Star among Colored People*.

10. Martin Summers's *Manliness and Its Discontents* is the only study to directly address the relationship between Eastern Star women and Prince Hall men. Maurice O. Wallace, who devotes a chapter to Prince Hall masonry and the construction of manhood therein, lingers on national spokesmen Prince Hall (founder of the Masonic group) and statesman Martin R. Delany; see *Constructing the Black Masculine*. Robert Kenzer's examination of North Carolina's black fraternal orders delves a bit into the early twentieth century, but the thrust of his analysis is primarily economic; see Kenzer, *Enterprising Southerners*. Similarly, David Hackett's work on the Prince Hall Masons in North Carolina focuses on links between secret societies and religion, primarily in the late nineteenth century; Hackett, "The Prince Hall Masons and the African American Church." More recently, Corey David Bazemore's

investigation of black freemasonry in Charlottesville, Virginia, from after emancipation to the turn of the century, has sought to reinterpret freemasonry as a "discursive space through which articulations of race, class, gender, and place are theorized and performed." See Bazemore, "The Freemasonry of the Race," vi.

11. Hackett, "The Prince Hall Masons and the African American Church," 800.

12. Fahey, *The Black Lodge in White America*, 7.

13. See Carnes, *Secret Ritual and Manhood*, 79; Hackett, "The Prince Hall Masons and the African American Church," 800; Fahey, *The Black Lodge in White America*, 7.

14. One of the most renowned early black organizations, Philadelphia's Free African Society, was founded in 1787 as a mutual aid organization after co-founder Absalom Jones and others were forcibly removed from prayer benches in St. George's Methodist Church, a white church. Jones and Richard Allen subsequently created the African Episcopal and the African Methodist Episcopal churches. See Nash, *Forging Freedom*, 98–104; and Horton, *Free People of Color*.

15. After a candidate was accepted as a Mason, he was "invested with a white apron in token of his newly attained purity." The ancient piece of apparel, which J. W. Hood maintains was worn by Adam and Eve before being thrust out of the Garden of Eden, made the initiate "feel his relationship to the fraternity." See Hackett, "The Prince Hall Masons and the African-American Church," 790–791.

16. Ibid., 782.

17. Ibid. For black men, white Masons' rejection of them as participants in freemasonry equated to a rejection of their manhood. Clawson, *Constructing Brotherhood*, 134–135.

18. It should be noted that the first black man to be initiated in North Carolina, William H. Hancock, a successful building contractor, received the degrees in the white St. John's Lodge No. 3 in Newberne. He served as tiler of the lodge for several years. Hancock, it was reported, was often seen leading his lodge with drawn sword in ceremonial processions. Overall, however, the state's white Masonic lodges refused to recognize the legitimacy of black freemasonry. See Davis, *A History of Freemasonry among Negroes in America*.

In the South, Prince Hall Lodges were founded in Maryland (1845), Louisiana (1863), Kentucky (1866), North Carolina (1870), Tennessee (1870), Alabama (1870), Florida (1870), South Carolina (1872), Virginia (1875), Mississippi (1876), Arkansas (1878), and West Virginia (1881). See Muraskin, *Middle-Class Blacks in a White Society*, 38n108.

19. Hood's successors as Grand Master through 1930 were James Telfair (1883–1886), Stewart Ellison (1886–1890), George White (1890–1896), James H. Young (1896–1898), J. J. Worlds (1898–1903), L. R. Randolph-Preston (1903–1908), R. B. McCrary (1908–1920), James E. Shepard (1920–1928), and L. B. Capehart,

(1928–1933). See Muraskin, *Middle-Class Blacks in a White Society*, 38; and Hackett, "The Prince Hall Masons and the African American Church," 773–774. For a comprehensive biography of Hood's life and career, see Martin, *For God and Race*.

20. *Proceedings of the Twenty-Eighth Annual Communication of the Most Worshipful Grand Lodge of North Carolina, Free and Accepted Ancient Masons, Wilson, N.C., December 14–17, 1897* (Goldsboro, N.C.: Nash Bros., Printers and Binders, 1897). Calvin Scott Brown played prominent roles in masonry, serving as general secretary from 1903 to 1928 and as grand master from 1933.

21. Historian Evelyn Brooks Higginbotham acknowledges the importance of feminist theology for black Baptist women. She asserts that "feminist theology had significant implications for black Baptist women's future work. It buttressed their demand for more vocal participation and infused their growing ranks with optimism about the dawning twentieth century. It also encouraged women to establish and control their own separate conventions at the state and national levels." Higginbotham, "The Feminist Theology of the Black Baptist Church," 283.

22. *Proceedings of the Fortieth Annual Communication of the Most Worshipful Grand Lodge of North Carolina, Free and Accepted Ancient Masons, Wilmington, N.C., December 14–16, 1909* (Goldsboro, N.C.: Nash Bros., Printers and Binders, 1909).

23. Ibid. See also R. Kelley Bryant, interviewed by Paul Ortiz, Durham, N.C.

24. Although the name "Electa" is not mentioned in the Bible, the apostle John refers to "the elect lady" in his second epistle. See 2 John, chapter 1.

25. Dr. Morris has been called the poet laureate of masonry. See "The Order of the Eastern Star," available online at http://gcoesphanc.org/faq.htm. See also Clawson, *Constructing Brotherhood*, 188.

26. White women struggled in their attempts to secure recognition from America's fraternal groups. The Knights of Pythias recognized its women's auxiliary, the Order of Pythian Sisters, only after twenty-seven years of struggle by women. The Masons have yet to officially recognize the Order of the Eastern Star as Masonic in character, despite its more than 100-year existence. See Clawson, *Constructing Brotherhood*, 200; and Carnes, *Secret Ritual and Manhood*, 79.

27. Other black orders, such as the True Reformers, supported women's auxiliaries. See Fahey, *The Black Lodge in White America*; and Martin, *For God and Race*, 163–175.

28. See "Address Delivered by Mrs. S. Joe Brown before Ninth Biennial Conference, Pittsburgh, Pennsylvania, August 1924," reprinted in Brown, *History of the Order of the Eastern Star among Colored People*, 37–38. Local chapters of black Eastern Star groups organized much earlier. Queen Esther Chapter No.1 in Washington, D.C., formed in 1874. The first worthy matron was Sister Martha Welch; Jackson served as the first worthy patron. On 28 April 1890, Queen of Sheba Chapter No. 3 of the Order of the Eastern Star was founded in the District of Columbia; later

that year, Gethsemane Chapter No.4 of Washington, D.C., was founded. Jackson also helped establish chapters in Alexandria, Virginia; Maryland; and Pennsylvania. Each time a chapter organized, it was adopted by a regularly constituted Masonic lodge. Brown, *History of the Order of the Eastern Star*, 15–16.

29. In 1994, this list was expanded to include nieces, daughters-in-law, and grandmothers. See "The Order of the Eastern Star," available online at http://gcoesphanc.org/oeshistory.htm.

30. The need for Eastern Star women to be protected speaks to the obligation Masonic men assumed to respect black womanhood. This included refuting racist discourses that asserted black women's promiscuity and seeing to black women's benevolent needs. This mutual aid consisted of burial expenses, insurance policies, and economic assistance to widows and orphans. Prince Hall freemasonry also provided an institutional outlet for women's labor. But protection also entailed black women's containment. Because men belonged to the OES, black women were aware of expectations that they conform to conventional gender behavior. For many black Masonic chapters across the country, "female protection is her [the Masons'] great pride and glory . . . [and] each Mason is a sworn protector of womanhood." See Muraskin, *Middle-Class Blacks in a White Society*, 72.

31. The father of York Garrett Jr., David Garrett York, Sr., was a grocery merchant in Tarboro who lived in Princeville, an all-black township founded by free blacks. David York belonged to the Masons and the Grand United Order of Odd Fellows, among other fraternal organizations. His wife, Sarah Frances Garrett, was a member of the Eastern Star and Household of Ruth fraternal auxiliaries. Like the Eastern Star, the Household of Ruth "had to have a man" in it. York Garrett recalls his father criss-crossing the state due to his Masonic activity. "The secret societies, that was his life," he said. Unfortunately, for his son, it wasn't. York "never took a part of any of it," though he did join a medical fraternity. See York Garrett, interviewed by Kara Miles, Durham, N.C.

32. Brown, *History of the Order of the Eastern Star*, 19.

33. Brown, *The History of the Order of the Eastern Star among Colored People*. By 1925, thirty-five Grand Lodges existed with 3,500 chapters whose combined membership was more than 100,000. Their combined treasuries totaled about half a million dollars.

34. Clawson, *Constructing Brotherhood*, 202–203.

35. Brown, *The History of the Order of the Eastern Star among Colored People*, 37.

36. *Proceedings of the Twenty-Eighth Annual Communication of the Most Worshipful Grand Lodge of North Carolina* (1897), 28.

37. Ayers, *Promise of the New South*, 301–304. See also Litwack, *Trouble in Mind*, 315–316.

38. *Proceedings of the Twenty-Ninth Annual Communication of the Most Worship-*

ful Grand Lodge of North Carolina, Free and Accepted Ancient Masons, Oxford, N.C., 13–15, 1898 (Goldsboro, N.C.: Nash Bros., Printers and Binders, 1898).

39. *Proceedings of the Thirty-First Annual Communication of the Most Worshipful Grand Lodge of North Carolina, Free and Accepted Ancient Masons, Asheville, N.C., 11–13, 1900* (Goldsboro, N.C.: Nash Bros., Printers and Binders, 1900); *Proceedings of the Forty-First Annual Communication of the Most Worshipful Grand Lodge of North Carolina, Free and Accepted Ancient Masons, Raleigh, N.C., December 13–15, 1910* (Goldsboro, N.C.: Nash Bros., Printers and Binders, 1910). Even in the racially turbulent 1890s, the number of Prince Hall Masons was a respectable 1,231. See Kenzer, *Enterprising Southerners*, 69. In 1902, Booker T. Washington recorded twenty national black secret societies. These included the Masons, the True Reformers, the Odd Fellows, the Knights of Pythias, the Elks, the Knights of Tabor, and the Mosaic Templars of America. Of these, the three wealthiest were the Odd Fellows ($2,500,000), the Masons ($1,000,000), and the True Reformers ($800,000). See Palmer, "Negro Secret Societies," 210.

40. *Proceedings of the Forty-Third Annual Communication of the Most Worshipful Grand Lodge of North Carolina, Free and Accepted Ancient Masons, Asheville, N.C., December 10–12, 1912* (Goldsboro, N.C.: Nash Bros., Printers and Binders, 1912).

41. Ibid.

42. Simmons-Henry, *Culture Town*.

43. *Proceedings of the Twenty-Eighth Annual Communication of the Most Worshipful Grand Lodge of North Carolina* (1897); *Proceedings of the Twenty-Ninth Annual Communication of the Most Worshipful Grand Lodge of North Carolina* (1898); *Proceedings of the Thirty-Seventh Annual Communication of the Most Worshipful Grand Lodge of North Carolina, Free and Accepted Ancient Masons, Raleigh, N.C., December 8–11, 1908* (Goldsboro, N.C.: Nash Bros., Printers and Binders, 1908); *Proceedings of the Forty-First Annual Communication of the Most Worshipful Grand Lodge of North Carolina* (1910). See also Kenzer, *Enterprising Southerners*, 73–75.

44. *Proceedings of the Forty-Third Communication of the Most Worshipful Grand Lodge of North Carolina* (1912).

45. Ibid.

46. See Muraskin, *Middle-Class Blacks in a White Society*, 252–253. Muraskin posits that divisions within the black middle class—that is, the resentment of working-class Masons about having to answer to one of their own rather than to the "superior" race—accounts for the hostility. These internal divisions continue to resonate in historical portrayals of black masonry. See Fahey, *The Black Lodge in White America*.

47. *Proceedings of the Fortieth Annual Communication of the Most Worshipful Grand Lodge of North Carolina* (1909). Masons' use of the word "protection" generally meant providing for the Order's members, their families, and the extended black commu-

nity. Given Prince Hall's commitment to render financial and charitable assistance, the work of Masons also became gender laden as it provided for the care of sick fraternity members, families of deceased members, or needy individuals outside the fraternal body. See Brown, *History of the Order of the Eastern Star*, 19; and Summers, *Manliness and Its Discontents*, 26–27.

48. *Proceedings of the Forty-Third Communication of the Most Worshipful Grand Lodge of North Carolina* (1912).

49. *Proceedings of the Twenty-Ninth Annual Communication of the Most Worshipful Grand Lodge of North Carolina* (1898). These accolades by Prince Hall men are perhaps somewhat superficial. In her interviews with Prince Hall members, Loretta Williams discovered that "while most mentioned the women's auxiliaries, few thought that these would be of interest to me; or, it might be said, few thought that these were on the same level of import or interest as the male lodges." See Williams, *Black Freemasonry and Middle-Class Realities*, 136.

50. *Proceedings of the Thirty-Seventh Annual Communication of the Most Worshipful Grand Lodge of North Carolina* (1908). Badham's letter was dated 7 December 1908.

51. *Proceedings of the Fortieth Annual Communication of the Most Worshipful Grand Lodge of North Carolina* (1909).

52. *Proceedings of the Forty-First Annual Communication of the Most Worshipful Grand Lodge of North Carolina* (1910); *Proceedings of the Forty-Second Annual Communication of the Most Worshipful Grand Lodge of North Carolina, Free and Accepted Ancient Masons, Greensboro, N.C., December 12–14, 1911* (Goldsboro, N.C.: Nash Bros., Printers and Binders, 1911).

53. Ibid.

54. See Haley, *Charles N. Hunter and Race Relations in North Carolina*, 175, 205–206.

55. *Proceedings of the Fifty-Eighth Annual Communication of the Most Worshipful Grand Lodge of North Carolina, Free and Accepted Ancient Masons, Winston-Salem, N.C., December 11–13, 1928* (Raleigh, N.C.: Edwards & Broughton Co., 1928), 29–30.

56. Haley has discussed dimensions of loyalty pertaining to Charles Hunter and his race work in North Carolina. See Haley, *Charles N. Hunter and Race Relations in North Carolina*. Sarah Thuesen has also addressed aspects of black loyalty in her dissertation, "Classes of Citizenship: The Culture and Politics of Black Public Education in North Carolina, 1919–1960." For sympathetic treatments of the efforts of black community leaders to negotiate on behalf of black interests, see Moore, *Leading the Race*; Gilmore, *Gender and Jim Crow*; and Clark, *Defining Moments*.

57. *Proceedings of the Fifty-Eighth Annual Communication of the Most Worshipful Grand Lodge of North Carolina* (1928). Shepard's embrace and use of the concept of "black loyalty" occurred as part of his prolonged battle with North Carolina's Divi-

sion of Negro Education (headed by Nathan Carter Newbold) to procure financial and curriculum support for his school. In the power struggle, Shepard reluctantly relinquished his membership in the Masons, an organization that Newbold repeatedly cited as distracting Shepard from his school responsibilities. Shepard and the concept of black loyalty are discussed in Sarah C. Thuesen's "Bargaining for Black Loyalty." Many thanks to Sarah for sharing her insights on "black loyalty" and the connections between Shepard's educational and Masonic activities.

58. *Proceedings of the Fifty-Eighth Annual Communication of the Most Worshipful Grand Lodge of North Carolina* (1928).

59. The leaders of other Grand Lodge chapters also counseled subordinate branches to flex their political muscle by utilizing the ballot and campaigning for race reforms, including anti-lynching legislation. See Williams, *Black Freemasonry and Middle-Class Realities*, 116.

60. Brown, *The History of the Order of the Eastern Star among Colored People*, 174. Introduced by Republican Congressman Leonidas C. Dyer on 19 May 1919, the NAACP-backed Dyer bill would have made lynching a federal offense. The Dyer anti-lynching bill passed the House of Representatives by a vote of 231 to 119 on 16 January 1922, but it was defeated in the Senate by a Democratic filibuster. Ferrell, *Nightmare and Dream*, 298–300.

61. See Summers, *Manliness and Its Discontents*, 36–37.

62. "Deficit Facing Negro Pythians," *News & Observer* (Raleigh), 31 January 1928, Charles N. Hunter Scrapbooks, Box 15, Folder 4, Charles N. Hunter Papers.

63. *Proceedings of the Fifty-Ninth Annual Communication of the Most Worshipful Grand Lodge of North Carolina, Free and Accepted Ancient Masons, Rocky Mount, N.C., December 10–12, 1929* (Raleigh, N.C.: Edwards & Broughton Co., 1930).

64. *Proceedings of the Sixty-Fourth Annual Communication of the Most Worshipful Grand Lodge of North Carolina, Free and Accepted Ancient Masons, Burlington, N.C., December 13–15, 1933* (Raleigh, N.C.: Edwards & Broughton Co., 1933).

65. Ibid.

66. Ibid. When he assumed his duties as Grand Master, Brown found himself "bare-handed, without a cent to begin with, and no office supplies, except a seal and a few old minutes" (15).

67. Ibid. Despite these sentiments, Brown had come to believe, after investigating the Lodge's defunct endowment department, that most of the blame for the fraternity's condition lay not with Masonic officers but with the "havoc that the 'depression' had brought to all business institutions in general" (16).

68. *Proceedings of the Fifty-Eighth Annual Communication of the Most Worshipful Grand Lodge of North Carolina* (1928).

69. Ibid. Capehart noted the negative reaction of Eastern Star officials to the policy change.

70. See Muraskin, *Middle-Class Blacks in a White Society*, 169.

71. *Proceedings of the Sixty-Fourth Annual Communication of the Most Worshipful Grand Lodge of North Carolina* (1933)

72. Palmer, "Negro Secret Societies," 210.

73. *Proceedings of the Forty-Seventh Annual Communication of the Most Worshipful Grand Lodge of North Carolina, Free and Accepted Ancient Masons, Rocky Mount, N.C., December 11–13, 1916* (Washington, N.C.: Nash Bros., Printers and Binders, 1916).

Chapter 4. "Let the white man put himself in the negro's place"

1. "How to Solve the Problem Discussed at YMI," *Asheville Citizen*, 22 March 1904. "The problem" refers to how race relations would be defined in the post-Reconstruction era. The concept of race relations as a "problem" held currency in and outside the black community. Though reports of the YMI event do not record if whites attended, it is likely that some were there; the YMI typically invited members of the white community to share in its community programs.

2. Ibid.

3. "Grand Celebration of the Emancipation of the Negro," *Asheville Citizen*, 2 January 1904. Members of the Emancipation Day Committee were credited for the success of the event, especially YMI general secretary W. J. Trent, who was singled out for his efforts. Special mention was also given to Douglas Clark and Benjamin Jackson for their planning of the musical offerings. It is uncertain whether any women members were on that year's Emancipation Day Committee.

4. Savage women were aggressive, according to social theories that equated white racial superiority with the advanced civilizations. Savage men lacked self-restraint and were overly emotional; they failed to protect their children and raped women instead of protecting them. See Bederman, *Manliness and Civilization*, 24; and Bederman, "The Decline of Middle-Class Manliness and Ida B. Wells's Anti-Lynching Campaign," 29.

5. Crowds sometimes rejected emancipation rhetoric in favor of leisure-time pursuits such as barbecues, baseball games, and bands. See Blight, *Race and Reunion*, 370–371.

6. An exception to this is Haley, *Charles N. Hunter and Race Relations in North Carolina*, which discusses the race cooperation aspects of both Emancipation Day ceremonies and the state fair. His analysis, however, does not address the gendered components of the events. David Blight also acknowledges the interracial composition of these events, though his observations largely predate the Jim Crow era. See Blight, *Race and Reunion*. Mitch Kachun focuses on the changes to Emancipation Day ceremonies over time, assessing how shifting social, cultural, and political contexts led to increased debate in black communities over public conduct and political

orientation. He notes the gradual decline of Emancipation Day ceremonies overall in the early twentieth century, except in the rural South, but does not analyze their biracial constituency. See Kachun, *Festivals of Freedom*, 1–15. In assessing the biracial and gendered aspects of emancipation ceremonies, Kathleen Clark examines race and gender subjectivity among Emancipation Day participants, though her discussion largely occurs outside the Jim Crow period. Clark assesses the complex organizational and rhetorical strategies inherent in commemoration ceremonies, which included "black and white, male and female, northern and southern, rural and urban, adult and child, freeborn and former slave." See Clark, *Defining Moments*, 6–7.

7. Kachun, *Festivals of Freedom*, 7. Kachun argues that at the onset of the Jim Crow period, Emancipation Day ceremonies became more "racially circumscribed events" (ibid.). See also Clark, "Celebrating Freedom," 125.

8. Clark argues that scholarly critiques of so-called accommodationists for their misplaced "confidence" in white southerners and "distrust" of working-class blacks have undercut the significance of their achievements during the Jim Crow period. Clark, *Defining Moments*, 6.

9. See Wiggins, *O Freedom!* 1–50.

10. Weare, "New Negroes for a New Century," 94–95.

11. Ibid., 98.

12. The racial and gendered dimensions of the exposition movement are analyzed in Bederman, *Manliness and Civilization*, 31–41.

13. Weare, "New Negroes for a New Century," 96–100. See Rydell, *All the World's a Fair*.

14. Ibid.

15. R. R. Wright Jr., "Forty Years of Negro Progress," *Southern Workman* (May 1908): 157–163. R. R. Wright's father, Major R. R. Wright, a veteran of the Spanish-American War, led a fund-raising campaign to host a national Emancipation Day exhibition in Savannah. The bill for a federally funded exhibit failed to pass both houses of Congress. See Wiggins, *O Freedom!*

16. "Constitution of the North Carolina Industrial Association," Box 12, Charles N. Hunter Papers.

17. Quotes in Connor and Poe, *The Life and Speeches of Charles Brantley Aycock*, 163. See also Newby, *In Jim Crow's Defense*, 14.

18. Ibid.

19. Racial demographics might have factored into the sympathy of Aycock and other white elites toward blacks. With a black population steadily hovering at 30 percent, North Carolina's race relations picture was considerably less hot than that of other southern states, particularly those in the lower South, which had substantially higher black populaces. See Williamson, *A Rage for Order*.

20. Aycock, who served as governor from 1901–1906, was regarded the "father of

the State's consolidated school program"; "Aycock Hoped to Admit Negroes, Graham Says," *Asheville Citizen*, 10 April 1951, in North Carolina Collection Biographical Clipping File through 1975, vol. 5, 192.

21. See "Emancipation Day Celebrated Here," 2 January 1917, Charles N. Hunter Scrapbooks, Box 15, Folder 1, Charles N. Hunter Papers; and "North Carolina Leads," in "Race Relations" file, *Tuskegee Institute News Clipping File*, Reel 26, Frame 1027.

22. To some white elites, political equality for blacks did not naturally lead to demands for social equality. President Theodore Roosevelt and southern moderate George Washington Cable, while strongly resistant to social integration of the races, actively supported black men's right to vote. See Newby, *In Jim Crow's Defense*, 146.

23. Key, *Southern Politics*; Gaston, *The New South Creed*, 42. For the concepts of "civility" and the "myth of progressive race relations" as applied to the modern Civil Rights Movement, see Chafe, *Civilities and Civil Rights*, 2–12.

24. "A Note of Warning: Let the Negro Race Beware of the Danger Line," and "An Omen of Ill: The White Man Who Induces a Negro to Vote Is Sowing Dragon's Teeth," both in *News & Observer* (Raleigh), 30 September 1903, Charles N. Hunter Scrapbooks, Box 14, Folder 1, Charles N. Hunter Papers. The "divided mind" of the South and its implications for race relations at the turn of the century has been explicated by a number of historians, including Woodward, *Origins of the New South*; and Williamson, *A Rage for Order*.

25. "Booker Washington's Ideas of Education," *Morning Post* (Raleigh), 31 October 1903, Charles N. Hunter Scrapbooks, Box 14, Folder 1, Charles N. Hunter Papers. See also Crow, Escott, and Hatley, "Black Life in the Age of Jim Crow," 122.

26. Kantrowitz, *Ben Tillman and the Reconstruction of White Supremacy*.

27. "Lauds Recent Race Conference: Prof. Charles N. Hunter Writes Letter to Superintendent of Education," *News & Observer* (Raleigh), 27 October 1919, Charles N. Hunter Scrapbooks, Box 15, Folder 2, Charles N. Hunter Papers. Hunter's position on race progress appeared in his *Journal of Industry*, the publishing organ of the North Carolina Industrial Association. In keeping with his varied approaches to the race question over the years, Hunter sometimes judged it practical for the race to pursue electoral politics.

28. See Weare, "New Negroes for a New Century," 110. Hunter's professional career was quite diverse and at times erratic. This was partially due to a drinking problem. See Haley, *Charles N. Hunter and Race Relations in North Carolina*, 132–134. Hunter's 42-year teaching career included posts in Goldsboro, Raleigh, and Durham. He founded the Berry O'Kelly Training and Industrial School at Method and served as its principal for nine years, and for several years he held the post of recording secretary of the black North Carolina State Teachers' Association (founded

in 1881 to promote the educational interests and secure the overall welfare of the state's black residents). During World War I, Hunter worked at the Norfolk Navy Yard. After the war, he took positions in schools in seven different communities.

29. Ibid.

30. The recurring debate about the merits of segregated fairs resonated in southern black communities, especially the cities of Atlanta (1895), Nashville (1897), Charleston (1902), and Jamestown, Virginia (1907). Weare posits that the debate over segregated fairs in the South ebbed after the Jamestown Exposition due to the location of black fairs and exhibitions in black rather than white settings See Weare, "New Negroes for a New Century," 112. Yet the issue continued to ferment in local southern communities. In North Carolina, the controversy persisted and intensified until the demise of black fairs in 1931.

31. Haley, *Charles N. Hunter and Race Relations in North Carolina*, 245.

32. President Theodore Roosevelt's discharge in 1906 of 170 black troops of the army's Twenty-Fifth Infantry (which was stationed in Brownsville) was denounced at Raleigh's Emancipation Day gathering as "executive lynch law." See "Emancipation Day," *Baptist Sentinel*, 10 January 1907, Charles N. Hunter Scrapbooks, Box 14, Folder 2, Charles N. Hunter Papers. Among attendees at the ceremony were students from local black schools and colleges.

33. Earl Lewis argues that the alignment and realignment of Hunter's self was dependent on a convergence of factors, including time, space, and memory. For his discourse on the multiple constructions of identity, see Lewis, "Invoking Concepts, Problematizing Identities," 292–308.

34. "Birthday of the Negro's Freedom," *News & Observer* (Raleigh), 2 January 1906. Emancipation ceremonies held these dinners as well. See, for example, "Emancipation Day Dinner for Slaves," *News & Observer* (Raleigh), 2 January 1924.

35. "The Negroes Discuss Their Grievances," *Raleigh Post*, 3 January 1905, Charles N. Hunter Scrapbooks Box 14, Folder 2, Charles N. Hunter Papers.

36. "Outlook Bright for Negro Fair: Opening Address by Berry O'Kelley," *News & Observer* (Raleigh), 27 October 1915; Robert R. Moton, "Signs of Growing Cooperation," *Southern Workman* (October 1914): 552–559.

37. "Bickett Talked to Negroes Here," *The Independent*, 11 April 1919, in "Emancipation," *Tuskegee Institute News Clipping File*, Reel 240, Frame 878.

38. Rolinson, *Grassroots Garveyism*, 138.

39. Ibid., 68.

40. Ibid.

41. W. J. Trent, "Emancipation Day: An Excellent Address, Musical Features," *Star of Zion*, 15 January 1903.

42. "Negroes Stage Annual Program," *Charlotte News*, 1 January 1925; "Negroes

Hear Cotton Speak," 2 January 1925, both in "Emancipation," *Tuskegee Institute News Clipping File*, Reel 240, Frame 893.

43. "Plan Celebration for Negroes Here," *Durham Herald*, 2 July 1930 in "Emancipation File," *Tuskegee Institute News Clipping File*, Reel 240, Frame 929; "Second Day Events of Colored Fair," *News & Observer* (Raleigh), 29 October 1903, Charles N. Hunter Scrapbooks, Box 14, Folder 1, Charles N. Hunter Papers.

44. Several black women were members of Emancipation Day committees. For example, Mary E. Gray was the corresponding secretary of the Emancipation Day committee in High Point in 1928. See "Emancipation Day Service Attended by Large Number," *High Point Enterprise*, 2 January 1928, in "Emancipation," *Tuskegee Institute News Clipping File*, Reel 240, Frame 920. The Black Women's Congress assembled at Tuskegee Institute on the fiftieth anniversary of emancipation. The estimated 500 women in attendance discussed the black woman's role in the advancement of her race and country. "The Great Emancipation Celebration Jubilee," 13 September 1913, *Tuskegee Institute News Clipping File*, Reel 240, Frame 834.

45. All quotes in this paragraph from "The Great Negro Fair. Bulletin No. 2. Raleigh, North Carolina, October, 1904," available online at http://docsouth.unc.edu/nc/fair/fair.html.

46. "Emancipation Address Stirs Raleigh Folks: Mrs. Charlotte Hawkins Brown Declares the Time Has Come for the Race to Put on the New Freedom," *Norfolk Journal and Guide*, 8 January 1926, in "Emancipation," *Tuskegee Institute News Clipping File*, Reel 240, Frame 905. See also White, *Too Heavy a Load*, 36–37. See note 109 of Chapter 2 for more information about Brown.

47. Black male and female representatives of the YMCA and YWCA, respectively, promoted a series of studies, programs, and conferences designed in part to increase black and white southern students' sympathies regarding interracial and international problems. State conferences held in Virginia and North Carolina in 1925 drew 300 and 200 delegates, respectively. The clearinghouse for the Christian association of black and white students in the South, the Council of Christian Associations for the South, held its second annual session at Black Mountain, North Carolina. "North Carolina Leads," *Pittsburgh Courier*, 30 January 1926, in "Race Relations," *Tuskegee Institute News Clipping File*, Reel 26, Frame 1027; "Colored Student Speaks at North Carolina University," 16 October 1926, in "Race Relations," *Tuskegee Institute News Clipping File*, Reel 26, Frame 1019.

48. See Gilmore, *Gender and Jim Crow*, 212–213.

49. "Emancipation Address Stirs Raleigh Folks," *Norfolk Journal and Guide*, 9 January 1926.

50. "Address Sent Forth by the Negroes of Wake County on the Occasion of the Celebration of the 44th Anniversary of the Proclamation of Emancipation," 1 January 1907, handwritten document, Correspondence Files, Box 3 (1906–1909), Charles N. Hunter Papers.

51. "'No Africa for Us': Raleigh All Right: Colored People of City on Emancipation Day," 2 January 1907, *News & Observer* (Raleigh), Charles N. Hunter Scrapbooks, Box 15, Folder 1, Charles N. Hunter Papers. At the ceremony, resolutions were approved in which "thanks were given the white people for their friendship."

52. D. Hiden Ramsey, "A Neglected Phase of the Negro Question," *Southern Workman* (December 1914): 693–694.

53. "Ex-Slaves' Reunion—A Call," *Raleigh Times*, 16 September 1913, Box 14, Folder 3, and "Colored Fair Opened Today; Weather Ideal," 27 October 1916, Box 15, Folder 1, both in Charles N. Hunter Scrapbooks, Charles N. Hunter Papers.

54. The Jamestown Exposition commemorated the founding of America's first permanent English settlement. The U.S. Congress appropriated $100,000 to erect a separate exhibit displaying black progress. Haley, *Charles N. Hunter and Race Relations in North Carolina*, 158.

55. "Address Sent Forth by the Negroes of Wake County on the Occasion of the Celebration of the 44th Anniversary of the Proclamation of Emancipation."

56. "The Negro Semi-Centennial Exposition," 18 May 1910, Charles N. Hunter Scrapbooks, Box 14, Folder 3, Charles N. Hunter Papers.

57. "Governor Glenn at the Negro Building," *Raleigh Evening Times*, 24 August 1907, Charles N. Hunter Scrapbooks, Box 14, Folder 2, Charles N. Hunter Papers. The Jamestown Exposition was held from April through November 1907. The Exposition designated August 3rd as "Negro Day"; black attendees were treated to a parade, fireworks, a military drill, a concert by the Fisk Jubilee Singers and the Hampton Institute band, and an appearance by Booker T. Washington. August 12–18 was dubbed North Carolina Week. See Haley, *Charles N. Hunter and Race Relations in North Carolina*, 163–165.

58. See Haley, *Charles N. Hunter and Race Relations in North Carolina*, 163–164.

59. Weare, "New Negroes for a New Century," 119–121; Haley, *Charles N. Hunter and Race Relations in North Carolina*, 162–165.

60. Haley, *Charles N. Hunter and Race Relations in North Carolina*, 162.

61. C. N. Hunter to Professor W. Saunders, 16 March 1907, Correspondence Files, Box 3, Hunter Papers.

62. "Negro Life in North Carolina Illustrated," Correspondence Files, Box 3, Charles N. Hunter Papers.

63. "Chas. N. Hunter Planning Intimate Story of Negro," *Raleigh Times*, 31 October 1927, Box 15, Folder 3, in Charles N. Hunter Scrapbooks.

64. Blight, *Race and Reunion*, 367.

65. Carter G. Woodson, "Some Things Negroes Need to Do," *Southern Workman* (January 1922): 33–36.

66. Thomas L. Dabney, "The Importance of Negro History," *Southern Workman* (December 1929): 558, 561. Dabney noted that the survey of students found that the majority were enrolled in the eighth and ninth grades. Of students surveyed, 119 did

not know who the founder of Tuskegee Institute was, 380 did not know what the purpose and activities of the National Association for the Advancement of Colored People were, and only sixty-six were familiar with the objectives of the Brotherhood of Sleeping Car Porters. Only thirty-seven students claimed to have read one or more black books. Only twenty-three students of the nineteen schools surveyed said that they read Du Bois's *Crisis* regularly. Such lamentable disclosures were evidence to Dabney of "the great failing of Negro students in race history" (561).

67. "Negro History in North Carolina," *News & Observer* (Raleigh), 23 November 1927, Charles N. Hunter Scrapbooks, Box 15, Folder 3, Charles N. Hunter Papers; Bruce Cotten to Charles Hunter, 21 July 1928, Box 9, Correspondence Files, Charles N. Hunter Papers. See also Haley, *Charles N. Hunter and Race Relations in North Carolina*, 269–272.

68. Haley, *Charles N. Hunter and Race Relations in North Carolina*, 154; Fairclough, "'Being in the Field of Education and Also Being a Negro . . . Seems . . . Tragic,'" 75.

69. Clark, *Defining Freedom*, 219–221.

70. Wormser, *The Rise and Fall of Jim Crow*.

71. "Negroes Entirely Loyal," *News & Observer* (Raleigh), 6 April 1917. Shepard's words were buttressed by Dr. Plato T. Durham, dean of Atlanta's Emory College, who maintained that "for every man in white who fell in Picardy a man in black also fell and that the negroes of America are the only people who gave one dollar out of every five earned for the support of the war chest." See "Dr. Durham Pays Tribute to Negro: Dean of Methodist University Pleads for Better Understanding between Races," *News & Observer* (Raleigh), 28 May 1921.

72. Kate M. Herring, "The Negro and War Savings in North Carolina," *South Atlantic Quarterly* 18 (January 1919): 36–40. Other leading black men active in war savings work included Calvin Scott Brown, general secretary of the Baptist State Convention and principal of the Waters Normal School; Bishop George W. Clinton of the A.M.E. Church in Charlotte; Henry McCrory, president of Biddle University in Charlotte; Col. James Young; and John Merrick, North Carolina Mutual Insurance Company executive. Also see "Influence of Southern White Women," *Southern Workman* (May 1919): 216–217; Gilmore, *Gender and Jim Crow*, 178; "'No Africa for Us': Raleigh All Right," *News & Observer* (Raleigh), 2 January 1917.

73. Poe proposed a rural segregation plan for blacks inspired by South Africa's apartheid system. To stem white out-migration from the countryside, Poe rationalized an arrangement whereby black and white communities would be wholly separate. In practice this would have meant that blacks could not buy land among white farmers; they would have been isolated in their own communities. Despite objections from large landowners and other employees dependent on black labor, Poe's plan reached the North Carolina legislature as an amendment to the state constitution in 1915 with petitions from 6,000 white farmers supporting its implementation.

The proposed amendment failed by two votes. Ayers, *The Promise of the New South*, 429.

74. "Negroes to Wage Bitter Fight on Naming of Linney," *News & Observer* (Raleigh), 21 May 1921, Box 15, Folder 2; and "Says His Attitude on Race Question Is Misrepresented: Editor Clarence Poe, Leading Exponent of Segregation of Races in Rural Districts," *Norfolk Journal and Guide*, 27 March 1915, Box 15, Folder 1, both in Charles N. Hunter Scrapbooks, Charles N. Hunter Papers; Crow, Escott, and Hatley, "Black Life in the Age of Jim Crow," 126. In 1918, four more local groups were founded in Fayetteville, Winston-Salem, Rocky Mount, and Asheville. A year later, branches were established in Wilmington, Charlotte, and Lexington. See Gavins, "The NAACP in the Age of Segregation."

75. The Twentieth Century Voters Club was comprised of eligible black voters and taxpayers. The club resolved that "as our government is now administered we are specifically excluded from any active participation in its affairs.... If we continue to remain quiescent under present conditions, the day will come, as it has already in many sections of our country, when property rights, so far as we are concerned, will pass away and be reduced to a condition of vassalage." See "Negroes of City Have Organized Political Clubs: Organize for Purpose of Effective Use of Right of Franchise," *Raleigh Times*, 3 November 1916, Charles N. Hunter Scrapbooks, Box 15, Folder 1, Charles N. Hunter Papers.

76. "Negro Leader Is Speaker Here: Dr. W. E. B. Du Bois, of New York, Delivers Address in City Auditorium," *News & Observer* (Raleigh), 11 May 1918.

77. Johnson's southern tour also included addresses to interracial audiences. In Asheville, his speech, which was held in a packed Young Men's Institute, was attended by U.S. attorney general George W. Wickersham. "Says Carolina Race Relation Is Improving," *Norfolk Journal and Guide*, 10 May 1924, Charles N. Hunter Scrapbooks, Box 15, Folder 3, Charles N. Hunter Papers.

78. "Conference on Race Relations," *Southern Workman* (June 1920): 243–245.

79. *Raleigh Times*, 17 July 1917, Charles N. Hunter Scrapbooks, Box 15, Folder 1, Charles N. Hunter Papers.

80. Ibid.

81. J. A. Rogers, "Who Is the New Negro, and Why?" *The Messenger* (March 1927).

82. "'No Africa for Us': Raleigh All Right," *News & Observer* (Raleigh), 2 January 1917. The notion that black identity was both American and southern has increasingly captured scholars' attention and imagination. While some intellectuals have stressed African Americans' cultural distinctiveness, others point to "nonracial features of the American South and to regional attachment" that, despite subjection to Jim Crow and other forms of discrimination, have kept blacks rooted to the Southland. See Franklin, "Black Southerners, Shared Experience, and Place"; Painter, "'The South' and 'The Negro'"; Davis, "Expanding the Limits."

83. "Negroes Protest Jim Crow Laws," *News & Observer* (Raleigh), 2 January 1919.

84. The pageant also featured a black figure labeled "Jim Crow" who passed down a line of figures, pushing and shoving them roughly. See "Negroes Protest Jim Crow Laws," *News & Observer* (Raleigh), 2 January 1919.

85. "Negroes Ask That Lynching Be Made Capital Offense," *News & Observer* (Raleigh), 2 January 1920.

86. Monroe N. Work, "Inter-racial Cooperation," *Southern Workman* (April 1920): 156–160.

87. Frank Trigg, president of Bennett College, a Methodist college for black women in Greensboro, also banned Du Bois's *Crisis* from the campus because he deemed it too "radical." Reflecting the tightrope black leaders sometimes walked between racial accommodation and protest when courting white support, W. S. Turner's address also included a "tribute" to the late Governor Thomas Bickett, whom he maintained had ascended to the governership "without having breathed vitriolic anathema against the negro" and had been "noble, fair, courteous and freely just with the instincts of a true gentleman." It is unclear if whites attended the Emancipation Day ceremony; if they did, their presence may have contributed to Turner's bold proclamation of Bickett as "the spokesman for the negro." At any rate, Turner made sure that a copy of the resolutions attesting to blacks' high esteem of Bickett was forwarded to the governor's widow. See "Negroes Hold New Year Event," *News & Observer* (Raleigh), 3 January 1922, Charles N. Hunter Scrapbooks, Box 7, Folder 1, Charles N. Hunter Papers.

88. For example, "Emancipation Day to Be Observed in City," *News & Observer* (Raleigh), 1 January 1928; "Negroes Stage Annual Program," *Greensboro Daily News*, 1 January 1925, in "Emancipation," *Tuskegee Institute News Clipping File*, Reel 240, Frame 893; "Negroes Protest Jim Crow Laws," *News & Observer* (Raleigh), 2 January 1919.

89. "Are Negroes Satisfied?" *Star of Zion*, 9 November 1920.

90. See "Prof. Jackson Speaks on the Negro Question: Points Out Where People of the City May Help Lessen Racial Friction," *Greensboro Daily News*, 13 July 1924, Charles N. Hunter Scrapbooks, Box 15, Folder 3, Charles N. Hunter Papers.

91. Mt. Lebanon was reportedly overflowing, as "crowds swarmed in the streets in front of the church." Emancipation Day festivities also included a massive parade that featured a 24-piece band from Norfolk. The parade was an "orderly procession, well marshaled and thoroughly dignified." See "Bickett Talked to Negroes Here," *The Independent*, 11 April 1919, in "Emancipation," *Tuskegee Institute News Clipping File*, Reel 240, Frame 878.

92. Haley, *Charles N. Hunter and Race Relations in North Carolina*, 247; and *News & Observer* (Raleigh), 27 October 1921.

93. Crow, Escott, and Hatley, "Black Life in the Age of Jim Crow," 134.

94. "Talk That Keeps Alive Old Emphasis on Negro Slavery," *Raleigh Times*, 4 January 1927, in "Emancipation," *Tuskegee Institute News Clipping File*, Reel 240, Frame 916.

95. Crow, Escott, and Hatley, "Black Life in the Age of Jim Crow," 134.

96. Hunter to the editor of Norfolk *Virginia Pilot*, 30 March 1921, in Correspondence Files, Box 6, Charles N. Hunter Papers. Also see Haley, *Charles N. Hunter and Race Relations in North Carolina*, 228–229.

97. Haley, *Charles N. Hunter and Race Relations in North Carolina*, 282.

98. "Wants Negro to Drop Isolation," *Macon News*, 3 January 1928, Reel 240, Frame 924; and "Demands Place for Negro Race in Government," *Raleigh Times*, 3 January 1927, Reel 240, Frame 915, both in "Emancipation," *Tuskegee Institute News Clipping File*.

99. "Demands Place for Negro Race in Government," *Raleigh Times*, 3 January 1927, Reel 240, Frame 915.

100. "Emancipation Act Did Not Free Negroes, Says Pastor," *News & Observer* (Raleigh), 3 January 1928.

101. Haley, *Charles N. Hunter and Race Relations in North Carolina*, 214–215.

102. "The Negroes of Raleigh Repudiate the Proclamation of Emancipation?" *Norfolk Journal and Guide*, 17 March 1928, Charles N. Hunter Scrapbooks, Box 15, Folder 4, Charles N. Hunter Papers.

103. See "Emancipation Day Service Attended by Large Number: Many White People Attend Service at American Theatre," 2 January 1928 in "Emancipation," *Tuskegee Institute News Clipping File*, Reel 240, Frame 920. See also "Emancipation Day Dinner for Slaves: Interesting Feature of 60th Annual Celebration of Lincoln Proclamation," *News & Observer* (Raleigh), 2 January 1924. The celebration combined the singing of the Negro National Anthem and the honoring of more than fifty former slave men and women in Wake County.

104. "Celebrating the Emancipation Proclamation," in "Emancipation," *Tuskegee Institute News Clipping File*, Reel 240, Frame 841.

105. "Emancipation Act Did Not Free Negroes," *News & Observer* (Raleigh), 3 January 1928.

106. Hunter's racial philosophy continues to evoke discomfort from some modern scholars. Historian Walter B. Weare, for example, described as "pathetic" Hunter's efforts to resurrect white support for the North Carolina Industrial Association and the state fair just prior to his death in 1931. See Weare, "New Negroes for a New Century," 104.

107. Ibid. See also "Negroes Get Sum for Civic Fairs: No Negro State Fair This Year, But Four Community Fairs Are to Be Staged," *News & Observer* (Raleigh), 8 September 1926, Charles N. Hunter Scrapbooks, Box 15, Folder 3, Charles N.

Hunter Papers; and Haley, *Charles N. Hunter and Race Relations in North Carolina*, 280–283.

Conclusion

1. Williams, "The Woman's Part in a Man's Business," 544–545. This sentiment was voiced much earlier by Robert Purvis, son-in-law of black abolitionist James Forten, Sr. Purvis stated that "the relation is perfectly reciprocal. God has given to both man and women the same intellectual capacities, and made them subject to the same moral argument." See Giddings, *When and Where I Enter*, 59.

2. "The Useful Man or Woman," in John M. Avery Scrapbook. See also "John Moses Avery: A Biographical Sketch," *Whetstone*, 1951; and "John Moses Avery," *The Mutual* (November 1923), both in John M. Avery Scrapbook, Series 8, Folder 347, William Kennedy Jr. Papers, Southern Historical Collection. Avery's life narrative has at its center the racial ideology of self-help. Avery is cast as the "self-made man" who used determination and the help of good Samaritans to attend Kittrell College in North Carolina. Quickly realizing that "life without a wife" was a mere existence, he married Lula Aiken, also a Kittrell College graduate, in April 1903 in Reidsville, North Carolina. The couple operated Waters' Academy in the mountain village of Adako. His wife, whom he respectfully called Partner, cooked for the boarding students, taught classes, served as matron, and fulfilled all other duties necessary for the operation of the academy.

3. Young, *Black Writers of the Thirties*.

Bibliography

Archival Material

Unpublished

Buncombe County Public Library, Asheville, N.C.
 Young Men's Institute (YMI) Clipping File
D. H. Ramsey Library Special Collections, University of North Carolina at Asheville
 Asheville YWCA Archive
 Heritage of Black Highlanders Collection
 Southern Highlands Research Center Oral History Collection
Louis Round Wilson Library, University of North Carolina, Chapel Hill, North Carolina
 North Carolina Collection
 Negroes in North Carolina. Biographical clipping file, 4 vols.
 Southern Historical Collection, Wilson Library, University of North Carolina, Chapel Hill, North Carolina
 John M. Avery Scrapbook
 William J. Kennedy Jr. Papers
 George Clayton Shaw Papers (unpublished microfilm)
Pack Memorial Library, Asheville, North Carolina
 Pack Vertical File
Rare Books, Manuscripts, and Special Collections Library, Duke University, Durham, North Carolina
 Behind the Veil Oral History Collection
 Charles N. Hunter Papers
 William G. Pearson Papers
 C. C. Spaulding Papers
Richard B. Harrison Public Library, Raleigh, N.C.
 Mollie Lee Collection
Robinson-Spangler Carolina Room, Charlotte Public Library, Charlotte, N.C.
 Charlotte Young Women's Christian Association File

Privately Held

M. T. Pope Papers, in possession of Kenneth Zogry

Proceedings of the Most Worshipful Grand Lodge of North Carolina (1897–1933), headquarters of the Most Worshipful Grand Lodge of North Carolina, Durham, N.C.

Oral Histories

R. Kelley Bryant, interviewed by Paul Ortiz, Durham, N.C., 12/7/94, 2/20/95, and 3/28/96. Behind the Veil: Documenting African-American Life in the Jim Crow South, Center for Documentary Studies at Duke University, Rare Book, Manuscript, and Special Collections Library, Duke University.

York Garrett, interviewed by Kara Miles, Durham, N.C., 6/3/93. Behind the Veil: Documenting African-American Life in the Jim Crow South, Center for Documentary Studies at Duke University, Rare Book, Manuscript, and Special Collections Library, Duke University.

Henry M. Houston, Charlotte, North Carolina, 29 August 1939. WPA Life Histories Collection Project, available at http://www.cmstory.org/aaa2/places/brook_010.htm.

Mr. and Mrs. (Magnolia Thompson) Ernest McKissick, Asheville, North Carolina, 2 August 1977. Interviewed by Dr. Louis D. Silveri. In Southern Highlands Research Center Oral History Collection.

Published Microfilm

African-American Baptist Annual Reports, North Carolina, 1865–1990. Rochester, N.Y.: American Baptist–Samuel Colgate Historical Library, 1997.

Charlotte Hawkins Brown Papers. Cambridge, Mass.: Schlesinger Library, Radcliffe College, 1992.

Claude A. Barnett Papers. Part 1. *Associated Negro Press News Releases, 1928–1964*. Chicago: Chicago Historical Society, 1986.

Tuskegee Institute News Clipping File, 1899–1966. Sanford, N.C.: Microfilming Corporation of America, 1976.

Newspapers and Magazines Consulted

AME Zion Quarterly Review (Salisbury, N.C.), 1899–1900

Asheville Citizen and *Citizen-Times* (Asheville, N.C.), 1890–1928, 1930–1977, 1983–2002

Carolina Times (Durham, N.C.), 1929

Charlotte Observer (Charlotte, N.C.), 1900

Durham Herald (Durham, N.C.), 1930

Greensboro Daily News (Greensboro, N.C.), 1924–1925

Independent (New York, N.Y.), 1919

The Messenger (Charlotte, N.C.), 1883
The Messenger (New York, N.Y.), 1927
Morning Post (Raleigh, N.C.), 1900
The Mutual (Durham, N.C.), 1923
News & Observer (Raleigh, N.C.), 1900–1930
Norfolk Journal and Guide (Norfolk, Va.), 1915–1928
Opportunity (New York), 1923
Shaw University Journal (Raleigh, N.C.), 1928
Southern Workman (Hampton, Va.), 1906–1929
Star of Zion (Charlotte, N.C.), 1900–1906, 1920
Times (Raleigh, N.C.), 1913, 1915–1917, 1927
Voice of the Negro (Atlanta, Ga.), 1904–1906
Washington Post (Washington, D.C.), 1986
Whetstone (Durham, N.C.), 1951

Published Primary Sources

Asheville City Directory. Asheville, N.C.: Piedmont Directory Co., 1905–1906.
Boyer, Marie Louise. *Early Days: All Souls' Church and Biltmore Village*. Asheville, N.C.: Biltmore, 1933.
Brinton, Hugh P. "The Negro in Durham: A Study of Adjustment to Town Life." Ph.D. diss., University of North Carolina, Chapel Hill, 1930.
Brown, Charlotte Hawkins. *The Correct Thing, to Do, to Say, to Wear*. Boston: Christopher Publishing House.
Brown, Sue M. Wilson *The History of the Order of the Eastern Star among Colored People*. Des Moines, Iowa: The Bystander Press, 1924.
Bruce, John Edward. *Prince Hall, the Pioneer of Negro Masonry*. New York, 1921. Electronic edition: Chapel Hill: Academic Affairs Library, University of North Carolina, Chapel Hill. Available at http://docsouth.unc.edu/neh/bruceje/bruceje.html.
Caldwell, A. B., ed. *History of the American Negro: North Carolina Edition*. Atlanta, Ga. A. B. Caldwell, 1921.
Dancy, John C. "How to Save Our Youth." In *The United Negro: His Problems and His Progress*, ed. I. Garland Penn and J. W. E. Bowen. Atlanta, Ga.: D. E. Luther Publishing, 1902.
Du Bois, W. E. B. *The Philadelphia Negro: A Social Study*. 1899; reprint, Philadelphia, Pa.: Benjamin Bloom, 1967.
Floyd, Silas X. *Floyd's Flowers, or Duty and Beauty for Colored Children*. Washington, D.C.: Hertel, Jenkins, 1905.
Forbush, William Byron. *The Boy Problem*. 6th ed. Boston: Pilgrim Press, 1907.
Ford, Silas. "Duty of the Church to the Young Man." In *The United Negro: His Prob-*

lems and His Progress, ed. I. Garland Penn and J. W. E. Bowen. Atlanta, Ga.: D. E. Luther Publishing, 1902.

Gibson, J. W. and W. H. Crogman, eds. Progress of a Race, or the Remarkable Advancement of the American Negro, from the Bondage of Slavery, Ignorance, and poverty to the Freedom of Citizenship, Intelligence, Affluence, Honor and Trust. Naperville, Ill.: J. L. Nichols & Co., 1929.

Harris, Eugene. Two Sermons on the Race Problem Addressed to Young Colored Men, by One of Them. Nashville, Tenn.: University Press, 1895.

Harris, Fenton H. Short History and Report of Young Men's Institute. Asheville, N.C.: YMI, 1937.

Moton, Robert R. "Signs of Growing Cooperation," Southern Workman (October 1914): 552–559.

Neely, Thomas B. "Men and the Church." In The United Negro: His Problems and His Progress, ed. I. Garland Penn and J. W. E. Bowen. Atlanta, Ga.: D. E. Luther Publishing, 1902.

Odum, Howard. Social and Mental Traits of the Negro: Research into the Conditions of the Negro in Southern Towns. New York: Columbia University Press, 1910.

Penn, Mrs. Garland. "How Can Mothers Teach Their Daughters and Sons Social Purity." In The United Negro: His Problems and His Progress, ed. I. Garland Penn and J. W. E. Bowen. Atlanta, Ga.: D. E. Luther Publishing, 1902.

Proceedings of the Twenty-Eighth Annual Communication of the Most Worshipful Grand Lodge of North Carolina, Free and Accepted Ancient Masons, Wilson, N.C., December 14–17. Goldsboro, N.C.: Nash Bros., Printers and Binders, 1897.

Ramsey, D. Hiden. "A Neglected Phase of the Negro Question." Southern Workman (December 1914).

Thomas, William Hannibal. The American Negro: What He Was, What He Is, and What He May Become: A Critical and Practical Discussion. New York: Negro Universities Press, 1901.

Watson, C. H. Colored Charlotte. Charlotte, N.C.: A.M.E. Zion Job Print, 1915.

White, Walter Francis. Rope and Faggot: A Biography of Judge Lynch. 1929. Reprint, New York: Arno Press, 1978.

Whitted, J. A. A History of the Negro Baptists of North Carolina. Raleigh, N.C.: Edwards & Broughton, 1908.

———. "The Duty of the Church to the Young." In The United Negro: His Problems and His Progress, ed. I. Garland Penn and J. W. E. Bowen. Atlanta, Ga.: D. E. Luther Publishing, 1902.

Williams, Fannie Barrier. "The Woman's Part in a Man's Business." Voice of the Negro (November 1904): 544–545.

Williams, M. W., and George W. Watkins. Who's Who among North Carolina Baptists, with a Brief History of Negro Baptist Organizations. N.p.: N.p., 1940.

Wolfe, Thomas. *Look Homeward Angel: A Story of the Buried Life.* New York: Charles Scribner's Sons, 1957.

Work, Monroe N. "Secret Societies as Factors in the Social and Economical Life of the Negro." In *Democracy in Earnest*, ed. James E. McCulloch. Washington, D.C.: Southern Sociological Congress, 1918.

Wright, R. R., Jr. "Forty Years of Negro Progress." *Southern Workman* (May 1908).

Secondary Sources

Alexander, Ruth. *The "Girl Problem": Female Sexual Delinquency in New York, 1900–1930.* Ithaca, N.Y.: Cornell University Press, 1995.

Anderson, Eric. *Race and Politics in North Carolina, 1872–1901: The Black Second.* Baton Rouge: Louisiana State University Press, 1981.

Anderson, James D. *The Education of Blacks in the South, 1860–1935.* Chapel Hill: University of North Carolina Press, 1988.

Awkward, Michael. "Black Male Trouble: The Challenges for Rethinking Masculine Differences." In *Masculinity Studies and Feminist Theory: New Directions*, ed. Judith Kegan Gardiner. New York: Columbia University Press, 2002.

Ayers, Edward. *The Promise of the New South: Life after Reconstruction.* Oxford: Oxford University Press, 1992.

Baker, Paula. "The Domestication of Politics: Women and Political Society, 1780–1920." *American Historical Review* 89 (1984): 620–647.

Bazemore, Corey David. "The Freemasonry of the Race": The Cultural Politics of Ritual, Race, and Place in Postemancipation Virginia." Ph.D. diss., College of William and Mary, 2001.

Bederman, Gail. "The Decline of Middle-Class Manliness and Ida B. Wells's Anti-Lynching Campaign (1892–94)." In *Gender and American History since 1890*, ed. Barbara Melosh. New York: Routledge, 1993.

———. *Manliness and Civilization: A Cultural History of Gender and Race in the United States, 1880–1917.* Chicago: University of Chicago Press, 1995.

———. "'The Women Have Had Charge of the Church Work Long Enough': The Men and Religious Forward Movement of 1911–12 and the Masculinization of Middle Class Protestantism." *American Quarterly* 41 (September 1989): 432–461.

Bell, Hazel Ruth. "Why Adults Attend Sunday School in Southern Baptist Churches." Ph.D. diss., University of Oklahoma, 1988.

Belton, Don., ed. *Speak My Name: Black Men on Masculinity and the American Dream.* New York: Beacon Press, 1995.

Bercaw, Nancy. *Gendered Freedoms: Race, Rights and the Politics of Household in the Delta, 1861–1875.* Gainesville: University Press of Florida, 2003.

The Black Public Sphere Collective, ed. *The Black Public Sphere: A Public Culture Book*. Chicago: University of Chicago Press Journals, 1995.

Black, Daniel P. *Dismantling Black Manhood: An Historical and Literary Analysis of the Legacy of Slavery*. New York: Garland Publishing, Inc., 1997.

Blassingame, John W. *The Slave Community: Plantation Life in the Antebellum South*. New York: Oxford University Press, 1972.

Blight, David. *Race and Reunion: The Civil War in American Memory*. Cambridge: Harvard University Press, 2001.

Boydston, Jeanne. *Home & Work: Housework, Wages, and the Ideology of Labor in the Early Republic*. New York: Oxford University Press, 1990.

Brawley, Benjamin. *Negro Builders and Heroes*. Chapel Hill: University of North Carolina Press, 1937.

Brian, Philip. *Are We Not Men? Masculine Anxiety and the Problem of African-American Identity*. Oxford: Oxford University Press, 1998.

Brown, Elsa Barkley. "Negotiating and Transforming the Public Sphere: African American Political Life in the Transition from Slavery to Freedom." *Public Culture* 7, no. 1 (Fall 1994): 107–146.

———. "Uncle Ned's Children: Negotiating Community and Freedom in Post-emancipation Richmond, Virginia." Ph.D. diss., Kent State University, 1994.

———. "Womanist Consciousness: Maggie Lena Walker and the Independent Order of St. Luke." *Signs* 14 (Spring 1989): 610–633.

Brown, Elsa Barkley, and Greg Kimball. "Mapping the Terrain of Black Richmond." *Journal of Urban History* 21 (March 1993): 296–346.

Buggs, Patricia. "The Negro in Charlotte: North Carolina as Reflected in the *Charlotte Observer* and Related Sources, 1900–1910." M.A. thesis, Atlanta University, 1976.

Bullock, Steven C. *Revolutionary Brotherhood: Freemasonry and the Transformation of the American Social Order, 1730–1840*. Chapel Hill: University of North Carolina Press, 1996.

Bynum, Carolyn. *Gender and Religion: On the Complexity of Symbols*. Boston: Beacon Press, 1986.

Campbell, Gavin. *Music and the Making of a New South*. Chapel Hill: University of North Carolina Press, 2004.

Carbado, Devon, ed. *Black Men on Race, Gender, and Sexuality: A Critical Reader*. New York: New York University Press, 1999.

Carby, Hazel. "Policing the Black Woman's Body in an Urban Context." *Critical Inquiry* 18 (Summer 1992): 738–755.

———. *Race Men*. Cambridge: Harvard University Press, 1998.

Cecelski, David S., and Timothy B. Tyson. *Democracy Betrayed: The Wilmington*

Race Riot of 1898 and Its Legacy. Chapel Hill: University of North Carolina Press, 1998.

Chafe, William, Raymond Gavins, Robert Korstad, and the Behind the Veil Project, eds. *Remembering Jim Crow: African Americans Tell about Life in the Segregated South*. New York: New Press, 2001.

Chafe, William. *Civilities and Civil Rights: Greensboro, North Carolina, and the Black Struggle for Freedom*. New York: Oxford University Press, 1980.

Clark, Kathleen. "Celebrating Freedom: Emancipation Day Ceremonies and African-American Memory in the Early Reconstruction South." In *Where These Memories Grow: History, Memory, and Southern Identity*, ed. W. Fitzhugh Brundage. Chapel Hill: University of North Carolina Press, 2000.

———. *Defining Moments: African-American Commemoration and Political Culture in the South, 1863–1913*. Chapel Hill: University of North Carolina Press, 2005.

Clawson, Mary Ann. *Constructing Brotherhood: Class, Gender, and Fraternalism*. Princeton, N.J.: Princeton University Press, 1989.

Connor, R. D. W., and Clarence Hamilton Poe. *The Life and Speeches of Charles Brantley Aycock*. Garden City, N.Y.: Doubleday, Page & Co., 1912.

Cott, Nancy. *The Bonds of Womanhood: "Woman's Sphere" in New England, 1780–1835*. New Haven, Conn.: Yale University Press, 1977.

Crow, Jeffrey J., Paul D. Escott, and Flora J. Hatley. "Black Life in the Age of Jim Crow." In *Black Americans in North Carolina and the South*, ed. Jeffrey J. Crow and Flora J. Hatley. Chapel Hill: University of North Carolina Press, 1984.

Davis, Harry. *A History of Freemasonry among Negroes in America*. N.p. 1946.

Davis, Lenwood. *The Black Heritage of Western North Carolina*. Asheville: University of North Carolina at Asheville, 1986.

Davis, Thadious. "Expanding the Limits: The Intersection of Race and Region." *Southern Literary Journal* 20 (Spring 1988): 3–11.

Dodson, Jualynne. *Engendering Church: Women, Power, and the AME Church*. Lanham, Md.: Rowman & Littlefield Inc., 2002.

———. "Nineteenth Century A.M.E. Preaching Women: Cutting Edge of Women's Inclusion in Church Polity." In *Women in New Worlds*, vol.1, ed. Hilah F. Thomas and Rosemary Skinner Keller. Nashville, Tenn.: Abingdon Press, 1981.

Dray, Philip. *At the Hands of Persons Unknown: The Lynching of Black America*. New York: Modern Library, 2003.

Edmonds, Helen G. *The Negro and Fusion Politics in North Carolina, 1894–1901*. Chapel Hill: University of North Carolina Press, 1951.

Edwards, Laura F. *Gendered Strife and Confusion: The Political Culture of Reconstruction*. Urbana: University of Illinois Press, 1997.

Escott, Paul. *Many Excellent People: Power and Privilege in North Carolina, 1850–1900*. Chapel Hill: University of North Carolina Press, 1985.

Fahey, David. *The Black Lodge in White America: "True Reformer Brown" and His Economic Strategy*. Dayton, Ohio: Wright State University Press, 1994.

Fairclough, Adam. "'Being in the Field of Education and Also Being a Negro . . . Seems . . . Tragic': Black Teachers in the Jim Crow South." *Journal of American History* 87, no. 1 (2000): 65–91.

Feimster, Crystal. "'Ladies and Lynching': The Gendered Discourse of Mob Violence in the New South, 1880–1930." Ph.D. diss., Princeton University, 2000.

Felski, Rita. *Beyond Feminist Aesthetics: Feminist Literature and Social Change*. Cambridge: Harvard University Press, 1989.

Ferguson, Roderick. "African American Masculinity and the Study of Social Formations." *American Quarterly* 58, no. 1 (2006): 213–219.

Ferrell, Claudine L. *Nightmare and Dream: Anti-Lynching in Congress, 1917–1922*. New York: Garland Publishing, 1986.

Filene, Peter G. *Him/Her/Self: Sex Roles in Modern America*. Baltimore, Md.: Johns Hopkins University Press, 1986.

Fogel, Robert, and Stanley Engerman, *Time on the Cross: The Economics of American Negro Slavery*. Boston: Little, Brown, 1974.

Fox-Genovese, Elizabeth. *Within the Plantation Household: Black and White Women of the Old South*. Chapel Hill: University of North Carolina Press, 1988.

Frankel, Noralee, and Nancy S. Dye, eds. *Gender, Class, Race, and Reform in the Progressive Era*. Lexington: University of Kentucky Press, 1991.

Franklin, Jimmie. "Black Southerners, Shared Experience, and Place: A Reflection." *Journal of Southern History* 60 (February 1994): 3–18.

Franklin, John Hope. *From Slavery to Freedom: A History of Negro Americans*. 3rd ed. New York: Knopf, 1967.

Fraser, Nancy. "Rethinking the Public Sphere: A Contribution to the Critique of Actually Existing Democracy." In *Habermas and the Public Sphere*, ed. Craig Calhoun. Cambridge, Mass.: MIT Press, 1992.

Frederickson, Mary. "'Each One Is Dependent on the Other': Southern Churchwomen, Racial Reform, and the Process of Transformation, 1880–1940." In *Visible Women: New Essays on American Activism*, ed. Nancy Hewitt and Suzanne Lebsock. Urbana: University of Illinois Press, 1993.

Freedman, Estelle. "Separatism as Strategy: Female Institution Building and American Feminism, 1870–1930." *Feminist Studies* 5, no. 3 (Fall 1979): 512–529.

Friend, Craig Thompson and Lorri Glover, eds. *Southern Manhood: Perspectives on Masculinity in the Old South*. Athens: University of Georgia Press, 2004.

Gaines, Kevin. "Black Americans' Racial Uplift Ideology as 'Civilizing Mission': Pauline E. Hopkins on Race and Imperialism." In *Cultures of United States Imperial-*

ism, ed. Amy Kaplan and Donald E. Pease. Durham, N.C.: Duke University Press, 1994.

———. *Uplifting the Race: Black Leadership, Politics, and Culture in the Twentieth Century*. Chapel Hill: University of North Carolina Press, 1996.

Gaston, Paul M. *The New South Creed: A Study in Southern Mythmaking*. New York: Knopf, 1970.

Gavins, Raymond. "The NAACP in the Age of Segregation." In *New Directions in Civil Rights Studies*, ed. Armstead L. Robinson and Patricia Sullivan. Charlottesville: University Press of Virginia, 1991.

Gibbs, Jewelle. "Young Black Males in America: Endangered, Embittered, and Embattled." In *Men's Lives*, ed. Michael Kimmel and Michael Messner. New York: Macmillan/Maxwell, 1991.

Giddings, Paula. *When and Where I Enter: The Impact of Black Women on Race and Sex in America*. New York: Quill, 1984.

Gilkes, Cheryl Townsend. "The Politics of 'Silence': Dual-Sex Political Systems and Women's Traditions of Conflict in African-American Religion." In *African-American Christianity: Essays in History*, ed. Paul E. Johnson. Berkeley: University of California Press, 1994.

———. "Something Within: Social Change and Collective Endurance in the Sacred World of Black Christian Women." In *Women and Religion in America, 1900–68*, vol. 3, ed. Rosemary Ruether and Rosemary S. Keller. San Francisco: Harper and Row, 1986.

Gilmore, Glenda. *Gender and Jim Crow: Women and the Politics of White Supremacy in North Carolina, 1896–1920*. Chapel Hill: University of North Carolina Press, 1996.

Greenwood, Janette Thomas. *Bittersweet Legacy: The Black and White "Better Classes" in Charlotte, 1850–1910*. Chapel Hill: University of North Carolina Press, 1994.

Gregory, James. *Southern Diaspora: How the Great Migrations of Black and White Southerners Transformed America*. Chapel Hill: University of North Carolina Press, 2007.

Grimshaw, William. *Official History of Freemasonry among the Colored People of North America*. 1903; Reprint, New York: Negro Universities Press, 1969.

Gutman, Herbert. *The Black Family in Slavery and Freedom, 1750–1925*. New York: Pantheon Books, 1976.

Guy-Sheftall, Beverly. *Daughters of Sorrow: Attitudes toward African-American Women, 1880–1920*. Brooklyn: Carlson Publishing, Inc., 1990.

Habermas, Jurgen. *The Structural Transformation of the Public Sphere: An Inquiry into a Category of Bourgeois Society*. Cambridge, Mass.: MIT Press, 1962.

Hackett, David. "The Prince Hall Masons and the African American Church: The

Labors of Grand Master and Bishop James Walker Hood, 1831–1918." *The American Society of Church History* 69 (December 2000): 770–802.

Hahn, Steven. *A Nation under Our Feet: Black Political Struggles in the Rural South from Slavery to the Great Migration.* Cambridge, Mass.: Harvard University Press, 2003.

Haley, John. *Charles N. Hunter and Race Relations in North Carolina.* Chapel Hill: University of North Carolina Press, 1987.

Hall, Jacquelyn Dowd. "Private Eyes, Public Women: Images of Class and Sex in the Urban South, Atlanta, Georgia, 1913–15." *Atlanta History* 36 (Winter 1993): 24–39.

———. *Revolt against Chivalry: Jessie Daniel Ames and the Women's Campaign against Lynching.* New York: Columbia University Press, 1993.

Harley, Sharon, and Rosalyn Terborg-Penn, eds. *The Afro-American Woman: Struggles and Images.* Port Washington, N.Y.: Kennikat Press, 1978.

Harper, Philip Brian. *Are We Not Men? Masculine Anxiety and the Problem of African-American Identity.* New York: Oxford University Press, 1996.

Harvey, Paul. *Redeeming the South: Religious Cultures and Racial Identities among Southern Baptists, 1865–1925.* Chapel Hill: University of North Carolina Press, 1997.

Henry, Philip, and Carol Speas, eds. *The Heritage of Blacks in North Carolina.* Vol. 1. Raleigh: North Carolina African-American Heritage Foundation, 1990.

Higginbotham, Evelyn Brooks. "Beyond the Sound of Silence: Afro-American Women in History." *Gender & History* 1 (Spring 1989): 50–67.

———. "The Feminist Theology of the Black Baptist Church, 1880–1900." In *Religion and American Culture: A Reader,* ed. David G. Gillard and David G. Hackett. New York: Routledge, 2003.

———. *Righteous Discontent: The Women's Movement in the Black Baptist Church, 1880–1920.* Cambridge, Mass.: Harvard University Press, 1993.

Hine, Darlene Clark, and Earnestine Jenkins, eds. *A Question of Manhood: A Reader in U.S. Black Men's History.* Bloomington: Indiana University Press, 1999.

Horton, James Oliver. *Free People of Color: Inside the African American Community.* Washington, D.C.: Smithsonian Institute, 1993.

Hunter, Andrea, and James Earl Davis. "Constructing Gender: An Exploration of Afro-American Men's Conceptualization of Manhood." *Gender and Society* 6 (September 1992): 464–479.

———. "Hidden Voices of Black Men: The Meaning, Structure, and Complexity of Manhood." *Journal of Black Studies* 25 (September 1994): 20–40.

Hunter, Tera. "The Correct Thing: Charlotte Hawkins Brown and the Palmer Institute." *Southern Exposure* (September/October 1983): 37–43.

————. *To 'Joy My Freedom: Southern Black Women's Lives and Labors after the Civil War*. Cambridge, Mass.: Harvard University Press, 1997.

Hutchinson, George. *The Harlem Renaissance in Black and White*. Cambridge, Mass.: Harvard University Press, 1995.

Jackson, Jerma. *Singing in My Soul: Black Gospel Music in a Secular Age*. Chapel Hill: University of North Carolina Press, 2004.

Janiewski, Dolores. "Seeking 'a New Day and a New Way': Black Women and Unions in the Southern Tobacco Industry." In *"To Toil the Livelong Day": America's Women at Work, 1780–1980*, ed. Carol Groneman and Mary Beth Norton. Ithaca, N.Y.: Cornell University Press, 1987.

Johnson, Joan Marie. *Southern Ladies, New Women: Race: Region, and Clubwomen in South Carolina, 1890–1930*. Gainesville: University Press of Florida, 2004.

Jones, Jacqueline. *Labor of Love, Labor of Sorrow: Black Women, Work and the Family from Slavery to the Present*. New York: Basic Books, 1985.

Kachun, Mitch. *Festivals of Freedom: Memory and Meaning in African American Emancipation Celebrations, 1808–1915* Amherst: University of Massachusetts Press, 2003.

Kantrowitz, Stephen. *Ben Tillman and the Reconstruction of White Supremacy*. Chapel Hill: University of North Carolina Press, 2000.

Kasson, John F. *Amusing the Millions: Coney Island at the Turn of the Century*. New York: Hill and Wang, 1978.

Kenzer, Robert. *Enterprising Southerners: Black Economic Success in North Carolina, 1865–1915*. Charlottesville: University Press of Virginia, 1997.

Key, V. O. *Southern Politics in State and Nation*. New York: Vintage Books, 1949.

Kimmel, Michael. *Manhood in America: A Cultural History*. New York: The Free Press, 1966.

Knoff, Gerald E. *The World Sunday School Movement: The Story of a Broadening Mission*. New York: Seabury Press, 1979

Kunjufu, Jawanza. *Countering the Conspiracy to Destroy Black Boys*. Chicago: University of Chicago Press, 1983.

Kunzel, Regina. *Fallen Women, Problem Girls: Unmarried Mothers and the Professionalization of Social Work, 1890–1945*. New Haven, Conn.: Yale University Press, 1993.

Landry, Bart. *The New Black Middle Class*. Berkeley: University of California Press, 1987.

Laqueur, Thomas Walter. *Religion and Respectability: Sunday Schools and Working Class Culture, 1780–1850*. New Haven, Conn.: Yale University Press, 1976.

Levine, Lawrence. *Black Culture and Black Consciousness: Afro-American Folk Thought from Slavery to Freedom*. New York: Oxford University Press, 1977.

Lewis, Earl. *In Their Own Interests: Race, Class, and Power in Twentieth-Century Norfolk, Virginia*. Berkeley: University of California Press, 1991.

———. "Invoking Concepts, Problematizing Identities: The Life of Charles N. Hunter and the Implications for the Study of Gender and Labor." *Labor History* 34 (Spring/Summer 1993): 292–308.

Leyburn, James G. *The Way We Lived: Durham, 1900–1920*. Eliston, Va.: Northcross House Publishers, 1989.

Lindquist, Malinda. "The Gender of Racial Science: Modern Black Manhood and Its Making, 1890–2000." Ph.D. diss., Princeton University, 2004.

Litwack, Leon. *Trouble in Mind: Black Southerners in the Age of Jim Crow*. New York: Knopf, 1998.

Macleod, David I. *Building Character in the American Boy: The Boy Scouts, YMCA, and Their Forerunners, 1870–1920*. Madison: University of Wisconsin Press, 1983.

Maffly-Kipp, Laurie. "Mapping the World, Mapping the Race: The Negro Race History, 1874–1915." *Church History* 64 (December 1995): 610–626.

Majors, Richard, and Janet Billson. *Cool Pose: The Dilemmas of Black Manhood in America*. New York: Touchstone, 1992.

Marby, William. *The Negro in North Carolina Politics since Reconstruction*. Durham, N.C.: Duke University Press, 1940.

Martin, Sandy Dwayne. *For God and Race: The Religious and Political Leadership of A.M.E.Z. Bishop James Walker Hood*. Columbia: University of South Carolina Press, 1999.

McGerr, Michael. "Political Style and Women's Power, 1830–1930." *Journal of American History* 77 (December 1990): 864–885.

McMillen, Sally G. *To Raise Up the South: Sunday Schools in Black and White Churches, 1865–1915*. Baton Rouge: Louisiana State University Press, 2001.

Meier, August, and Elliot Rudwick. "The Boycott Movement against Jim Crow Streetcars in the South, 1900–1906." *Journal of American History* 55 (March 1969): 756–775.

Mitchell, Michele. "The Black Man's Burden: African Americans, Imperialism, and Notions of Racial Manhood 1890–1910." *International Review of Social History* 44 Supplement 7 (1999): 77–99.

———. *Righteous Propagation: African Americans and the Politics of Racial Destiny after Reconstruction*. Chapel Hill: University of North Carolina Press, 2004.

Mjagkij, Nina. *Light in the Darkness: African Americans and the YMCA, 1852–1946*. Lexington: University Press of Kentucky, 1994.

———. "True Manhood: The YMCA and Racial Advancement, 1890–1930." In *Men and Women Adrift: The YMCA and the YWCA in the City*, ed. Nina Mjagkij and Margaret Spratt. New York: New York University Press, 1997.

———. "Young Men's Christian Association, Colored Department." In *Organizing*

Black America: An Encyclopedia of African-American Associations, ed. Nina Mjagkij. New York: Garland Publishing Co., 2001.

Montgomery, William E. *Under Their Own Vine and Fig Tree: The African-American Church in the South, 1865–1900*. Baton Rouge: Louisiana State University Press, 1993.

Moore, Jacqueline M. *Leading the Race: The Transformation of the Black Elite in the Nation's Capital, 1880–1920*. Charlottesville and London: University of Virginia Press, 1999.

Moose, Walter J. "Sunday School Work as Promoted by the Baptist State Convention of North Carolina, 1830–1930." M.A. thesis, Wake Forest College, 1930.

Moseley-Edington, Helen. *Angels Unaware: Asheville Women of Color*. Asheville, N.C.: Home Press, 1996.

Moses, Wilson J. *Alexander Crummell: A Study of Civilization and Discontent*. New York: Oxford University Press, 1989.

Mossell, N. F. *The Work of the Afro-American Woman*. New York: Oxford University Press, 1988.

Muraskin, William. *Middle-Class Blacks in a White Society*. Berkeley: University of California Press, 1975.

Nash, Gary B. *Forging Freedom: The Formation of Philadelphia's Black Community*. Cambridge, Mass.: Harvard University Press, 1988.

Neverdon-Morton, Cynthia. *Afro-American Women of the South and the Advancement of the Race, 1895–1925*. Knoxville: The University of Tennessee Press, 1989.

———. "The Black Woman's Struggle for Equality in the South, 1895–1925." In *The Afro-American Woman: Struggles and Images*, ed. Sharon Harley and Rosalyn Terborg-Penn. Port Washington, N.Y.: Kennikat Press, 1978.

Newby, I. A. *In Jim Crow's Defense: Anti-Negro Thought in America, 1900–1930*. Baton Rouge: Louisiana State University Press, 1965.

Nimmons, Julius F. "Social Reform and Moral Uplift in the Black Community, 1890–1910: Social Settlements, Temperance, and Social Purity." Ph.D. diss., Howard University, 1981.

Odem, Mary. *Delinquent Daughters: Protecting and Policing Adolescent Female Sexuality in the United States, 1885–1920*. Chapel Hill: University of North Carolina Press, 1995

Packard, Jerrold M. *American Nightmare: The History of Jim Crow*. New York: St. Martin's Press, 2002.

Painter, Nell Irvin. "'The South' and 'The Negro': The Rhetoric of Race Relations and Real Life." In *The South for Southerners*, ed. Paul D. Escott and David Goldfield. Chapel Hill: University of North Carolina Press, 1991.

Palmer, Edward. "Negro Secret Societies." *Social Forces* 23 (December 1944): 207–212.

Parker, Inez Moore, and Helen Vassy Callison. *The Biddle-Johnson C. Smith University Story*. Charlotte, N.C.: Charlotte Publishing, 1975.

Payne, Charles. *I've Got the Light of Freedom: The Organizing Tradition and the Mississippi Freedom Struggle*. Berkeley: University of California Press, 1995.

Prather, Henry Leon. *We Have Taken a City: Wilmington Racial Massacre and Coup of 1898*. Rutherford, N.J.: Associated Universities Press, 1984.

Rabinowitz, Howard. "A Comparative Perspective on Race Relations in Southern and Northern Cities, 1860–1900, with Special Emphasis on Raleigh." In *Black Americans in North Carolina*, ed. Jeffrey Crow and Flora Hatley. Chapel Hill: University of North Carolina Press, 1984.

Raper, Arthur F. *The Tragedy of Lynching*. Chapel Hill: University of North Carolina Press, 1933.

Rolinson, Mary. *Grassroots Garveyism: The Universal Negro Improvement Association in the Rural South, 1920–1927*. Chapel Hill: University of North Carolina Press, 2007.

Rosen, Hannah. "The Gender of Reconstruction: Rape, Race and Citizenship in the Post-Emancipation South." Ph.D. diss., University of Chicago, 1999.

Rotundo, Anthony. *American Manhood: Transformations in Masculinity from the Revolution to the Modern Era*. New York: Basic Books, 1993.

———. "Boy Culture: Middle-Class Boyhood in Nineteenth-Century America." In *Meanings for Manhood: Constructions of Masculinity in Victorian America*, ed. Mark C. Carnes and Clyde Griffen. Chicago: University of Chicago Press, 1990.

Rouse, Jacqueline. *Lugenia Burns Hope, Black Southern Reformer*. Athens: University of Georgia Press, 1989.

Ruether, Rosemary, and Eleanor McLaughlin. "Women's Leadership in the Jewish and Christian Traditions: Continuity and Change." In *Women of Spirit: Female Leadership in the Jewish and Christian Traditions*, ed. Rosemary Radford Ruether and Eleanor McLaughlin. New York: Simon and Schuster, 1979.

Ryan, Mary. *Civic Wars: Democracy and Public Life in the American City during the Nineteenth Century*. Berkeley: University of California Press, 1997.

Rydell, Robert. *All the World's a Fair: Visions of Empire at American International Expositions, 1876–1916*. Chicago: University of Chicago Press, 1984.

Rydell, Robert, John E. Findling, and Kimberly D. Pelle. *Fair America: World's Fairs in the United States*. Washington, D.C.: Smithsonian Institution Press, 2000.

Salem, Dorothy. *To Better Our World: Black Women in Organized Reform, 1890–1920*. Brooklyn: Carlson Publishing, 1990.

Scott, Anne Firor. *From Pedestal to Politics, 1830–1930*. Chicago: University of Chicago Press, 1970.

———. "Most Invisible of All: Black Women's Voluntary Associations." *Journal of Southern History* 56 (February 1990): 3–22.

Scott, Joan Wallach. *Gender and the Politics of History.* New York: Columbia University Press, 1988.

Shaw, Stephanie. "Black Club Women and the Creation of the National Association of Colored Women." *Journal of Women's History* 3 (Fall 1991): 10–25.

———. *What a Woman Ought to Be and to Do: Black Professional Women Workers during the Jim Crow Era.* Chicago: University of Chicago Press, 1996.

Simmons-Henry, Linda. *Culture Town: Life in Raleigh's African-American Communities.* Raleigh, N.C.: Raleigh Historic Districts Commission, 1993.

Singal, Daniel. "Towards a Definition of American Modernism." *American Quarterly* 39 (Spring 1987): 7–26.

Smith, Jessie Carney, ed. *Notable Black American Women.* Detroit: Gale Press, 1992.

Smooth, Wendy G., and Tamelyn Tucker. "Behind But Not Forgotten: Women and the Behind-the-Scenes Organizing of the Million Man March." In *Still Lifting, Still Climbing: African American Women's Contemporary Activism,* ed. Kimberly Springer. New York: New York University Press, 1999.

Steelman, Joseph F. *North Carolina's Role in the Spanish-American War.* Raleigh: North Carolina Department of Cultural Resources, 1975.

Summers, Martin. *Manliness and Its Discontents: The Black Middle Class and the Transformation of Masculinity, 1900–1930.* Chapel Hill: University of North Carolina Press, 2004.

Thuesen, Sarah C. "Bargaining for Black Loyalty: Postwar State Involvement in Black Education and the Embattled Dream of James E. Shepard, 1919–1926." Paper presented at the annual meeting of the Southern Historical Association, Baltimore, Maryland, 9 November 2002.

———. "Classes of Citizenship: The Culture and Politics of Black Public Education in North Carolina, 1919–1960." Ph.D. diss., University of North Carolina at Chapel Hill, 2003.

Trotter, Joe. *Coal, Class, and Color: Blacks in Southern West Virginia.* Urbana: University of Illinois Press, 1990.

Wallace, Maurice O. *Constructing the Black Masculine: Identity and Ideality in African American Men's Literature and Culture, 1775–1995.* Durham, N.C.: Duke University Press, 2002.

Watson, Clifford. *Educating African American Males: Detroit's Malcolm X Academy Solution.* Chicago: Third World Press, 1996.

Weare, Walter B. "New Negroes for a New Century: Adaptability on Display." In *The Adaptable South: Essays in Honor of George Brown Tindall,* ed. Elizabeth Jacoway, Dan T. Carter, Lester C. Lehman, and Robert C. McMath, Jr. Baton Rouge: Louisiana State University Press, 1991.

Welter, Barbara. "The Feminization of American Religion: 1800–1860." In *Clio's Consciousness Raised: New Perspectives in the History of Women*, ed. Mary S. Hartman and Lois Banner. New York: Harper and Row, 1974.

White, Deborah Gray "The Cost of Club Work, the Price of Black Feminism." In *Visible Women: New Essays on American Activism*, ed. Nancy A. Hewitt and Suzanne Lebsock. Urbana: University of Illinois Press, 1993.

———. "Female Slaves: Sex Roles and Status in the Antebellum Plantation South." *Journal of Family History* 8, no. 3 (Fall 1983): 248–261.

———. *Too Heavy a Load: Black Women in Defense of Themselves, 1894–1994.* New York: Norton, 1999.

Wiggins, William H., Jr. *O Freedom! Afro-American Emancipation Celebrations.* Knoxville: University of Tennessee Press, 1987.

Williams, Loretta. *Black Freemasonry and Middle-Class Realities.* Columbia: University of Missouri Press, 1980.

Williamson, Joel. *A Rage for Order: Black/White Relations in the American South since Emancipation.* New York: Oxford University, Press, 1986.

Woodward, C. Vann. *Origins of the New South, 1877–1913.* 1971; reprint, Baton Rouge: Louisiana State University Press, 1994.

Wormser, Richard. *The Rise and Fall of Jim Crow.* New York: St. Martin's Press, 2004.

Wright, George C. *Life behind a Veil: Blacks in Louisville, Kentucky, 1865–1930.* Baton Rouge: Louisiana State University Press, 1985.

Young, James. *Black Writers of the Thirties.* Baton Rouge: Louisiana State University Press, 1973.

Index

Page numbers in *italics* refer to illustrations.

CPSIA information can be obtained
at www.ICGtesting.com
Printed in the USA
JSHW022058061221
21027JS00001B/33